Super Sweet Treats for Diabetics

By Mary Jane Finsand,
Karin Cadwell, Ph.D., R.N.

Main Street
A division of Sterling Publishing Co., Inc.
New York

10 9 8 7 6 5 4 3 2 1

Published by Main Street, a division of Sterling Publishing Co., Inc.
387 Park Avenue South, New York, NY 10016
This book is comprised of material from the following Sterling titles:
Diabetic Sweet Tooth Cookbook © 1993 by Mary Jane Finsand
Delicious Diabetic Desserts © 1997 by Karin Cadwell

© 2003 by Sterling Publishing Co., Inc.
Distributed in Canada by Sterling Publishing
c/o Canadian Manda Group, One Atlantic Avenue, Suite 105
Toronto, Ontario, Canada M6K 3E7
Distributed in Great Britain and Europe by Cassell PLC
Wellington House, 125 Strand, London WC2R 0BB, England
Distributed in Australia by Capricorn Link (Australia) Pty. Ltd.
P.O. Box 6651, Baulkham Hills, Business Centre, NSW 2153 Australia

Manufactured in the United States of America
All rights reserved

ISBN 1-4027-1084-4

Contents

Foreword 4

Introduction 5

Drinks 11

Mostly Fruit 25

Ice Cream & Frozen Treats 34

Ice Box Pies 56

Phyllo Dough 70

Pudding 82

Roll-Ups 94

Pancakes & Waffles 104

Meringues 111

Cream Puffs 124

Dressed-Up Angels 131

Baked Goodies 140

    Cakes 140

    Pies 188

    Cookies & Bars 202

Candy 217

Sauces 223

Glazes & Frostings 228

Food Exchange Lists 233

Index 248

Foreword

Unlike short-term crash diets, which have proven to be ineffective in the long run, changes in eating habits are a positive step toward a healthier, happier life. They make you look and feel better and significantly reduce the risk of a variety of illnesses. Far from being a punishment, they reap innumerable rewards. For example, a recent nationwide study indicated that when blood sugars were lowered, people with type I diabetes reduced diabetic eye complications by 54 to 76 percent, kidney complications by 39 to 54 percent, and nerve problems by 60 percent.

Many patients who are diabetic or who, for other reasons, have problems controlling their blood pressure, blood sugar levels, cholesterol, or weight have come to my office looking for solutions to their health problems. Most of them have already tried a variety of "quick fix" schemes and have either given up all hope of living a so-called "normal" life or are still searching for a magic panacea. They fear being put on the dreaded "diet," considering it to be more of a punishment than a cure. They couldn't be more wrong.

Let's not forget that a diet that's good for someone with diabetes is good for someone with a heart condition, a cholesterol problem, or a weight problem. In fact, it's just plain good for everyone!

As Karin Cadwell and Mary Jane Finsand proves in this remarkable cookbook, choosing a more healthful eating plan does not mean you have to sacrifice taste, satisfaction, or fun. Packed with mouthwatering desserts, this volume is a powerful tool to help anyone, diabetic or not, in developing a more healthful way of living. The recipes are easy to follow and yield delicious, wholesome results that the whole family will love.

Enjoy!

—JOHN F. COUGHLIN, M.D., PH.D.
MEDICAL DIRECTOR
JOSLIN DIABETES CENTER/FALMOUTH

Introduction

Super Sweet Treats for Diabetics is probably different from other cook-books for diabetics you've read or used, because I believe that just about everyone can benefit from low-fat, low-calorie, controlled-carbohydrate desserts. The recipes in this book are meant to be served to your whole family, everyone at the birthday party, or dis-played with pride at the potluck supper. I think you will find these desserts delicious enough, attractive enough, and easy enough to make so that you will no longer make two desserts—one for the dia-betic and one for everyone else. I make one fabulous dessert every-one can enjoy.

My thinking about diabetic desserts began when I was a young girl and my grandfather "got sugar diabetes," as the family said. As a result, my grandmother brought my grandfather's desserts, wrapped in waxed paper, whenever they went out to dinner. My grandmoth-er was a renowned cook and over the years developed many special recipes my grandfather enjoyed, but they weren't shared around. Dinners and special occasions were two-dessert affairs, often plain cake for my grandfather and homemade pastry for the rest of us.

Tom Martin, my parents' good friend, has been on a diabetic diet for as long as I can remember. Over the years there have been count-less occasions, from Cub Scout "Blue and Golds" to 50th anniver-saries, that feature desserts and sweet treats. At buffets especially, Tom's wife, Jean, or my mother would peruse the possibilities and tell Tom what he could eat. Often the news was that unless Jean had brought something, Tom was out of luck. Other friends would try to come up with something for Tom when he was going to be a din-ner guest. My mother, whose father was on a strict diabetic diet for many years, often got telephone calls asking: "Jean and Tom are com-ing for dinner this weekend. Do you have any ideas about dessert for Tom?" Often, if the hostess spent her creative talents on the rest of the guests, Tom ended up with "diet" gelatin dessert.

Recently, my mother turned 75. She's been on a diabetic diet for many years, and, when I was planning her big party, a major consid-eration was that I wanted her to be able to choose from attractive and delicious treats. After all, it was her birthday. So, I made only desserts and treats suitable for her fairly strict diet. She was thrilled and so were her guests, all of whom appreciated being treated to luscious low-fat, low-calorie, limited-carbohydrate party food. Many of those recipes are in this book.

Many of the recipes in this book are from scratch. They call for everyday ingredients, many of which you probably already have on hand. They don't usually demand a trip to the supermarket. Other recipes require convenience foods, such as pudding, gelatin mixes, or frozen low-fat, non-dairy topping. I have only used ingredients I feel sure are available in every grocery store. I also tried to make your treat-making easier by using appropriate "ready made" foods, such as angel food cakes. Supermarket angel food cakes are very low in fat and (compared to other dessert foods) low in carbohydrates, because they are mostly egg whites and air. Dressing up angel food cakes is a fast and foolproof way to a sweet treat.

Although many of the recipes are quick and easy, some, such as tiramisu, are more complex. Don't be put off by the length of the list of ingredients or the directions. Take the recipes step-by-step and you'll be thrilled with the results. This book has a whole chapter on meringues, featuring the classic Pavlova. This is an ideal dessert, tempting and beautiful, yet easy and healthful. Even if you have never seen a Pavlova before, try it. You'll be delighted. Just be sure to read the introductory recipe or section at the beginning of each chapter to orient you and point out any special considerations.

This book is organized by the central technique or ingredient featured in each chapter. Phyllo dough, for example, is a great ingredient for diabetic desserts, but please follow my low-fat, low-calorie instructions, not the melted-butter ones on the phyllo box!

So that beginner cooks will be able to prepare these wonderful treats, I have tried not to use specialized equipment.

I've tried to give you a choice about which sugar substitute to use. In many cases, any of the three available basic substitutes will work: aspartame (Nutrasweet, Equal); saccharin (Sweet 'n Low, Sugar Twin); acesulfame-K or Ace-K (Sweet-One). Some people prefer one taste over another and when it doesn't matter, I just call for sugar substitute. Other times, especially when heat or freezing is involved, I indicate the one that works best when I prepare the recipes. These chemicals can change flavor and become bitter with different temperatures. There is a chart on page 10 that will help you make substitutions.

Please keep in mind that aspartame (marketed as Equal or NutraSweet) must be added after cooking. I like to store aspartame with a vanilla bean in little covered containers. I do this with Equal Measure (a concentrated form of aspartame) and NutraSweet Spoonful (the measures-like-sugar type of aspartame).

If your supermarket doesn't carry Acesulfame-K, which is marketed as Sweet One, you can call 1-800-544-8610, or write to Stadt Corporation, 60 Flushing Avenue, Brooklyn, NY 11205, for information about how to get it.

One of the reasons I use different sugar substitutes is that my taste testers tend to find that heat-treated foods containing aspartame taste bitter. In most recipes you can substitute one brand of sugar substitute for another according to your individual preference.

Outside the United States, the same artificial sweeteners tend to be available and are frequently marketed with the same brand names mentioned above. A choice may be a mix of sweeteners marketed in a blend and may include cyclamate. In all cases, these products are reasonably the same equivalents as those listed here. Just be sure to choose a concentrated variety where about one-fifth to one-quarter of a teaspoon is equivalent to two teaspoons of sugar. If the product is sold in a jar, use a quarter of a teaspoon to equal a packet.

I hope you enjoy making and serving these sweet treats. I know you'll be proud to serve them.

Basic Pantry Tips

Below you will find instructions to follow when working with phyllo dough and meringues.

Phyllo Dough

Phyllo dough is a paper thin pastry made in the Mediterranean since ancient times. In most recipes phyllo dough is layered and baked to a golden-brown color. Because it has virtually no fat, phyllo is an ideal dough for diabetic desserts and sweet treats.

General Instructions

- Buy phyllo or "Fillo" dough in the freezer section of the super market. The dough comes in large rectangular sheets.
- Store the box in the freezer until the day before you want to use it.
- Transfer the unopened box to the refrigerator to thaw overnight.

- Choose a large work surface, such as a kitchen table.
- Wet a dish towel and ring it out thoroughly. You will also need a piece of plastic. I usually use an unused plastic trash bag.
- Open the phyllo dough box and carefully unroll the dough onto your work surface.
- Cover the dough immediately with the plastic and spread the damp towel over on top. This is the key to working with phyllo dough. Don't let it dry out! Don't leave the pile uncovered except when you are removing one sheet from it.
- Roll any unused sheets of phyllo in the plastic it was originally packaged in and refreeze. I usually add an extra plastic layer of wrapping to be sure the sheets don't dry out in the freezer.
- Work phyllo dough one layer at a time. Uncover the pile, remove one sheet, and cover the pile again.
- Use butter-flavored vegetable cooking spray instead of melted butter. This will really help cut down on calories. Start by spraying around the edges. This will help to avoid cracking. Work toward the center. Spray the sheet evenly. You generally put 4 sheets on top of one another. Don't forget to spray the last sheet. Cut through all four sheets to form 16 rectangular piles each four sheets high. Place these stacks on ungreased cookie sheets (or whatever the recipe calls for) and bake them in a preheated oven. Cool completely.

In the following recipes you'll often use three of these rectangular stacks together with fillings between the stacks to form each napoleon.

I've included some of my favorite phyllo recipes. I think you'll find them easy and delicious.

Meringues

Some recipes in this book are based on meringue—beaten egg whites slowly baked. They are low in fat and very elegant. You might think meringues are beyond your capabilities—they are not! It's hard to go wrong if you follow a few simple rules.

General Instructions

- Don't use plastic when you beat the egg whites. Glass or metal bowls give the most fluff from egg whites.

- Be sure your utensils are spotless. For egg whites to beat up, the bowls, blades, and scrapers should be grease free.

- Be sure no bits of yolks are mixed in with the whites. Separate whites and yolks into small cups or bowls, and put only pure egg whites into the mixing bowl. Should the yolk break during the separation process, put that egg aside and use another one.

- Don't bake meringues on wax paper or plain cookie sheets. Use parchment paper or the inside of clean brown paper grocery bags.

- Recognize that humidity changes meringues. On high-humidity days, meringues are chewy. On low-humidity days, meringues are dry and crispy.

- Never open the oven, even to peek, until the stated time has elapsed.

- Use reconstituted "Just Whites" powdered egg whites if you have no use for leftover yolks. They may be found in your supermarket, health food store, or gourmet shop.

- Even though egg substitutes are mostly egg whites, they don't work for meringues.

- Freeze meringues after you've made them or store them at room temperature. Always keep meringues in air tight containers.

❖ GUIDE TO APPROXIMATE EQUIVALENTS ❖

Amount of Artificial Sweeteners to Substitute for Sugar

SUGAR	ACESULFAME-K	ASPARTAME	SACCHARIN
2 teaspoons	1 packet	1 packet or $1/4$ teaspoon	1 packet or $1/5$ teaspoon
1 tablespoon	$1^{1/4}$ packets	$1^{1/2}$ packets or $1/2$ teaspoon	$1^{1/3}$ packets or $1/3$ teaspoon
$1/4$ cup	3 packets	6 packets or $1^{3/4}$ teaspoons	3 packets or $1^{1/6}$ teaspoons
$1/3$ cup	4 packets	8 packets or $2^{1/2}$ teaspoons	4 packets or $1^{1/4}$ teaspoons
$1/2$ cup	6 packets	12 packets or $3^{1/2}$ teaspoons	6 packets or 2 teaspoons
$2/3$ cup	8 packets	16 packets or 5 teaspoons	8 packets or $2^{1/2}$ teaspoons
$3/4$ cup	9 packets	18 packets or $5^{1/4}$ teaspoons	9 packets or $3^{1/2}$ teaspoons
1 cup	12 packets	24 packets or $7^{1/4}$ teaspoons	12 packets or 4 teaspoons

DRINKS

❖ Banana Tofu Cream ❖

2 SERVINGS

1/2 cup	skim milk	125 mL
1	banana	1
1 teaspoon	vanilla extract	3 mL
3 envelopes	aspartame sweetener	3 envelopes
1/2 package	firm tofu (10.5-ounce)	1/2 package (297 g)
	ground nutmeg	

Combine skim milk and banana in a blender. Process until smooth. Add vanilla and aspartame sweetener. Process to mix. Add tofu. Process until smooth. Pour into two white-wine glasses. (A champagne flute can also be used.) Sprinkle surface with nutmeg.

EACH SERVING CONTAINS: CALORIES: 122 ▲ CARBOHYDRATES: 18 G ▲ EXCHANGE: 1 1/2 SKIM MILK, 1 FAT

❖ Banana Yogurt Nog ❖

4 SERVINGS

1	banana	1
1 1/2 cups	skim milk	375 mL
8 ounces	nonfat plain yogurt	227 g
2 teaspoons	vanilla extract	10 mL
4 envelopes	aspartame sweetener	4 envelopes
	or	
1 1/2 tablespoons	granulated sugar replacement	21 mL
3	ice cubes	3

Combine banana, milk, yogurt, vanilla extract, and sweetener of your choice in a blender. Process until smooth. With the motor running, add ice cubes, one at a time, through the feed tube in the lid. Blend until smooth. Pour into decorative red-wine glasses.

EACH SERVING CONTAINS: CALORIES: 86 ▲ CARBOHYDRATES: 14 G ▲ EXCHANGE: 1 SKIM MILK

❖ Black-Raspberry Tofu Cream ❖

2 SERVINGS

1 cup	fresh or frozen black raspberries	250 mL
1/2 cup	skim milk	125 mL
1 teaspoon	vanilla extract	5 mL
3 envelopes	aspartame sweetener	3 envelopes
1/2 package	(10.5 ounces) firm tofu	1/2 package (297 g)

Combine black raspberries and skim milk in a blender. Process until smooth. Add vanilla and aspartame sweetener. Process to mix. Add tofu. Process until smooth. Pour into two white-wine glasses.

EACH SERVING CONTAINS: CALORIES: 157 ▲ CARBOHYDRATES: 14 G ▲ EXCHANGE: 1 SKIM MILK, 1 MEDIUM-FAT MEAT

❖ Butter-Almond Frappé ❖

1 SERVING

Do you like butter-almond ice cream? This is a wonderful substitute!

1 cup	frozen fat-free non-dairy whipped topping	250 mL
1/2 teaspoon	butter extract	3 mL
1/2 teaspoon	almond extract	3 mL
1 cup	crushed ice	250 mL

Put all ingredients into a food processor blender. Blend at the highest speed until the ice is liquefied.

EACH SERVING CONTAINS: CALORIES: 125 ▲ CARBOHYDRATES: 20 G ▲ EXCHANGE: 1 FRUIT

❖ Chocolate Frappé ❖

A wonderful chocolaty taste.

1 envelope	hot chocolate mix, no sugar added	1 envelope
3 tablespoons	hot water	45 mL
1 cup	skim milk	250 mL
1 cup	crushed ice	250 mL

In a small bowl, combine the hot chocolate mix and water until a smooth paste forms. Put the milk and crushed ice into a food processor or blender. Using a rubber scraper, pour the chocolate paste over the milk and ice mixture. Process at the highest speed until the ice is liquefied. Serve in tall glasses.

EACH SERVING CONTAINS: CALORIES: 73 ▲ CARBOHYDRATES: 11 G ▲ EXCHANGE: 1 MILK

❖ Chocolate Mint Dessert Drink ❖

4 SERVINGS

2 cups	low-fat ice cream	500 mL
2 tablespoons	chocolate flavoring or extract	30 mL
2 tablespoons	mint flavoring or extract	30 mL
1 tablespoon	chunky peanut butter	15 mL
4	fresh mint sprigs (optional)	4

Combine the ice cream, flavorings, and peanut butter in a blender. Blend until smooth and creamy. Pour into four wine glasses. If desired, garnish each with a mint sprig.

EACH SERVING CONTAINS: CALORIES: 116 ▲ CARBOHYDRATES: 15 G ▲ EXCHANGE: 1 LOW-FAT MILK

❖ Coffee and Cream ❖

6 SERVINGS

1 envelope	(2 cups) nondairy whipped-topping powder	1 envelope (500mL)
3 tablespoons	lemon juice	45 mL
2 tablespoons	water	30 mL
4 envelopes	aspartame sweetener	4 envelopes
1 tablespoon	instant-coffee powder	15 mL
2 cups	cracked ice	500 mL
1 cup	diet ginger ale	250 mL

Combine whipped-topping powder, lemon juice, water, aspartame sweetener, and instant-coffee powder in a blender. Process until foamy. Add ice and process using the off/on switch until smooth. Add ginger ale and process on low until blended.

EACH SERVING CONTAINS: CALORIES: 62 ▲ CARBOHYDRATES: 6 G ▲ EXCHANGE: 1 FAT, 1/4 FRUIT

❖ Cranberry Grapefruit Cooler ❖

6 SERVINGS

3 cups	unsweetened pink-grapefruit juice	750 mL
2 1/2 cups	low-calorie cranberry-juice cocktail	625 mL
2 tablespoons	granulated sugar replacement	30 mL
	or	
5 envelopes	aspartame sweetener	5 envelopes
3 cups	cracked ice	750 mL
6	thin slices of lime	6

Combine pink-grapefruit juice, cranberry juice, and sweetener of your choice in a large pitcher. Stir to dissolve sweetener. Divide the cracked ice equally among six glasses. Pour juice mixture into glasses. Garnish each glass with a slice of lime. This makes a perfect dessert drink after a barbecue dinner on a warm night.

EACH SERVING CONTAINS: CALORIES: 63 ▲ CARBOHYDRATES: 16 G ▲ EXCHANGE: 1 FRUIT

❖ Double-Raspberry Cooler ❖

1 1/2 cups	cracked ice	375 mL
1 1/2 cups	fresh or frozen unsweetened raspberries	190 mL
4	thin slices of lemon	4
6 tablespons	low-calorie raspberry syrup	90 mL
2 cups	sparkling water	500 mL

Divide cracked ice and raspberries equally among four glasses. Add one lemon slice, 1 1/2 tablespoons (21 mL) of raspberry syrup, and 1/2 cup (125 mL) of sparkling water to each glass. Serve with spoons so that the fruit can be muddled.

EACH SERVING CONTAINS: CALORIES: 43 ▲ CARBOHYDRATES: 10 G ▲ EXCHANGE: 3/4 FRUIT

❖ Hot Cider ❖

2 SERVINGS

2 cups	apple cider	500 mL
2	(3-inch) cinnamon sticks	2 (7.5-cm)
1/2 teaspoon	whole cloves	2 mL
1/8 teaspoon	ground nutmeg	1/2 mL
2 envelopes	aspartame sweetener	2 envelopes
2 teaspoons	rum flavoring	10 mL

In a small saucepan, heat the apple cider, cinnamon sticks, whole cloves, and nutmeg until boiling. Reduce heat and simmer gently for 5 to 6 minutes. Remove from heat; then remove cinnamon sticks and whole cloves. Stir in aspartame sweetener and rum flavoring. Pour into two preheated cups or mugs. (To preheat mugs: Pour boiling or very hot water into mugs, allow to stand for 1 to 2 minutes, then pour out hot water and fill with drink.)

EACH SERVING CONTAINS: CALORIES: 100 ▲ CARBOHYDRATES: 13 G ▲ EXCHANGE: 1 FRUIT

❖ Mango Cooler ❖

1 pound	mango	500 g
1/2 cup	fresh lemon juice	125 mL
1 tablespoon	rum flavoring	15 mL
1 tablespoon	granulated fructose	15 mL
	or	
6 envelopes	aspartame sweetener	6 envelopes
3 cups	cracked ice	750 mL

Peel, pit, and chop mango. Place mango pieces in a blender and process to a purée. Add lemon juice, rum flavoring, and sweetener of your choice. Then add the cracked ice and blend until smooth. Pour into chilled glasses.

EACH SERVING CONTAINS: CALORIES: 50 ▲ CARBOHYDRATES: 12 G ▲ EXCHANGE: 1 FRUIT

❖ Icy Eggnog ❖

Terrific for holiday get-togethers. Serve in punch cups sprinkled with nutmeg or cinnamon.

3 cups	skim milk	750 mL
3/4 cup	liquid egg substitute	185 mL
1 tablespoon	sugar	15 mL
2 packages	sugar substitute	2 packages
1 teaspoon	vanilla extract	5 mL
1 cup	crushed ice	250 mL

Put all the ingredients in a blender or food processor and process at the highest speed until the ice is liquefied.

EACH SERVING CONTAINS: CALORIES: 60 ▲ CARBOHYDRATES: 6 G ▲ EXCHANGE: 1/2 MILK

❖ Mocha Frappé ❖

As indulgent as those high-fat, fancy coffee drinks.

1 envelope	sugar-free hot chocolate mix	1 envelope
3 tablespoons	hot coffee	45 mL
1 cup	skim milk	250 mL
1 cup	crushed ice	250 mL

Put all the ingredients into a food processor or blender. Process at the highest speed until the ice is liquefied.

EACH SERVING CONTAINS: CALORIES: 86 ▲ CARBOHYDRATES: 12 G ▲ EXCHANGE: 1 MILK

❖ Orange Banana Smoothie ❖

4 SERVINGS

As good as it can be. Use sweet oranges and remove the white skin.

2	oranges, peeled and cut into chunks	2
1	ripe banana, peeled and sliced	1
1/2 cup	skim milk	125 mL
1 package	aspartame sweetener	1 package
1/4 teaspoon	almond extract	2 mL
3	ice cubes	3

Put all ingredients into a blender or food processor. Blend at the highest speed until smooth. Pour into four glasses. Serve cold.

EACH SERVING CONTAINS: CALORIES: 69 ▲ CARBOHYDRATES: 16 G ▲ EXCHANGE: 1 STARCH/BREAD

❖ Orange Sipper ❖

1 1/2 cups	buttermilk	375 mL
1/3 cup	orange-juice concentrate, undiluted	90 mL
2 tablespoons	granulated sugar replacement	30 mL
1 teaspoon	vanilla extract	5 mL
3	ice cubes	3

Combine buttermilk, orange-juice concentrate, sweetener of your choice, and vanilla. Blend until completely mixed. With blender running, drop ice cubes, one at a time, into the liquid. Blend until smooth. (Extra amount of drink can be frozen for later use. Place in freezer container. Allow to thaw slightly before using, then process in blender.)

EACH SERVING CONTAINS: CALORIES: 87 ▲ CARBOHYDRATES: 17 G ▲ EXCHANGE: 2/3 SKIM MILK, 1/2 FRUIT

❖ Party Pineapple Punch ❖

2	bananas	2
3 cups	unsweetened pineapple juice	750 mL
1 can	(6 ounces) orange-juice concentrate	178 g can
3 cups	cold water	750 mL
2 tablespoons	lemon juice	30 mL
5 envelopes	aspartame sweetener	5 envelopes
1 quart	diet lemon-lime soda	1 liter

Cut bananas into chunks and place in a blender. Add 1 cup (250 mL) of the pineapple juice and orange-juice concentrate. Blend until smooth. Transfer to large bowl. Add the remaining 2 cups (500 mL) of the pineapple juice and the cold water, lemon juice, and aspartame sweetener. Stir to completely mix. Pour into a large metal baking pan. Place in freezer and allow to freeze into a slush. Scoop into a punch bowl. Pour the lemon-lime soda down the sides of the bowl. Stir gently to mix. Serve in small punch cups.

EACH SERVING CONTAINS: CALORIES: 39 ▲ CARBOHYDRATES: 9 G ▲ EXCHANGE: 2/3 FRUIT

❖ Peach Slush ❖

1 SERVING

1 1/2 cups	frozen, unsweetened peach slices	375 mL
1/2 cup	skim milk	125 mL
3 envelopes	aspartame sweetener	3 envelopes
1	fresh mint sprig (optional)	1

Allow peach slices to thaw slightly. Pour milk into a blender or food processor. With the motor running, gradually add the peach slices (keeping top of blender covered to prevent splashing). Process into a slush. Blend in aspartame sweetener. Pour into a decorative glass. If desired, garnish with a sprig of mint.

EACH SERVING CONTAINS: CALORIES: 143 ▲ CARBOHYDRATES: 30 G ▲ EXCHANGE: 1 1/2 FRUIT, 1/2 SKIM MILK

❖ Peach Smoothie ❖

4 SERVINGS

1 1/4 cups	nonfat plain yogurt	310 mL
1 pound	ripe peaches	500 g
2 tablespoons	fresh lemon juice	30 mL
2 tablespoons	liquid fructose	30 mL
1/4 teaspoon	vanilla extract	1 mL

Divide 1 cup (250 mL) of the yogurt among 8 to 10 sections of an ice-cube tray. Freeze hard (at least 4 to 5 hours). Peel, pit, and slice peaches. Combine peach slices and lemon juice in a blender. Process until almost a purée. Add the remaining 1/4 cup yogurt and the liquid fructose and vanilla. Process into a purée. Add frozen yogurt cubes and process until smooth. Pour into four decorative glasses.

EACH SERVING CONTAINS: CALORIES: 81 ▲ CARBOHYDRATES: 16 G ▲ EXCHANGE: 1 FRUIT, 1/2 SKIM MILK

❖ Pineapple-Mint Drink ❖

6 SERVINGS

If you don't have a fresh pineapple, used canned pineapple packed in its own juice. Drain it first.

1/2 cup	water (or drained pineapple juice)	125 mL
1 cup	pineapple, cut into pieces	250 mL
3	whole oranges, seeded andchopped	3
1 cup	crushed ice	250 mL
1/2 teaspoon	mint extract	3 mL

Put all ingredients into a blender or food processor. Blend at the highest speed until the ice is liquefied.

EACH SERVING CONTAINS: CALORIES: 44 ▲ CARBOHYDRATES: 11 G ▲ EXCHANGE: 3/4 FRUIT

❖ Prince Alex After-Dinner Drink ❖

1 SERVING

2 tablespoons	water	30 mL
2 tablespoons	low-fat ice cream	30 mL
1 tablespoon	liquid nondairy creamer	15 mL
1 teaspoon	chocolate flavoring	5 mL
	ground nutmeg	

Shake ingredients (except nutmeg) with ice cubes in a shaker jar. Place one ice cube into a chilled cocktail glass. Strain mixture over ice cube in glass. Dust with nutmeg.

EACH SERVING CONTAINS: CALORIES: NEGLIGIBLE ▲ CARBOHYDRATES: NEGLIGIBLE ▲ EXCHANGE: NEGLIGIBLE

❖ Quick Cappuccino ❖

3 cups	hot strong coffee*	750 mL
3 cups	scalded skim milk	750 mL
12 envelopes	aspartame sweetener	12 envelopes
	unsweetened cocoa powder	

★ To brew strong coffee, use double the amount of coffee that you would normally use.

Pour scalded milk into a blender. Place hot pad over blender cover to protect yourself against burning. Process the milk until frothy. Pour 1/2 cup (500 mL) of the strong coffee into each of six cups or mugs. Pour 1/2 cup (500 mL) of the hot milk into each of the cups. Stir two envelopes of aspartame sweetener into each cup. Sprinkle with a small amount of unsweetened cocoa. Serve immediately.

EACH SERVING CONTAINS: CALORIES: 50 ▲ CARBOHYDRATES: 6 G ▲ EXCHANGE: 1/2 LOW-FAT MILK

❖ Raspberry Frappé ❖

1 SERVING

Raspberry extract makes all the difference. Buy it at a specialty food shop since supermarkets carry only the most ordinary flavors.

1 cup	raspberry sugar-free soda	250 mL
1/3 cup	plain yogurt	80 mL
1 package	sugar substitute	1 package
1 teaspoon	raspberry extract	5 mL
1/2 tablespoon	vanilla extract	7.5 mL

Put all the ingredients into a blender or food processor. Blend or process at the highest speed until the ice is liquefied.

EACH SERVING CONTAINS: CALORIES: 63 ▲ CARBOHYDRATES: 5 G ▲ EXCHANGE: 1 VEGETABLE, 1/2 FAT

❖ Strawberry Slush ❖

1 SERVING

1 1/2 cups	frozen, unsweetened whole strawberries	375 mL
1/2 cup	buttermilk	125 mL
1 tablespoon	granulated fructose	15 mL

Allow strawberries to thaw slightly. Reserve one or two of the larger strawberries. Combine buttermilk and fructose in a blender or food processor. With the motor running, gradually add the strawberries (keeping top of blender covered to prevent splashing). Process into a slush. Pour into a decorative glass. Cut reserved strawberries into medium-sized pieces. Stir into strawberry slush.

EACH SERVING CONTAINS: CALORIES: 105 ▲ CARBOHYDRATES: 21 G ▲ EXCHANGE: 1 FRUIT, 1/2 SKIM MILK

❖ Strawberry Smoothie ❖

4 SERVINGS

I've used frozen berries in this with excellent results.

1 cup	skim milk	250 mL
3/4 cup	fresh or sugar-free whole frozen strawberries	185 mL
1 package	sugar substitute	1 package
1/2 teaspoon	lemon extract	3 mL
1 cup	crushed ice	250 mL

Put all the ingredients in a blender or food processor. Blend at the highest speed until the ice is liquefied.

EACH SERVING CONTAINS: CALORIES: 31 ▲ CARBOHYDRATES: 5 G ▲ EXCHANGE: 1 VEGETABLE

❖ Strawberry Yogurt Nog ❖

4 SERVINGS

1 1/2 cups	fresh or frozen unsweet-ened strawberries	375 mL
1 1/2 cups	skim milk	375 mL
8 ounces	nonfat plain yogurt	227 g
1 teaspoon	vanilla extract	5 mL
1 teaspoon	strawberry flavoring	5 mL
6 envelopes	aspartame sweetener or	6 envelopes
1 tablespoon	granulated fructose	15 mL
3	ice cubes	3

(If you are using fresh strawberries, you might want to set four aside for garnish.) Combine strawberries, milk, yogurt, vanilla extract, strawberry flavoring, and sweetener of your choice in a blender. Process until smooth. With the motor running, add ice cubes, one at a time, through the feed tube in the lid. Blend until smooth. Pour into decorative red-wine glasses. (Cut reserved fresh strawberries into a fan. Lay on top of nog.)

EACH SERVING CONTAINS: CALORIES: 76 ▲ CARBOHYDRATES: 10 G ▲ EXCHANGE: 1 SKIM MILK

❖ Tropical Punch ❖

6 SERVINGS

1 cup	mango nectar	250 mL
1 cup	unsweetened pineapple juice	250 mL
3/4 cup	guava nectar	190 mL
1/4 cup	lime juice	60 mL
6 1/2 cups	cracked ice	1,625 mL

Mix juices in a large pitcher. Combine 1 cup (250 mL) of the punch with 2 cups (500 mL) of the cracked ice in a blender. Blend until smooth. Pour into two glasses. Repeat procedure with remaining punch in batches.

EACH SERVING CONTAINS: CALORIES: 69 ▲ CARBOHYDRATES: 17 G ▲ EXCHANGE: 1 FRUIT

❖ Vanilla Shake ❖

As good as those in your favorite fast–food restaurant.

1/2 cup	skim milk	125 mL
1 cup	frozen, fat-free non-dairy whipped topping	250 mL
1 tablespoon	vanilla extract	15 mL
1/2 cup	crushed ice	125 mL

Place all ingredients in a blender or food processor. Process at the highest spped until liquefied. Serve immediately.

EACH SERVING CONTAINS: CALORIES: 165 ▲ CARBOHYDRATES: 26 G ▲ EXCHANGE: 1 1/2 STARCH/BREAD

❖ Virgin Piña Colada ❖

This is thick and frothy; imagine yourself sitting beside a pool in the topics sipping it.

1 cup	frozen, fat-free non-dairy whipped topping	250 mL
2 tablespoons	crushed pineapple in juice, drained	30 mL
1 teaspoon	rum extract	5 mL
1 teaspoon	coconut extract	5 mL
1 cup	crushed ice	250 mL

Place all the ingredients in a food processor or blender. Process at the highest speed until the ice is liquefied.

EACH SERVING CONTAINS: CALORIES: 40 ▲ CARBOHYDRATES: 30 G ▲ EXCHANGE: 1 1/2 FRUIT

MOSTLY FRUIT

❖ Bananas and Yogurt ❖

The yogurt is like sweetened whipped cream.

4	ripe bananas, peeled	4
3 packages	sugar substitute	3 packages
1 cup	nonfat vanilla yogurt	250 mL
2 tablespoons	walnuts, chopped (optional)	30 mL

Slice the bananas in half lengthwise. Cut into chunks and place one banana in each serving dish. In a mixing bowl, combine the sugar substitute, yogurt, and vanilla. Put one quarter of the yogurt mixture over the bananas in each dish.

Chill for one hour before serving. Sprinkle with nuts, if desired.

EACH SERVING CONTAINS: CALORIES: 159 ▲ CARBOHYDRATES: 37 G ▲ EXCHANGE: 1 STARCH/BREAD, 1 1/2 FRUIT

❖ Peach Clafouti ❖

YIELD: 6 SERVINGS

Clafouti is like a cobbler. It's just one dish, easy with fruit and pastry.

1 pound	peaches, sliced	450 g
1 cup	skim milk	250 mL
2	whole eggs or equivalent egg substitute	2 whole
2 tablespoons	peach-flavored brandy (optional)	30 mL
2 tablespoons	sugar	30 mL

2 packages	acesulfame-K	2 packages
1/2 cup	flour	125 mL
1/4 teaspoon	nutmeg	2 mL

Coat a one-quart (1 L) shallow baking dish with non-stick vegetable cooking spray. Arrange peach slices evenly on the bottom of it.

Put the milk, eggs, brandy (if you are using it), sugar, and acesulfame-K in a blender or food processor. Use a tablespoon (15 mL) measure and remove 1 tablespoon (15 mL) flour from the half-cup (125 mL) measure and mix in the nutmeg. Set aside. Add the 1/2 cup minus 1 tablespoon (125 mL minus 15 mL) flour to the mixture in the blender or food processor and process until smooth. Pour over the peaches.

Sprinkle with the flour-nutmeg mixture. Bake in a preheated 350° F (180°C) oven for 30 to 35 minutes. The topping will be golden and puffed.

EACH SERVING CONTAINS: CALORIES: 126 ▲ CARBOHYDRATES: 23 G ▲ EXCHANGE: 1 1/2 STARCH/BREAD

❖ Peach Crème Fraîche ❖

YIELD: 4 SERVINGS

20 ounces	peach slices in juice	550 g
1 cup	frozen, low-fat non-dairy whipped topping	250 mL
1 teaspoon	almond extract	5 mL
1 envelope	plain gelatin	1 envelope
3 tablespoons	water	45 mL

Drain the peaches. Reserve four slices for garnish. Discard the juice or reserve it for another use. Put the peaches, whipped topping, and almond extract in a blender or food processor. Blend until smooth. In a small saucepan, mix together the gelatin and water. Let stand five minutes. Heat over low flame, stirring constantly until the gelatin is dissolved. Add to the peach mixture. Blend another few seconds. Spoon into four dessert dishes. Refrigerate until serving time. Garnish with the reserved peach slices and additional whipped topping, if desired.

EACH SERVING CONTAINS: CALORIES: 114 ▲ CARBOHYDRATES: 22 G ▲ EXCHANGE: 1 STARCH/BREAD; 1/2 FRUIT

❖ Individual Banana Soufflés ❖

Serve these right away!

6	medium bananas, ripe and peeled	6
1 tablespoon	cornstarch	15 mL
1/2 cup	skim milk	125 mL
1 teaspoon	almond extract or	5 mL
1 tablespoon	almond liqueur	15 mL
2	egg yolks	2
3	egg whites	3
1/2 teaspoon	confectioners' sugar	3 mL

Purée the bananas. Measure 2 cups (500 mL) for use in this recipe. Combine the cornstarch and skim milk and cook in a heavy-bottomed medium saucepan. Stir constantly until the mixture thickens. Continue stirring and add the extract or liqueur, banana pureé, and egg yolks. Bring to a boil. Transfer to a mixing bowl. Cool. Beat the egg whites until stiff but not dry. Fold them into the banana mixture carefully. Spoon the mixture into individual soufflé dishes that have been coated with non-stick vegetable cooking spray. Place them in a preheated 350°F (180°C) oven for 10 to 15 minutes. Try not to open the oven door during this time. The tops should be brown and the soufflés puffed. Sprinkle the tops with confectioners sugar.

EACH SERVING CONTAINS: CALORIES: 147 ▲ CARBOHYDRATES: 29 G ▲ EXCHANGE: 2 STARCH/BREAD

❖ Yogurt Orange Whip ❖

4	oranges, peeled	4
3 packages	sugar substitute	3 packages
2 cups	lemon or vanilla nonfat yogurt	500 mL
2 tablespoons	walnuts (optional)	30 mL

Chop the oranges coarsely. Place them in a blender or food processor. Add the sugar substitute and yogurt and process at a high speed until ingredients are well combined. Pour into four dessert dishes. Chill for an hour or two. Just before serving, sprinkle the tops with walnuts if desired.

EACH SERVING CONTAINS: CALORIES: 65 ▲ CARBOHYDRATES: 16 G ▲ EXCHANGE: 1 FRUIT

❖ Fried Spiced Apples ❖

YIELD: 4 SERVINGS

This is a wonderfully satisfying dessert for a winter evening.

4	large cooking apples, peeled and cored	4
1 teaspoon	sugar	5 mL
1/4 teaspoon	ginger	2 mL
1/4 teaspoon	cinnamon	2 mL
2 tablespoons	butter or margarine	30 mL
1 cup	frozen low-fat non-dairy whipped topping	250 mL

Cut the apples into 1/4-inch (6 mm) thick slices. On a dinner plate, mix together the sugar, ginger, and cinnamon. In a large, heavy-bottomed frying pan, melt the butter or margarine. Dip the apple slices in the sugar and cinnamon mixture. Fry 3–5 minutes on each side or until lightly browned. Remove slices to a serving dish. Serve immediately with whipped topping.

EACH SERVING CONTAINS: CALORIES: 176 ▲ CARBOHYDRATES: 26 G ▲ EXCHANGE: 2 FRUIT, 1 1/2 FAT

❖ Frozen Bananas ❖

YIELD: 8 SERVINGS

Keep these in a plastic bag in the freezer for instant snacks.

2	medium firm bananas	2
1/3 cup	sugar-free chocolate candy, broken up	80 mL
2 tablespoons	creamy peanut butter	30 mL
2 tablespoons	nuts, chopped and toasted	30 mL

Cut the bananas into four pieces each. Put the pieces on a pan in the freezer for 30 minutes. Melt the chocolate over a very low flame in a small saucepan. Add the peanut butter and stir. Put the chocolate mixture on one plate and the nuts on another. Roll the banana pieces in the chocolate and then the nuts. Return to the freezer to harden the chocolate. Store the pieces in the freezer in a plastic bag.

EACH SERVING CONTAINS: CALORIES: 101 ▲ CARBOHYDRATES: 14 G ▲ EXCHANGE: 1 STARCH/BREAD, 1 FAT

❖ Marinated Blueberries ❖

YIELD: 4 SERVINGS

Delicious when blueberries are fresh and plentiful.

2 cups	fresh blueberries	500 mL
1 teaspoon	grated orange rind	5 mL
2 tablespoons	Triple Sec or other orange-flavored liqueur	30 mL
2 teaspoons	sugar	10 mL
1/2 cup	frozen, low-fat non-dairy whipped topping	125 mL

In a shallow mixing bowl, combine the blueberries, orange rind, Triple Sec, and sugar. Toss to coat the berries. Cover loosely and refrigerate for an hour or more. Before serving, mix a few times. Serve with whipped topping.

EACH SERVING CONTAINS: CALORIES: 69 ▲ CARBOHYDRATES: 14 G ▲ EXCHANGE: 1 STARCH/BREAD

❖ Oranges and Grapes ❖

YIELD: 4 SERVINGS

Make a glamorous-looking fresh dessert with fresh winter fruits.

4	oranges, peeled	4
1 cup	grapes, halved and seeded, if necessary	250 mL
1/4 cup	water	60 mL

| 1 teaspoon | rum flavoring | 5 mL |
| 2 packages | sugar substitute | 2 packages |

Slice the oranges into layers. Arrange with grape halves in a glass serving dish. Mix together the water, flavoring, and sugar substitute.

Pour the mixture over the fruit. Cover the bowl and refrigerate for at least an hour before serving.

EACH SERVING CONTAINS: CALORIES: 90 ▲ CARBOHYDRATES: 23 G ▲ EXCHANGE: 1 STARCH/BREAD, 1/2 FRUIT

❖ Fruit Platter with Mango Sauce ❖

YIELD: 12 SERVINGS

2	large mangos, pitted	2
1/3 cup	unsweetened pineapple juice	90 mL
2 tablespoons	fresh lime juice	30 mL
1 tablespoon	granulated fructose	15 mL
2	papayas (peeled, seeded, and cut into 12 slices)	2
1	pineapple (peeled, cored, and cut into 12 slices)	1
1	honeydew melon (peeled and cut into 12 wedges)	1
1 tablespoon	grated lime peel	30 mL

Cut away mango flesh from skin. Combine mango, pineapple juice, lime juice, and fructose in a blender. Process to a purée. Cover and refrigerate. Arrange papaya slices, pineapple slices, and honeydew wedges on a large platter. Pour mango sauce over fruit. Sprinkle with lime peel.

EACH SERVING CONTAINS: CALORIES: 126 ▲ CARBOHYDRATES: 26 G ▲ EXCHANGE: 2 FRUIT

❖ Fruit Chutney ❖

YIELD: 20 SERVINGS

| 1 cup | raspberry vinegar | 250 mL |
| 1/2 cup | red-wine vinegar | 125 mL |

2 cups	dry white wine	500 mL
1/2 cup	frozen orange-juice concentrate	125 mL
1 cup	crushed pineapple in juice	250 mL
1 cup	diced apple	250 mL
2/3 cup	diced papaya	180 mL
2/3 cup	diced mango	180 mL
1/2 cup	thinly sliced green bell pepper	125 mL
1/2 cup	thinly sliced red bell pepper	125 mL
1/2 cup	thinly sliced yellow bell pepper	125 mL
1/2 cup	granulated sugar replacement	60 mL
6	whole peppercorns	6
1	bay leaf	1
2	tablespoons minced fresh mint	30 mL

Combine vinegars in a large saucepan. Bring to a boil, reduce heat, and simmer to reduce liquid to about 1/2 cup (125 mL). Add wine, orange-juice concentrate, fruit, bell peppers, sugar replacement, peppercorns, and bay leaf. Cook until fruit is soft. Transfer fruit and bell peppers to a bowl. Simmer liquid for about 5 minutes. Return fruit and bell peppers to saucepan. Cook over low heat, stirring occasionally, and reduce mixture to about 2 1/2 cups (725 mL). Remove from heat. Remove peppercorns and bay leaf. Stir in mint. Cover and chill.

EACH SERVING CONTAINS: CALORIES: NEGLIGIBLE ▲ CARBOHYDRATES: NEGLIGIBLE ▲ EXCHANGE: NEGLIGIBLE

❖ Glazed Apricots ❖

YIELD: 8 SERVINGS

1/2 cup	water	125 mL
2 tablespoons	all-natural orange marmalade	30 mL
16	moist dried apricots	16

Combine water and marmalade in a small nonstick saucepan. Heat and stir over medium heat until marmalade is melted. Add apricots. Reduce heat; then cover and simmer until apricots are tender and syrup is reduced and coats apricots (about 20 to 25 minutes). Cool apricots in syrup. Remove apricots from syrup. Drain to remove excess syrup.

EACH SERVING CONTAINS: CALORIES: 24 ▲ CARBOHYDRATES: 6 G ▲ EXCHANGE: 1/2 FRUIT

❖ Cranberry and Raspberry Fool ❖

YIELD: 6 SERVINGS

1 1/2 cups	fresh cranberries	375 mL
1 1/2 cups	fresh raspberries	375 mL
1/4 cup	granulated fructose	60 mL
1/4 cup	raspberry juice	60 mL
2 cups	prepared nondairy whipped topping	500 mL

Combine cranberries, raspberries, and fructose in a food processor or blender. Process into a purée. Transfer to a nonstick saucepan. Stir in raspberry juice. Cook and stir over medium heat until mixture is a thick purée. If desired, press through a sieve to remove seeds. Transfer mixture to a large bowl. Cover and chill mixture thoroughly. To serve: Swirl nondairy whipped topping into cranberry-raspberry mixture. Do not mix thoroughly. Divide evenly among six decorative glasses. Serve immediately.

EACH SERVING CONTAINS: CALORIES: 69 ▲ CARBOHYDRATES: 4 G ▲ EXCHANGE: 1/3 FRUIT, 1 FAT

❖ Poached Bananas in Apple Juice ❖

YIELD: 8 SERVINGS

2 cups	apple juice	500 mL
2 tablespoons	raisins	30 mL
1 tablespoon	vanilla extract	15 mL
1 stick	cinnamon	1 stick
4	firm ripe bananas, cut in half	4
8 tablespoons	nonfat plain yogurt	120 mL

Combine apple juice, raisins, vanilla, and cinnamon in a saucepan. Bring to a light boil. Reduce heat and simmer for 5 minutes. Add bananas; then cover and simmer 6 to 8 minutes or until bananas are just tender. Spoon each half-banana into a small dessert bowl or plate. Remove cinnamon stick from sauce. Divide sauce evenly among the plates. Top each plate with 1 tablespoon (15 mL) of yogurt. Serve immediately.

EACH SERVING CONTAINS: CALORIES: 75 ▲ CARBOHYDRATES: 18 G ▲ EXCHANGE: 1 1/4 FRUIT

❖ Strawberries with Cinnamon Sauce ❖

YIELD: 2 SERVINGS

2/3 cup	water	180 mL
1 teaspoon	ground cinnamon	5 mL
1	cinnamon stick, (6 inches) broken in pieces	1 (9 cm)
1 tablespoon	cold water	15 mL
1 teaspoon	cornstarch	5 mL
3 envelopes	aspartame sweetener	3 envelopes
2 cups	frozen, unsweetened strawberries*	500 mL
2 tablespoons	prepared nondairy whipped topping	30 mL

★ This recipe can be made with fresh strawberries, but there will be less juice.

Combine the 2/3 cup (180 mL) of water, the ground cinnamon, and broken cinnamon pieces in a saucepan. Bring to a boil, reduce heat, and simmer until liquid is about 1/2 cup (125 mL). Remove cinnamon pieces. Dissolve the cornstarch in the 1 tablespoon (15 mL) of cold water. Pour into cinnamon water. Cook and stir until mixture becomes the consistency of a thin syrup. Remove from heat. Allow to cool until pan is cool enough to comfortably put on your hand. Stir in the aspartame sweetener. Place frozen strawberries in a narrow bowl. Pour warm cinnamon mixture over the strawberries. Cover and refrigerate until strawberries are thawed and liquid is chilled. To serve: Divide berries and juice evenly between two decorative glasses. Top each glass with 1 tablespoon (15 mL) of nondairy whipped topping.

EACH SERVING CONTAINS: CALORIES: 55 ▲ CARBOHYDRATES: 13 G ▲ EXCHANGE: 1 FRUIT

ICE CREAM & FROZEN TREATS

❖ Blackberry Buttermilk Sherbet ❖

YIELD: 10 SERVINGS

1 pound bag	frozen, unsweetened blackberries	1 bag (454 g)
1	egg	1
dash	salt	dash
5 envelopes	aspartame sweetener	5 envelopes
2 cups	buttermilk	500 mL

Slightly thaw blackberries. Transfer to a food processor or blender and process to purée. Set aside. Separate egg, setting the white aside. Combine egg yolk, salt, and aspartame sweetener in a bowl. Beat until thick and lemon-colored. Gradually beat in blackberry purée. Blend in buttermilk. Beat egg white until it holds a firm peak. Fold buttermilk-blackberry mixture into beaten egg white just enough to blend. Transfer mixture to an ice-cream freezer and freeze according to manufacturer's directions, or pour mixture into a 9-inch (23-cm) baking pan and place pan in freezer for 2 to 3 hours or until mixture is almost firm. Remove pan from freezer and break mixture into pieces. Place pieces in a chilled bowl. Beat with an electric mixer until smooth but not melted. Transfer back to pan. Cover and freeze until firm.

EACH SERVING CONTAINS: CALORIES: 52 ▲ CARBOHYDRATES: 13 G ▲ EXCHANGE: 1 FRUIT

❖ Blackberry Lemon Parfait ❖

1 package	(1 pound) frozen, unsweetened black-berries	1 package (456 g)
5 envelopes	aspartame sweetener	5 envelopes
1/2 teaspoon	lemon juice	2 mL
1 recipe	Real Lemon Sherbet (page 50)	1 recipe
	or	
1 quart	reduced-calorie lemon sherbet	1 L

Purée blackberries, aspartame sweetener, and lemon juice in a food processor or blender. Measure 1¹/4 cups (310 mL) of the blackberry purée and place in a heavy saucepan. Reserve remaining blackberry purée for the sauce. Cook and stir over medium heat until mixture is reduced to a scant 1 cup (250 mL). Transfer to a bowl and chill for at least 30 minutes. Line a 9 x 5 inch (23 x 12.5-cm) loaf pan with plastic wrap. Transfer 1¹/2 cups (375 mL) of the lemon sherbet to a large bowl. Fold in the reduced blackberry purée. Spread one-third of the remaining lemon sherbet in the bottom of the prepared loaf pan. Cover with the blackberry-lemon mixture. Top with the remaining lemon sherbet. Smooth the top and freeze overnight. When ready to serve, unmould parfait onto a decorative plate, allow to soften slightly, and pour reserved blackberry purée over the top. Slice into eight servings.

EACH SERVING CONTAINS: CALORIES: 27 ▲ CARBOHYDRATES: 7 G ▲ EXCHANGE: 1/2 FRUIT

❖ Blueberry Mountain Dessert ❖

1 package	frozen, unsweetened blueberries (1 pound)	1 package (456 g)
5 envelopes	aspartame sweetener	5 envelopes
1/2 teaspoon	lemon juice	2 mL
2 2/3 cups	reduced-calorie vanilla ice cream	680 mL

| 8 tablespoons | prepared nondairy whipped topping | 120 mL |

Remove 1/2 cup (125 mL) of the blueberries from the package. Set aside. Purée remaining blueberries, aspartame sweetener, and lemon juice in a food processor or blender. Pour the puréed blueberries into a heavy saucepan. Cook and stir over medium heat until mixture is very thick. Transfer to a bowl and chill for at least 30 minutes. Meanwhile, soften the ice cream. Line eight muffin or custard cups with plastic wrap. Pack each cup with 1/3 cup (90 mL) of ice cream. Freeze until firm. To serve: Turn cup upside down on a decorative plate. Remove cup and plastic wrap. Top with 1/8 of the blueberry puree. Top that with 1 tablespoon (15 ml) of the nondairy whipped topping. Garnish with a few of the reserved blueberries. Repeat this procedure with each ice-cream cup.

EACH SERVING CONTAINS: CALORIES: 90 ▲ CARBOHYDRATES: 21 G ▲ EXCHANGE: 2/3 BREAD, 2/3 FRUIT

❖ Blueberry Tofu Cream ❖

YIELD: 8 SERVINGS

1 1/2 cups	fresh or unsweetened frozen blueberries	375 mL
2 teaspoons	lemon juice	10 mL
1 envelope	unflavored gelatin	1 envelope
1/3 cup	water	90 mL
2/3 cup	granulated sugar replacement	180 mL
	or	
1/3 cup	granulated fructose	90 mL
1/2 package	firm tofu (10.5 ounces)	1/2 package (297 g)
1 1/2 cups	low-fat milk	375 mL
1 tablespoon	vanilla extract	15 mL
1/2 cup	prepared non-dairy whipped topping	125 mL

Purée blueberries in a blender. Transfer to a heavy saucepan, and bring to a boil. Reduce heat and simmer, uncovered, until blueberries are reduced to about 1/2 cup (125 mL). Stir in lemon juice and cool to room temperature. In a small saucepan, sprinkle gelatin over water. Allow to soften for 1 minute. Cook and stir over low heat until gelatin dissolves. Set aside to cool. When the gelatin is cooled, combine with sweetener of your choice and tofu in a blender. Blend until smooth. Pour in milk and vanilla. Blend until completely mixed. Add nondairy whipped topping and puréed blueberries. Blend just until mixed. Transfer to an ice-cream freezer or a 9-inch (23-cm) baking pan. Freeze according to freezer manufacturer's instructions or place pan in the freezer and freeze until firm. Break into pieces. Place in a large mixing bowl or food processor. With an electric mixer or food processor, beat mixture until smooth. Return it to the pan and refreeze. To serve: Score into eight equal servings, and place on chilled serving plates. Serve immediately (Tofu Cream softens quickly).

EACH SERVING CONTAINS, WITH GRANULATED SUGAR REPLACEMENT: CALORIES: 50 ▲ CARBOHYDRATES: 7 G ▲ EXCHANGE: 1/2 FRUIT, 1/3 LOW-FAT MILK

EACH SERVING CONTAINS WITH GRANULATED FRUCTOSE: CALORIES: 92 ▲ CARBOHYDRATES: 17 G ▲ EXCHANGE: 2/3 FRUIT, 1/2 LOW-FAT MILK

❖ Chocolate Graham Cracker ❖ Ice-Cream Pie

YIELD: 12 SERVINGS

| 1 quart | reduced-calorie chocolate ice cream | 1 L |
| 1 cup | graham-cracker crumbs | 250 mL |

Slightly soften the ice cream. Spread half of the ice cream in the bottom of an 8-inch (20-cm) pie pan. Sprinkle half of the graham-cracker crumbs over the surface of the ice cream. (If mixture is very soft, you might want to place in freezer until surface is firm before continuing.) Spread remaining softened ice cream over the crumb top. Sprinkle with remaining graham-cracker crumbs. Freeze pie until firm. Cut into 12 wedges to serve.

EACH SERVING CONTAINS: CALORIES: 82 ▲ CARBOHYDRATES: 14 G ▲ EXCHANGE: 1 BREAD

❖ Chocolate Ice-Cream Cake ❖

YIELD: 10 SERVINGS

| 1 | prepared, sugar-free chocolate cake (8 inches) | 1 (23 cm) |
| 2 1/2 cups | reduced-calorie chocolate ice cream | 625 mL |

Chill cake thoroughly. Cut cake in half horizontally. Slightly soften the ice cream. Spread 1 cup (250 mL) of the chocolate ice cream between the layers of the cake. Spread the remaining chocolate ice cream on the top of the cake. Freeze until firm. Allow cake to stand at room temperature for 10 minutes. Cut into 10 wedges to serve.

EACH SERVING CONTAINS: CALORIES: 150 ▲ CARBOHYDRATES: 21 G ▲ EXCHANGE: 1 1/2 BREAD, 1/2 FAT

❖ Double-Decker Mocha ❖ Ice-Cream Pie

YIELD: 8 SERVINGS

2 tablespoons	instant coffee powder	30 mL
1 tablespoon	boiling water	15 mL
1 quart	reduced-calorie vanilla ice cream	1 L
1	prepared chocolate pie crust (8 inches)	1 (20 cm)
1 quart	reduced-calorie chocolate ice cream	1 L
1 cup	prepared, nondairy whipped topping	250 mL

Dissolve the coffee powder in the boiling water. Allow to cool completely. Slightly soften the vanilla ice cream. Stir coffee liquid into vanilla ice cream. Freeze until almost firm. Spread coffee ice cream in the bottom of the chocolate crust. Slightly soften chocolate ice cream. Spread chocolate ice cream on top of coffee ice cream. Freeze until firm. Just before serving, spoon nondairy whipped topping into a pastry bag that has been fitted with a small star tip. Pipe rosettes decoratively on the top of the pie.

EACH SERVING CONTAINS: CALORIES: 205 ▲ CARBOHYDRATES: 29 G ▲ EXCHANGE: 2 BREAD, 1/2 FAT

❖ Fresh Apple Cinnamon Ice Cream ❖

YIELD: 16 SERVINGS

2 tablespoons	margarine	30 mL
3 large	Red Delicious apples (peeled, cored, and chopped)	3 large
1	cinnamon stick (2 inches)	1 (5 cm)
2 quarts	vanilla ice cream	2 L

Melt margarine in a heavy skillet over medium heat. Add apples and cinnamon stick. Sauté for 5 minutes. Remove from heat and cool completely. Soften the ice cream in the refrigerator until it can be whipped with an electric beater. Transfer the ice cream to a large mixing bowl. Whip the ice cream on low until smooth. Remove cinnamon stick. Fold the apple mixture into the ice cream. Transfer to a covered freezer container. Freeze for several hours before serving. If the ice cream becomes solid, soften it slightly in the refrigerator before serving.

EACH SERVING CONTAINS: CALORIES: 110 ▲ CARBOHYDRATES: 19 G ▲ EXCHANGE: 1 BREAD,1/4 FRUIT

❖ Fresh Raspberry Ice Cream ❖

YIELD: 16 SERVINGS

2 quarts	vanilla ice cream	2 L
1 quart	fresh raspberries	1 L
1 tablespoon	granulated fructose	15 mL

Soften the ice cream in the refrigerator until it can be whipped with an electric beater. Wash and clean the raspberries. Transfer to a medium sized bowl. With a fork, slightly crush raspberries. Sprinkle with fructose. Stir, cover, and allow to rest 30 minutes. Transfer the ice cream to a large mixing bowl. Whip the ice cream on low until smooth. Fold in the crushed raspberries, allowing the raspberries to marbleize the ice cream. Transfer the ice cream to a covered freezer container. Freeze for several hours before serving. If the ice cream becomes solid, soften it slightly in the refrigerator before serving.

EACH SERVING CONTAINS: CALORIES: 121 ▲ CARBOHYDRATES: 21 G ▲ EXCHANGE: 1 BREAD, 1/2 FRUIT

❖ Frozen Strawberry Mousse ❖

Lovely! You'll be proud to serve this.

2 cups	fresh strawberries, hulled	500 mL
1 tablespoon	sugar	15 mL
1/2 tablespoon	gelatin	7.5 mL
3 tablespoon	cold water	45 mL
5 packages	aspartame sweetener	5 packages
2 cups	frozen, low-fat non-dairy whipped topping	500 mL

Cut the strawberries into a medium bowl. Sprinkle with sugar and set aside. Sprinkle the gelatin over the cold water in the top of a double boiler. Bring the water to a boil in the bottom of the double boiler. Put on the top part of the double boiler and heat the gelatin mixture until it dissolves. Remove from heat. Mash the strawberries. Fold in the gelatin and the whipped topping. Freeze.

EACH SERVING CONTAINS: CALORIES: 60 ▲ CARBOHYDRATES: 9 G ▲ EXCHANGE: 1/2 FRUIT, 1/2 FAT

❖ Frozen Raspberry Mousse ❖
with Black–Raspberry Sauce

YIELD: 8 SERVINGS

2 packages	sugar-free raspberry gelatin (4 servings)	2 packages
2 cups	frozen black raspberries, slightly thawed	500 mL
1/4 cup	water	60 mL
1 tablespoon	cider vinegar	15 mL
1 stick	cinnamon	1 stick
1	egg white, beaten stiff	1
1 cup	prepared non-dairy whipped topping	250 mL

Prepare both packages of raspberry gelatin together, as directed on package. Allow to completely set. Meanwhile, combine 1 1/4 cups (310 mL) of the black raspberries, water, cider vinegar, and cinnamon stick in a saucepan. Bring to a boil, reduce heat, and simmer for 5 to 6 minutes. If desired, strain mixture to remove seeds. Cool completely. Remove cinnamon stick. Beat the set raspberry gelatin with a wire whisk or electric mixer. Then beat 1/4 cup (60 mL) of the black-raspberry sauce into the gelatin. Stir in the stiffly beaten egg white and the nondairy whipped topping. Spoon gelatin mixture into eight decorative glasses or bowls. Freeze until firm. To serve: top frozen gelatin mixture with the remaining black-raspberry sauce. Garnish with the reserved 3/4 cup (190 mL) of black raspberries.

EACH SERVING CONTAINS: CALORIES: 22 ▲ CARBOHYDRATES: 4 G ▲ EXCHANGE: 1/3 FRUIT

❖ Frozen Watermelon Pops ❖

YIELD: 8 SERVINGS

3 cups	puréed watermelon	750 mL
1 tablespoons	lemon juice	15 mL
1 envelope	unflavored gelatin	1 envelope
1 package	sugar-free strawberry gelatin powder	1 package
2 cups	frozen low-fat non-dairy whipped topping, softened	500 mL

In a saucepan, combine the watermelon puree, lemon juice, and unflavored gelatin. Set aside for five minutes. Heat over a low flame, stirring until the gelatin dissolves. Remove from the heat and stir in the strawberry gelatin. Mix until smooth and the gelatin is dissolved. Refrigerate for 15 minutes, to bring to room temperature. In a large mixing bowl, fold together the gelatin mixture and whipped topping. Distribute into eight 4-ounze (100 g) paper cups. Freeze. To serve, peel back the paper.

EACH SERVING CONTAINS: CALORIES: 66 ▲ CARBOHYDRATES: 9 G ▲ EXCHANGE: 1/2 FRUIT, 1/2 FAT

❖ Grand Marnier Ice Cream ❖

2 quarts	vanilla ice cream	2 L
1/3 cup	Grand Marnier	90 mL
1 recipe	Sweetened Citrus Peel (page 222; use orange peel)	1 recipe

Soften the ice cream in the refrigerator until it can be whipped with an electric beater. Transfer the ice cream to a large mixing bowl. Whip the ice cream on low until smooth. Beat in the Grand Marnier. Transfer the ice cream to a covered freezer container. Freeze for several hours before serving. If the ice cream becomes solid, soften it slightly in the refrigerator before serving. Garnish with Candied Orange Peel.

EACH SERVING CONTAINS: CALORIES: 135 ▲ CARBOHYDRATES: 22 G ▲ EXCHANGE: 1 1/2 BREAD

❖ Grape Sherbet ❖

1/2 cup	grape juice	125 mL
1/2 cup	low-fat milk	125 mL
1/2 teaspoon	vanilla extract	2 mL
1/3 cup	prepared, nondairy whipped topping	90 mL

Combine grape juice, milk, and vanilla in a bowl. (Mixture will appear to have curdled slightly.) Stir to combine ingredients. Place bowl in freezer and chill until mixture is almost firm. Remove bowl from freezer and break mixture into pieces. Beat with an electric mixer until smooth but not melted. Beat in nondairy whipped topping. Cover and freeze to desired consistency.

EACH SERVING CONTAINS: CALORIES: 108 ▲ CARBOHYDRATES: 13 G ▲ EXCHANGE: 1/2 FRUIT, 1/2 LOW-FAT MILK

❖ Honeydew Sherbet ❖

If you don't have an ice cream machine, this won't be as creamy, but it will still taste fabulous.

1/2	medium honeydew melon	1/2
1 3/4 cups	frozen, low-fat non-dairy whipped topping, thawed	435 mL
1 tablespoon	Triple Sec (optional)	15 mL
dash	aspartame sweetener to taste (optional)	dash

Cut the melon in half and remove the seeds. Peel the melon. Scoop the soft pulp into chunks. Purée in a food processor. Measure 1 3/4 cups (435 mL) of melon purée. Discard any extra, or reserve it for another use. Put the melon into a mixing bowl. Add the whipped topping. Mix to blend. Add the Triple Sec and aspartame, if desired. Process in an ice cream machine according to the manufacturer's directions.

EACH SERVING CONTAINS: CALORIES: 63 ▲ CARBOHYDRATES: 11 G ▲ EXCHANGE: 2/3 FRUIT, 1/2 FAT

❖ Ice-Cream Loaf with ❖ Raspberry Orange Sauce

YIELD: 12 SERVINGS

1 quart	reduced -calorie vanilla ice cream	1 L
1 package	frozen, unsweetened red raspberries (12 ounces)	1 package (340 g)
1 tablespoon	all natural apricot preserves	15 mL
1/3 cup	orange juice	90 mL
1 tablespoon	lemon juice	15 mL
1 1/3 cups	prepared nondairy whipped topping	340 mL
12	thinly sliced lemon-peel strips	12

Slightly soften ice cream. Line a 9 x 5-inch (23 x 12.5-cm) loaf pan with plastic wrap. Transfer softened ice cream to loaf pan. Freeze. Purée raspberries with the apricot preserves in a blender. If desired, strain to remove seeds. Add orange juice and lemon juice and stir to mix. Cover and refrigerate. To assemble: Unmould the ice cream onto a chilled platter. Spoon nondairy whipped topping into a pastry bag that has been fitted with a star tip. Pipe rosettes around base and 12 rosettes down middle of loaf of ice cream. Place a lemon strip on each of the middle rosettes. To serve: Spoon a small amount of raspberry orange sauce on one side of 12 chilled dessert plates. Cut ice-cream loaf into 12 slices. Place a slice of ice cream beside (not on top of) the raspberry orange sauce. Then drizzle the remaining sauce on each of the 12 slices.

EACH SERVING CONTAINS: CALORIES: 70 ▲ CARBOHYDRATES: 15 G ▲ EXCHANGE: 2/3 BREAD, 1/3 FRUIT

❖ Lemon Ice Cream ❖

YIELD: 4 SERVINGS

You don't need an ice cream machine for this one!

1 cup	skim milk	250 mL
1 package	lemon gelatin powder, sugar-free	1 package
1 tablespoon	lemon juice	15 mL
2 packages	sugar substitute	2 packages
1 cup	frozen low-fat non-dairy whipped topping	250 mL
1 teaspoon	vanilla extract	5 mL

Scald the milk in a medium saucepan. Stir in the lemon gelatin and the lemon juice. Mix to dissolve the powder. Put the saucepan in the refrigerator to cool but not to set, 15 to 20 minutes. Stir in the sugar substitute and lemon juice. Fold in the whipped topping and vanilla extract. Blend thoroughly. Freeze in an ice cube tray until set. Turn the frozen mixture into a food processor or electric mixer bowl. Process until light and fluffy. Return to the freezer tray. Freeze for an additional 3 hours.

EACH SERVING CONTAINS: CALORIES: 68 ▲ CARBOHYDRATES: 8 G ▲ EXCHANGE: 1/2 FRUIT, 1/4 HIGH FAT MEAT

❖ Luscious Lemon Ice-Cream Pie ❖

| 1 quart | reduced-calorie vanilla ice cream | 1 L |
| 1 package | (4 servings) sugar-free lemon-pudding mix, prepared | 1 package |

Slightly soften ice cream. Spread half of the ice cream on the bottom of an 8-inch (20-cm) pie pan. Spread half of the prepared lemon pudding on top of the ice cream. Spoon remaining ice cream over the top of the lemon pudding, spreading lightly. Spoon remaining lemon pudding over the top of the ice cream. Use a small knife to swirl the top pudding layer into the ice-cream layer below. Freeze until firm. Cut into 12 wedges to serve.

EACH SERVING CONTAINS: CALORIES: 50 ▲ CARBOHYDRATES: 9 G ▲ EXCHANGE: 2/3 BREAD

❖ Maple Ice-Cream Tart ❖

1 quart	reduced-calorie vanilla ice cream	1 L
1/2 cup	chopped toasted pecans	125 mL
2 teaspoons	caramel flavoring	10 mL
3/4 cup	sugar-free maple syrup	190 mL

Soften the ice cream just enough to stir. Stir in toasted pecans and caramel flavoring. Pack into a 9 inch (23-cm) tart pan with a removable bottom, lined with plastic wrap. Refreeze until firm. To serve: Carefully remove ice cream tart from pan by turning it upside down on a decorative plate. Remove plastic wrap. Pour maple syrup over top of ice cream tart. Serve immediately .

EACH SERVING CONTAINS: CALORIES: 92 ▲ CARBOHYDRATES: 10 G ▲ EXCHANGE: 2/3 BREAD, 2/3 FAT

❖ Mixed Fruit Sherbet ❖

YIELD: 8 SERVINGS

This is really different. If you like fruity desserts you'll love this one.

2 cups	fresh strawberries, or whole frozen, thawed	500 mL
1	ripe banana	1
1/2 cup	orange pieces	125 mL
6 packets	aspartame sweetener	90 mL
2 cups	frozen, low-fat non-dairy whipped topping, thawed	500 mL
1 1/2 cups	skim milk	375 mL

Wash, hull, and slice the strawberries. Put them in a mixing bowl. Peel and slice the banana. Mash the two fruits together with a fork. Stir in the remaining ingredients and mix until everything is evenly combined. Process in an ice cream machine according to manufacturer's directions.

EACH SERVING CONTAINS: CALORIES: 92 ▲ CARBOHYDRATES: 15 G ▲ EXCHANGE: 1 STARCH/BREAD

❖ Orange Frost ❖

YIELD: 4 SERVINGS

This recipe works best with the freezer turned to its coldest setting.

1 cup	orange juice	250 mL
2 tablespoons	lemon juice	30 mL
1 teaspoon	orange flavoring	5 mL
1 cup	frozen, low-fat non-dairy whipped topping, softened	250 mL

Combine the orange juice and lemon juice in a mixing bowl. Stir in the orange flavoring. Pour the mixture into four freezer-safe dessert dishes (i.e., paper, Pyrex, metal). Freeze. Serve with whipped topping.

EACH SERVING CONTAINS: CALORIES: 70 ▲ CARBOHYDRATES: 11 G ▲ EXCHANGE: 2/3 FRUIT, 1/2 FAT

❖ Orange Sherbet ❖

YIELD: 8 SERVINGS

3 1/2 cups	orange juice	875 mL
1 envelope	unflavored gelatin	1 envelope
5 envelopes	aspartame sweetener	5 envelopes
1 cup	low-fat milk	250 mL
	orange food coloring*	

* If you don't have orange food coloring, combine red and yellow to make orange.

In a saucepan, mix orange juice, unflavored gelatin, and aspartame sweetener. Heat and stir until gelatin and aspartame sweetener are dissolved and mixture is slightly warmed. Remove from heat. Stir in milk. (Mixture will appear to have curdled slightly.) Mix all ingredients. Freeze in an ice-cream freezer, according to manufacturer's directions, or pour mixture into a 9-inch (23-cm) baking pan and place pan in freezer for 2 to 3 hours or until mixture is almost firm. Remove pan from freezer and break mixture into pieces. Place pieces in a chilled bowl. Beat with an electric mixer until smooth but not melted. Transfer back to pan. Cover and freeze until firm.

EACH SERVING CONTAINS: CALORIES: 62 ▲ CARBOHYDRATES: 14 G ▲ EXCHANGE: 1 FRUIT

❖ Piña Colada Sherbet ❖

YIELD: 4 SERVINGS

You don't make this sherbet and freeze it; you freeze the pineapple ahead of time.

20 ounces	pineapple chunks in juice, no sugar added	550 g
2 teaspoons	coconut extract	10 mL
1 cup	frozen, low-fat non-dairy whipped topping	250 mL

Drain and freeze the pineapple chunks. Put them into a food processor. If the pineapple sticks to the container, run water on the outside.

Add the coconut extract and blend until mushy. Transfer to a medium mixing bowl. Fold in the whipped topping. Serve immediately.

EACH SERVING CONTAINS: CALORIES: 127 ▲ CARBOHYDRATES: 26 G ▲ EXCHANGE: 2 FRUIT, 1/2 FAT

❖ Pineapple Sherbet ❖

YIELD: 8 SERVINGS

3 1/4 cups	unsweetened pineapple juice	875 mL
1/4 cup	crushed pineapple in juice	60 mL
1 envelope	unflavored gelatin	1 envelope
5 envelopes	aspartame sweetener	5 envelopes
1 cup	low-fat milk	250 mL

In a saucepan, mix pineapple juice, crushed pineapple with juice, unflavored gelatin, and aspartame sweetener. Heat and stir until gelatin and aspartame sweetener are dissolved and mixture is slightly warmed. Remove from heat. Stir in milk. (Mixture will appear to have curdled slightly.) Mix all ingredients. Freeze in an ice-cream freezer, according to manufacturer's directions, or pour mixture into a 9-inch (23-cm) baking pan and place pan in freezer for 2 to 3 hours or until mixture is almost firm. Remove pan from freezer and break pineapple mixture into pieces. Place pieces in a chilled bowl. Beat with an electric mixer until smooth but not melted. Transfer back to pan. Cover and freeze until firm.

EACH SERVING CONTAINS: CALORIES: 76 ▲ CARBOHYDRATES: 15 G ▲ EXCHANGE: 1 FRUIT

❖ Pink 'n' Pretty ❖ Strawberry Frozen Dessert

YIELD: 10 SERVINGS

1 box	(8 ounce) sugar-free white cake mix	1 box (227 g)
1 package	(4 servings) sugar-free strawberry gelatin	1 package

1 cup	boiling water	250 mL
1 cup	frozen, unsweetened strawberries	250 mL
1	egg white, beaten stiff	1
1/4 cup	prepared, nondairy whipped topping	60 mL

Prepare cake mix as directed on package in a loaf pan. Cool in pan for 5 to 6 minutes. Move to rack and cool completely. Combine strawberry gelatin and boiling water in a mixing bowl. Stir to completely dissolve gelatin. Stir in strawberries. Allow to set. When gelatin has set, beat with an electric mixer. Stir in egg white and nondairy whipped topping. Chill until almost set. Cut cake into four layers. Divide the strawberry gelatin evenly among the layers and top. Freeze until firm (at least 6 hours). To serve: Heat a long knife in hot water, and wipe dry. Cut cake straight down (do not use a sawing back-and-forth motion). Clean knife between each serving.

EACH SERVING CONTAINS: CALORIES: 105 ▲ CARBOHYDRATES: 15 G ▲ EXCHANGE: 1 BREAD

❖ Quick Orange-Yogurt Pops ❖

YIELD: 8 SERVINGS

1 can	(6 ounces) orange-juice concentrate	1 can (210 g)
3/4 cup	water	190 mL
1 cup	plain low-fat yogurt	250 mL

Combine ingredients in a blender. Process until well blended. Divide mixture evenly among eight paper drinking cups. Place in freezer and freeze until frozen. If desired, when pops are partially frozen, place a wooden stick in middle of each pop. Freeze completely.

EACH SERVING CONTAINS: CALORIES: 68 ▲ CARBOHYDRATES: 9 G ▲ EXCHANGE: 1 FRUIT

❖ Real Lemon Sherbet ❖

YIELD: 8 SERVINGS

3 cups	water	750 mL
1 envelope	unflavored gelatin	1 envelope
5 envelopes	aspartame sweetener	5 envelopes
3/4 cup	fresh lemon juice	190 mL
1 cup	low-fat milk	250 mL
1 teaspoon	grated lemon peel	5 mL

In a saucepan, mix water, unflavored gelatin, and aspartame sweetener. Heat and stir until gelatin and aspartame sweetener are dissolved and mixture is slightly warmed. Remove from heat. Stir in lemon juice, milk, and lemon peel. (Mixture will appear to have curdled slightly.) Mix all ingredients. Freeze in an ice-cream freezer, according to manufacturer's directions, or pour mixture into a 9-inch (23-cm) baking pan and place pan in freezer for 2 to 3 hours or until mixture is almost firm. Remove pan from freezer and break mixture into pieces. Place pieces in a chilled bowl, and beat with an electric mixer until smooth but not melted. Or process pieces in a food processor in small batches using the pulse or on/off switch. Transfer back to pan. Cover and freeze until firm.

EACH SERVING CONTAINS: CALORIES: 15 ▲ CARBOHYDRATES: NEGLIGIBLE ▲ EXCHANGE: NEGLIGIBLE

❖ Strawberry Ice ❖

YIELD: 6 SERVINGS, WITH GRANULATED SUGAR REPLACEMENT

1 quart	fresh or frozen unsweetened strawberries	1 L
1/2 cup	water	125 mL
1/2 cup	granulated sugar replacement	125 mL
	or	
1/4 cup	granulated fructose	60 mL
2 tablespoons	lemon juice	30 mL

In a food processor or blender, process strawberries into a puree. Add water, sweetener of your choice, and lemon juice. Process to mix.

Pour mixture into a 9 inch (23-cm) baking pan. Freeze until firm. Remove from freezer and allow to stand at room temperature for 5 to 6 minutes. Break strawberry mixture into pieces and transfer to a large mixing bowl or food processor. Whip or process until smooth. Serve immediately or cover and refreeze. Before serving, allow mixture to stand at room temperature until slightly softened. Then scoop into six decorative glasses or bowls. (This dessert can also be frozen, in either six paper drinking cups or six cupcake cups lined with plastic wrap. At serving time, remove from cups.)

EACH SERVING CONTAINS: CALORIES: 36 ▲ CARBOHYDRATES: 8 G ▲ EXCHANGE: ²/₃ FRUIT

❖ Strawberry Sorbet ❖

YIELD: 8 SERVINGS

1 envelope	unflavored gelatin	1 envelope
1 1/2 cups	cool water	375 mL
1 package	(1 pound) frozen strawberries, slightly thawed	1 package (454 g)
1/2 cup	reduced-calorie cranberry-juice cocktail	125 mL
1/2 cup	granulated sugar replacement	125 mL
2 tablespoons	lemon juice	30 mL

In a medium-sized saucepan, sprinkle gelatin over cool water. Allow to soften for 1 minute. Cook and stir over low heat until gelatin has dissolved. Cool to room temperature. Meanwhile, combine strawberries and cranberry-juice cocktail in a blender or food processor. Process to a puree. Blend in sweetener of your choice and lemon juice. When gelatin has cooled, blend into strawberry mixture. Pour into a 9 inch (23-cm) baking pan; freeze until firm (about 3 hours). Break into pieces. Place in a large mixing bowl or food processor. With an electric mixer or food processor, beat mixture until smooth. Return to pan and refreeze. Before serving, allow sorbet to stand at room temperature for about 15 minutes or until slightly softened.

EACH SERVING CONTAINS: CALORIES: 24 ▲ CARBOHYDRATES: 4 G ▲ EXCHANGE: ¹/₃ FRUIT

❖ Strawberry–Banana Frozen Yogurt ❖

1 package	(4 servings) sugar-free strawberry-banana gelatin	1 package
1 cup	boiling water	250 mL
1/2 cup	cold water	125 mL
1 cup	fresh or frozen straw-berries, diced and mashed	250 mL
1 cup	low-fat vanilla yogurt	250 mL
2 cups	frozen, low-fat non-dairy whipped topping, thawed	500 mL

Put the gelatin into a mixing bowl. Add the boiling water. Stir to dissolve. Add the cold water and the strawberries. In another bowl, use a wire whisk to combine the yogurt and whipped topping. Pour the gelatin mixture into the yogurt mixture. Mix thoroughly. Process in an ice cream machine according to manufacturer's directions or pour into a brownie pan and freeze.

EACH SERVING CONTAINS: CALORIES: 129 ▲ CARBOHYDRATES: 10 G ▲ EXCHANGE: 1 MILK, 1 LEAN MEAT

❖ Tart–Cherry Ice Cream ❖

YIELD: 16 SERVINGS

2 quarts	vanilla ice cream	2 L
1 pound bag	frozen, unsweetened, pitted tart red cherries	1 bag (456 g)

Soften the ice cream in the refrigerator until it can be whipped with an electric beater. Meanwhile, thaw, drain, and pat the cherries dry with paper towels. Transfer the ice cream to a large mixing bowl. Whip the ice cream on low until smooth. Fold in the cherries. Transfer the ice cream to a covered freezer container. Freeze for several hours before serving. If the ice cream becomes solid, soften it slightly in the refrigerator before serving.

EACH SERVING CONTAINS: CALORIES: 98 ▲ CARBOHYDRATES: 15 G ▲ EXCHANGE: 1 BREAD

❖ Toasted-Walnut Chocolate-Chip ❖ Ice Cream

YIELD: 16 SERVINGS

2 quarts	vanilla ice cream	2 L
1 cup	English walnut pieces	250 mL
1/2 cup	mini-semisweet chocolate chips	125 mL

Soften the ice cream in the refrigerator until it can be whipped with an electric beater. Meanwhile, place walnuts in a nonstick skillet. Place over medium-low heat, and shake pan occasionally to toast the walnuts. Remove from heat and allow to cool completely. Transfer the ice cream to a large mixing bowl. Whip the ice cream on low until smooth. Fold in the toasted walnuts and chocolate chips. Transfer the ice cream to a covered freezer container. Freeze for several hours before serving. If the ice cream becomes solid, soften it slightly in the refrigerator before serving.

EACH SERVING CONTAINS: CALORIES: 166 ▲ CARBOHYDRATES: 14 G ▲ EXCHANGE: 1 BREAD, 1 1/2 FAT

❖ Tortoni ❖

YIELD: 4 SERVINGS

2/3 cup	ice water	165 mL
2/3 cup	dry skim milk	165 mL
1/4 cup	lemon juice	60 mL
3 packages	sugar substitute	3 packages
2 tablespoons	sherry	30 mL
1/2 teaspoon	vanilla extract	3 mL
1/2 teaspoon	almond extract	3 mL
1/4 cup	sliced toasted almonds (optional)	60 mL
6	maraschino cherries, chopped	6

In an electric mixer bowl or food processor, beat the ice water and dry milk until the mixture begins to thicken. Add the lemon juice and sugar substitute and beat until thick. Beat in the sherry and extracts. Fold in the toasted almonds, if you are using them, and the cherry pieces. Freeze.

EACH SERVING CONTAINS: CALORIES: 98 ▲ CARBOHYDRATES: 15 G ▲ EXCHANGE: 1 MILK

❖ Triple Sherbet Dessert ❖

YIELD: 12 SERVINGS

2 cups	reduced-calorie raspberry sherbet	500 mL
2 cups	reduced-calorie lemon sherbet	500 mL
2 cups	reduced-calorie lime sherbet	500 mL

Slightly soften raspberry sherbet. Spread into an 8-inch (20-cm) pie pan. Refreeze until firm. Slightly soften lemon sherbet. Spread over the surface of the raspberry sherbet. Refreeze. Slightly soften lime sherbet. Spread over the surface of the lemon sherbet. Refreeze until firm. Cut into 12 wedges to serve.

EACH SERVING CONTAINS: CALORIES: 52 ▲ CARBOHYDRATES: 9 G ▲ EXCHANGE: 2/3 BREAD

❖ Watermelon Sorbet ❖

YIELD: 8 SERVINGS

1 envelope	unflavored gelatin	1 envelope
1 1/2 cups	cool water	375 mL
1 1/2 quarts	watermelon cut in 1-inch (2.5-cm) chunks	1 1/2 L
1/2 cup	granulated sugar replacement	125 mL
2 tablespoons	lemon juice	30 mL

In a medium-sized saucepan, sprinkle gelatin over cool water. Allow to soften for 1 minute. Cook and stir over low heat until gelatin has dissolved. Cool to room temperature. Meanwhile, puree watermelon chunks in a blender or food processor. Blend in sweetener and lemon juice. When gelatin has cooled, blend into watermelon mixture. Pour into a 9 inch (23-cm) baking pan; freeze until firm (about 3 hours). Break into pieces. Place in a large mixing bowl or food processor. With an electric mixer or food processor, beat mixture until smooth. Return to pan and refreeze. Before serving, allow sorbet to stand at room temperature for about 15 minutes or until slightly softened.

EACH SERVING CONTAINS: CALORIES: 30 ▲ CARBOHYDRATES: 7 G ▲ EXCHANGE: 1/2 FRUIT

ICE BOX PIES

❖ Blueberry–Yogurt Pie ❖

YIELD: 8 SERVINGS

A substantial pie that works well after a light dinner.

1 tablespoon	unflavored gelatin	15 mL
1/4 cup	water	60 mL
2 large	egg yolks, slightly beaten	2 large
1 cup	fat-free cottage cheese	250 mL
1 cup	low-fat blueberry yogurt	250 mL
1 cup	frozen, low-fat non-dairy whipped topping, thawed	250 mL
4 teaspoons	aspartame sweetener	20 mL
1/2 cup	fresh or frozen blueberries	125 mL
1	frozen pie crust, baked	1

In a small saucepan, combine the gelatin and water. Stir. Let stand for a few minutes to soften. Add the egg yolks. Cook, stirring constantly, over low heat until the mixture begins to thicken. Set aside. Put the cottage cheese into a large mixing bowl. Stir in the gelatin mixture. Add the yogurt, whipped topping, and aspartame, stirring well after each ingredient. Turn into the pie shell. Refrigerate 6 to 8 hours before serving. Top with fresh blueberries and additional non-dairy topping, if desired.

EACH SERVING CONTAINS: CALORIES: 170 ▲ CARBOHYDRATES: 19 G ▲ EXCHANGE: 1 STARCH/BREAD, 1 HIGH FAT MEAT, 1 FAT

❖ Double Blueberry Pie ❖

YIELD: 8 SERVINGS

This is called double blueberry because you cook half the blueberries and not the other half. This makes for great flavor and texture.

6 ounces	fat-free cream cheese	160 g
2 tablespoons	skim milk	30 mL
1/2 teaspoon	lemon extract	3 mL
4 cups	fresh blueberries or frozen, unsweetened	1 L
1 tablespoon	lemon juice	15 mL
	water	
2 tablespoons	cornstarch	30 mL
7 teaspoons	aspartame sweetener	35 mL
1	frozen pie crust, baked	1

Put the cream cheese into a mixing bowl. Add the skim milk and lemon extract. With an electric mixer, whip until smooth and soft. Distribute the cream cheese mixture onto the bottom of the pie shell. Be careful not to damage the shell as you coat it with the cream cheese. Measure two cups (500 mL) of blueberries and put them on top of the cream cheese in the pie shell. Mash the remaining berries and put them into a two–cup (500 mL) measure. Add the teaspoon (30 mL) of lemon juice to the blueberries in the measuring cup. Add enough water so the combination of mashed blueberries, lemon juice, and water comes up to 1 1/2 cups (375 mL). Transfer this mixture to a small saucepan. Add the cornstarch and stir to blend. Place the pan over heat and bring to a boil. Stir constantly. Cook for a minute or two until the mixture is thick. Set aside to cool. When the mixture is lukewarm, stir in the aspartame. Spoon the sauce over the fresh blueberries in the pie crust. Refrigerate for at least 3 hours. Serve with dollops of your favorite white topping, if desired.

EACH SERVING CONTAINS: CALORIES: 157 ▲ CARBOHYDRATES (G): 23 G ▲ EXCHANGE: 1 STARCH/BREAD, 1/2 FRUIT, 1 FAT

❖ Apricot Cream Pie ❖

Try decorating the top with cut pieces of dried apricots.

2 large	egg yolks, beaten lightly	2 large
1 1/2 cups	apricot nectar with no added sugar	375 mL
1 envelope	unflavored gelatin	1 envelope
1 tablespoon	lemon juice (fresh is best)	15 mL
2 cups	frozen, low-fat non-dairy whipped topping, thawed	500 mL
1	frozen pie crust, baked	1

Put the egg yolks and apricot nectar into a medium saucepan. Use a wire whisk to blend the two. Cook over medium heat, stirring constantly, until slightly thickened. Remove from heat. In a small bowl, combine the gelatin and the lemon juice. Stir and let sit for a minute or two. Add to the hot mixture. Stir. Cool for 15 to 20 minutes. Pour into a mixing bowl. Stir in the whipped topping. Pour into the prepared pie shell. Refrigerate 3 to 4 hours or until set.

EACH SERVING CONTAINS: CALORIES: 165 ▲ CARBOHYDRATES: 20 G ▲ EXCHANGE: 1 STARCH/BREAD, 1/3 FRUIT, 1 1/2 FAT

❖ Lime Chiffon Pie ❖

1 package	(4 servings) sugar-free lime gelatin	1 package
1/2 cup	boiling water	125 mL
1 tablespoon	lime juice (Key lime is best)	15 mL
1/2 cup	cold water ice cubes	125 mL
2 cups	frozen, low-fat non-dairy whipped topping, thawed	500 mL
1	frozen pie crust, baked	1

Put the gelatin in a large mixing bowl. Add the boiling water and stir until it is dissolved. Add the lime juice. Put the cold water into a one-cup measuring cup. Add ice cubes until reaching the one-cup mark. Put this water and ice mixture into a blender or food processor. Add the gelatin mixture and blend until the ice has disappeared. Add the whipped topping. Blend again until mixed. Spoon into prepared pie crust. Refrigerate at least 1 hour before serving.

EACH SERVING CONTAINS: CALORIES: 124 ▲ CARBOHYDRATES: 13 G ▲ EXCHANGE: 1 STARCH/BREAD, 1 FAT

❖ Lemon Chiffon Pie ❖

YIELD: 8 SERVINGS

Prepare the Lime Chiffon Pie on page 58, substituting lemon gelatin for the lime, and lemon juice for the Key lime juice.

EACH SERVING CONTAINS: CALORIES: 124 ▲ CARBOHYDRATES: 13 G ▲ EXCHANGE: 1 STARCH/BREAD, 1 FAT

❖ Raspberry Shimmer Pie ❖

YIELD: 8 SERVINGS

This layered pie looks and tastes spectacular. Don't be overwhelmed by the length of the directions-there is nothing tricky to do.

4 cups	raspberries (fresh or frozen whole berries without syrup)	1 L
1 cup	water	250 mL
3 tablespoons	cornstarch	45 mL
2 teaspoons	lemon juice	10 mL
7 teaspoons	aspartame sweetener	35 mL
3 ounces	fat-free cream cheese	80 g
1 tablespoon	skim milk	15 mL
1	frozen pie crust, baked	1

Wash the fresh berries (if you are using them) very gently in cold water. Spread them to dry in a single layer on paper towels. Put 1 cup (250 mL) of the raspberries and 2/3 cup (165 mL) of the water into a small saucepan over medium heat. Simmer for 3 to 4 minutes. Strain the liquid to remove the seeds. Return the liquid to the saucepan. Add the remaining 1/3 cup (80 mL) water and the cornstarch. Stir. Cook until the mixture is thick, stirring constantly. Add the lemon juice. Stir. Set aside to cool. When cool, add the aspartame and mix thoroughly.

Put the cream cheese into a mixing bowl. Add the milk. Whip until soft. Spread the cream cheese mixture very gently over the bottom of the pie crust, being careful not to damage the crust. Spread most of the reserved berries (saving a few for garnish) over the cream cheese mixture in the pie shell. Put the cooled, cooked berry mixture over the fresh berries. Refrigerate 2 to 3 hours. Serve with your favorite white topping, if desired. Garnish with reserved raspberries.

EACH SERVING CONTAINS: CALORIES: 140 ▲ CARBOHYDRATES: 20 G ▲ EXCHANGE: 1 STARCH/BREAD, 1/2 FRUIT, 1 FAT

❖ Raspberry Ribbon Pie ❖

YIELD: 8 SERVINGS

The ribbon in the title refers to the red and white layers.

1 package	(4 servings) sugar-free raspberry gelatin mix	1 package
1 1/4 cups	boiling water	310 mL
10 ounces	frozen whole red raspberries	300 g
1 tablespoon	lemon juice	15 mL
3 ounces	fat-free cream cheese	80 g
2 teaspoons	aspartame sweetener	10 mL
1 teaspoon	vanilla extract	5 mL
1 cup	frozen, low-fat non-dairy whipped topping, thawed	250 mL
1	frozen pie crust, baked	1

To prepare the red layers: Put the raspberry gelatin mix into a mixing bowl. Add the boiling water. Add the frozen raspberries and lemon juice. Stir until the raspberries are defrosted. Refrigerate 1 to 2 hours until partially set.

To prepare the white layers: In a mixing bowl, combine the cream cheese, aspartame, and vanilla. Add a spoonful of the whipped topping. Fold to mix. Continue adding the topping spoonful by spoonful, folding in each addition. Refrigerate until the white layer is partially set.

Spread half the white mixture on the bottom of the pie shell. Cover with half the red gelatin mixture. Repeat with white and red layers, ending with the white mixture. Chill until set, 3 hours or more.

EACH SERVING CONTAINS: CALORIES: 132 ▲ CARBOHYDRATES: 16 G ▲ EXCHANGE: 1 STARCH/BREAD, 1 FAT

❖ Raspberry Cream Pie ❖

YIELD: 8 SERVINGS

Prepare this in the morning and let it freeze all day.

1 package	(4 servings) sugar-free raspberry gelatin	1 package
2/3 cup	boiling water	165 mL
1 1/2 cups	sugar-free, low-fat vanilla ice cream	375 mL
1 1/2 cups	frozen, low-fat non-dairy whipped topping, thawed	375 mL
1 cup	fresh or frozen (no sugar syrup) whole raspberries	250 mL
1	frozen pie crust, baked	1

Put the gelatin into a large mixing bowl. Add the boiling water. Stir until the gelatin is dissolved. Add the ice cream slowly. Stir until the mixture is smooth. Stir in the whipped topping. When well blended, add the raspberries. Transfer to the pie crust. Freeze until firm, an hour or more. For easiest cutting, run a sharp knife under hot running water between each cut. Top each slice with a dollop of whipped topping and raspberries.

EACH SERVING CONTAINS: CALORIES: 140 ▲ CARBOHYDRATES: 18 G ▲ EXCHANGE: 1 STARCH/BREAD, 1 1/2 FAT

❖ Hawaiian Pineapple Pie ❖

YIELD: 8 SERVINGS

20 ounces	crushed pineapple in juice	570 g
1 package	(4 servings) sugar-free vanilla pudding mix	1 package
1/2 cup	water	125 mL
1 teaspoon	butter or margarine	5 mL
1	frozen pie crust, baked	1
1/2 cup	frozen, low-fat non-dairy whipped topping	125 mL
2 tablespoons	coconut flakes (optional)	30 mL

Drain the can of pineapple pieces, saving the juice. In a saucepan, combine the pudding mix, water, and reserved pineapple juice. Cook over medium heat. Stir constantly. When mixture comes to a full boil, add the pineapple chunks and butter. Stir well. Pour into the pie crust. Cool. Just before serving, top with the non-dairy topping and sprinkle with coconut flakes, if desired.

EACH SERVING CONTAINS: CALORIES: 140 ▲ CARBOHYDRATES: 21 G ▲ EXCHANGE: 1 STARCH/BREAD, 1 FAT

❖ Peach Cream Cheese Pie ❖

YIELD: 8 SERVINGS

This pie is not very sweet. It's perfect after dinner on a hot summer evening.

1/2 cup	orange juice	125 mL
2 envelopes	plain gelatin	2 envelopes
2 teaspoons	orange extract	10 mL
1 cup	fat-free cream cheese	250 mL
1 cup	frozen, low-fat non-dairy whipped topping, thawed	250 mL
16 ounces	"lite" peach slices in juice, drained and chopped	450 g
1	frozen pie crust, baked	1

In a small saucepan, heat the orange juice until simmering. Pour into a blender or food processor. Add the gelatin and orange extract.

Blend for 30 seconds or so before adding the cream cheese, topping, and peaches. Blend until smooth, another 20 seconds or more. Pour quickly into the pie crust. Refrigerate 3 hours or so before serving.

EACH SERVING CONTAINS: CALORIES: 170 ▲ CARBOHYDRATES: 22 G ▲ EXCHANGE: 1 STARCH/BREAD, 1/2 FRUIT, 1 FAT

❖ Strawberry Ice Cream Pie ❖

YIELD: 8 SERVINGS

Let the ice cream soften before beginning the rest of the recipe.

1 package	(4 servings) sugar-free strawberry gelatin	1 package
2/3 cup	boiling water	165 mL
2 cups	sugar-free low-fat strawberry ice cream, softened	500 mL
1 cup	frozen, low-fat non-dairy whipped topping, thawed	250 mL
1	frozen pie crust, baked	1
1 cup	fresh or frozen (no sugar added) strawberries (optional)	250 mL

Put the gelatin into a large mixing bowl. Add the boiling water. Stir until gelatin is dissolved. Add the ice cream slowly. Stir until the mixture is smooth (except for the strawberry pieces, of course). Stir in the whipped topping by spoonfuls. Beat after each addition. A whisk works well. Spoon the mixture into the prepared pie crust. Freeze a few hours until firm. For easiest cutting, run a sharp knife under hot running water between each cut. Garnish with strawberries and whipped topping, if desired.

EACH SERVING CONTAINS: CALORIES: 128 ▲ CARBOHYDRATES: 17 G ▲ EXCHANGE: 1 STARCH/BREAD, 1 FAT

❖ Banana Cream and Strawberry Pie ❖

YIELD: 8 SERVINGS

1 package	(4 servings) sugar-free strawberry-banana gelatin	1 package
2/3 cup	boiling water	165 mL
2 cups	sugar-free low-fat vanilla ice cream, softened	500 mL
1 cup	frozen, low-fat non-dairy whipped topping, thawed	250 mL
1	frozen pie crust, baked	1
1	medium banana, sliced	1
1 cup	fresh strawberries, sliced	250 mL

Put the gelatin into a large mixing bowl. Add the boiling water and stir until it is dissolved. Add the ice cream slowly. Stir until smooth. Stir in the whipped topping by spoonfuls. Beat after each addition. Transfer to a prepared pie crust. Freeze until firm, at least one hour. For easiest cutting, run a sharp knife under hot running water between each cut. Just before serving, combine the banana and strawberry slices. Spoon over pie slices.

EACH SERVING CONTAINS: CALORIES: 147 ▲ CARBOHYDRATES: 22 G ▲ EXCHANGE: 1 1/2 FRUIT, 1 FAT

❖ Strawberry Cream Cheese Pie ❖

YIELD: 8 SERVINGS

The cream cheese adds a smooth and rich consistency.

1 cup	fat-free cream cheese	250 mL
1/4 cup	fruit-only strawberry jam	60 mL
1/2 teaspoon	almond extract	3 mL
	or	
1 tablespoon	almond-flavored liqueur	15 mL
1 cup	frozen low-fat non-dairy whipped topping, thawed	250 mL
1	frozen pie crust, baked	1
2 cups	fresh or frozen (without syrup) strawberries	500 mL

Use an electric mixer to beat together the cream cheese, jam, and almond extract or liqueur. Changing to the lowest speed, add the whipped topping. Mix until smooth. Transfer this mixture to the prepared pie crust. Smooth the top with a spoon. Cover with the strawberries. Freeze for an hour or more before serving.

EACH SERVING CONTAINS: CALORIES: 156 ▲ CARBOHYDRATES: 19 G ▲ EXCHANGE: 1 STARCH/BREAD, 1 FAT

❖ Strawberry Meringue Pie ❖

YIELD: 8 SERVINGS

A baked Alaska-style pie with strawberries. Dessert lovers will be delighted with the ice cream-meringue combination.

4 cups	sugar-free, low-fat vanilla ice cream, softened	1 L
1	frozen pie crust, baked	1
3 cups	fresh strawberries or frozen, unsweetened, thawed	750 mL
2 large	egg whites	2 large
1/4 teaspoon	cream of tartar	2 mL
1 1/2 teaspoons	aspartame sweetener	8 mL

Spread the ice cream into the pie shell, pushing it to the edges. Freeze all day or overnight. Just before serving, spread the strawberries on top of the ice cream and preheat the oven to 500°F (250°C). Put the egg whites, cream of tartar, and aspartame into an electric mixing bowl. Beat at high speed until the whites are stiff and form peaks but are not dry. Spoon this meringue on top of the strawberries using the spoon to make decorative peaks. Be sure all the surface is covered right up to the crust. Put the pie on a wooden bread board and place it in the oven. Bake for 5 minutes or so in the hot oven until meringue is lightly browned. Serve at once.

EACH SERVING CONTAINS: CALORIES: 150 ▲ CARBOHYDRATES: 24 G ▲ EXCHANGE: 1 STARCH/BREAD, 1/2 FRUIT, 1 FAT

❖ Pumpkin Ice Cream Pie ❖

If you like pumpkin, you'll enjoy this frozen ice cream pie.

2 cups	sugar-free low-fat vanilla ice cream, softened	500 mL
1	frozen pie crust, baked	1
5 teaspoons	aspartame sweetener	25 mL
1/2 teaspoon	cinnamon	3 mL
1/2 teaspoon	ginger	3 mL
1/4 teaspoon	nutmeg	2 mL
1 cup	canned pumpkin (not pumpkin pie filling)	250 mL
1 cup	frozen, low-fat non-dairy whipped topping, thawed	250 mL

Spread the softened ice cream in the bottom of the prepared pie shell, being careful not to damage the shell. Freeze. In a large mixing bowl combine the aspartame and spices. Blend in the pumpkin. Mix well. Add the non-dairy whipped topping. Fold until well mixed. Spread this mixture over the ice cream. Freeze 2 to 3 hours. Put out at room temperature for one-half hour before cutting.

EACH SERVING CONTAINS: CALORIES: 136 ▲ CARBOHYDRATES: 18 G ▲ EXCHANGE: 1 FRUIT, 1 1/2 FAT

❖ Frozen Pumpkin Pie ❖

2 cups	no-sugar low-fat vanilla ice cream or frozen yogurt, thawed	500 mL
2 cups	frozen low-fat non-dairy whipped topping, thawed	500 mL
1 cup	canned pumpkin	250 mL
2 teaspoons	aspartame sweetener	10 mL
1 teaspoon	cinnamon	5 mL
1/2 teaspoon	ginger	3 mL
1/2 teaspoon	cloves	3 mL
1	frozen pie crust, baked	1

Put the ice cream, topping, pumpkin, aspartame, and spices into a mixing bowl. Mix at medium speed until well blended. Pour into a pie shell. Freeze 3 hours or more, until firm.

EACH SERVING CONTAINS: CALORIES: 153 ▲ CARBOHYDRATES: 20 G ▲ EXCHANGE: 1 STARCH/BREAD, 1/2 FRUIT, 1 FAT

❖ Butterscotch Pie ❖

YIELD: 8 SERVINGS

Although this pie has pumpkin, the flavor of butterscotch is dominant and delicious.

1 tablespoon	unflavored gelatin	5 mL
1 1/2 cups	skim milk	325 mL
3 ounces	fat-free cream cheese	80 g
1 1/2 cups	canned pumpkin pie filling	325 mL
2 large	eggs or equivalent egg substitute	2 large
1 package	(4 servings) sugar-free butterscotch pudding mix (not instant)	1 package
2 cups	frozen, low-fat non-dairy whipped topping, thawed	500 mL
1	frozen pie crust, baked	1

Put the gelatin in a small mixing bowl. Add 1/2 cup (125 mL) milk and stir. Set aside while the gelatin softens. In the bowl of an electric mixer, combine the cream cheese, pumpkin, and eggs. Beat until smooth. In a heavy-bottomed saucepan, combine the remaining 1 cup (250 mL) of milk and the pudding mix. Add the pumpkin filling and the gelatin. Cook over medium heat until the mixture bubbles and thickens. Put the pan in the refrigerator to cool but do not allow it to set, 45 minutes or so. Fold in the whipped topping. Spoon into a prepared pie crust. Chill overnight or for several hours.

EACH SERVING CONTAINS: CALORIES: 179 ▲ CARBOHYDRATES: 17 G ▲ EXCHANGE: 1 HIGH-FAT MEAT, 1 FRUIT

❖ Chocolate Chocolate Pie ❖

1 1/2 cups	cold skim milk	375 mL
2 packages	(4-serving size) sugar-free instant chocolate pudding mix	2 packages
1 1/4 cups	water or skim milk	310 mL
1	frozen pie crust, baked	1
1/2 cup	fat-free cream cheese	125 mL
1 tablespoon	cold skim milk	15 mL
2 tablespoons	low-sugar no- fat chocolate syrup	30 mL
1 1/2 cups	frozen, low-fat non-dairy whipped topping	375 mL

Combine 1 1/2 cups (375 mL) milk and pudding mixes in a mixing bowl. Beat with an electric mixer on medium speed until very thick. Turn into pie crust. Put the cream cheese and 1 tablespoon (15 mL) of milk into a mixing bowl. Beat on high speed until the mixture is smooth. Using the lowest speed, mix in the syrup and whipped topping. Pour this mixture on top of the pudding mixture in the pie crust. Refrigerate 3 hours or more.

EACH SERVING CONTAINS: CALORIES: 151 ▲ CARBOHYDRATES: 18 G ▲ EXCHANGE: 1 STARCH/BREAD, 1 FAT

❖ Coffee-and-Cream Pie ❖

To cut the fat down to practically nothing, try fat-free whipped topping.

3 cups	frozen low-fat non-dairy whipped topping, thawed	750 mL
2 tablespoons	instant coffee powder	30 mL
1 teaspoon	vanilla	5 mL
1/4 cup	cold water	60 mL
1 envelope	unflavored gelatin	1 envelope
1	frozen pie crust, baked	1
1/2 cup	toasted coconut flakes (optional)	125 mL

Put the topping, coffee powder, and vanilla into a mixing bowl. Beat until blended. Put the cold water into a small saucepan. Sprinkle the gelatin onto the water. Let stand a minute or two. Put the saucepan over a low heat and stir until the gelatin is thoroughly dissolved. Pour the gelatin into the coffee mixture and beat again, until the gelatin is blended in. Pour the mixture into the pie crust. Sprinkle the coconut over the top, if desired. Refrigerate 1 hour or more before serving.

EACH SERVING CONTAINS: CALORIES: 160 ▲ CARBOHYDRATES: 15 G ▲ EXCHANGE: 1 STARCH/BREAD, 2 FAT

❖ Cocoa Chiffon Pie ❖

YIELD: 8 SERVINGS

This needs at least eight hours to chill. Prepare it the night before you plan to serve it or in the morning if you want to serve it in the evening. It's worth planning ahead.

1 envelope	unflavored gelatin	1 envelope
3 tablespoons	unsweetened cocoa powder	45 mL
1 3/4 cups	skim milk	435 mL
1 teaspoon	vanilla extract	5 mL
1 1/2 cups	frozen, low-fat non-dairy whipped topping, thawed	375 mL
1 1/2 teaspoon	aspartame sweetener	8 mL
1	frozen pie crust, baked	1

In a medium saucepan, mix together the gelatin, cocoa powder, and skim milk. Let stand for 5 minutes or so. Place over low heat. Stir with a wire whisk until the gelatin is dissolved, about 5 minutes. Remove from heat and stir in the vanilla. Refrigerate the mixture while preparing the rest of the pie. Put the whipped topping and aspartame in a mixing bowl. Mix to combine. Add the cocoa mixture. Mix at the lowest speed until blended. Turn into prepared pie crust. Refrigerate 8 hours or overnight before serving.

EACH SERVING CONTAINS: CALORIES: 145 ▲ CARBOHYDRATES: 16 G ▲ EXCHANGE: 1 STARCH/BREAD, 1 1/2 FAT

PHYLLO DOUGH

❖ Hawaiian Napoleon ❖

YIELD: 1 HAWAIIAN NAPOLEON

3 piles	phyllo dough napoleon rectangles (4 deep)	3 piles
1/4 cup	sugar-free vanilla pudding made with skim milk	60 mL
1 tablespoon	pineapple, crushed, in juice	15 mL
1 teaspoon	coconut flakes	25 mL
1 teaspoon	Strawberry-Kiwi Glaze (p. 232)	25 mL

Bake sheets of phyllo according to the instructions on page 7. Cut the pile of four sprayed sheets into 16 rectangles. Bake in a preheated 375°F (190°C) oven for 8 minutes. Three of these rectangular piles are used to make each napoleon.

Place one cooked and cooled four-layer rectangular stack on a dessert plate. Spread on the vanilla pudding. Place a second rectangular pile on top of the vanilla pudding. Top this layer with the crushed pineapple. Sprinkle on the coconut. Add the last layer of phyllo. Smooth on the Strawberry-Kiwi Glaze.

EACH SERVING CONTAINS: CALORIES: 105 ▲ CARBOHYDRATES: 21 G ▲ EXCHANGE: 1 FRUIT, 1/3 STARCH/BREAD

❖ Washington's Birthday Napoleon ❖

For each napoleon prepare the following:

3 piles	phyllo dough napoleon rectangles (4 deep)	3 piles
1/4 cup	sugar-free vanilla pudding, made with skim milk	60 mL
2	maraschino cherries, finely chopped	2
1 teaspoon	fruit-only cherry preserves	5 mL
1/2 teaspoon	Cherry Glaze (recipe follows)	3 mL

Bake sheets of phyllo according to the instructions on page 7. Cut the pile of four sprayed sheets into 16 rectangles. Bake in a preheated 375°F (190°C) oven for 8 minutes. Three of these rectangular piles are used to make each napoleon.

Arrange one phyllo dough rectangle on a dessert plate. Put the vanilla pudding in a small bowl. Add the maraschino cherries. Mix well. Spread the cherry preserves gently onto the phyllo rectangle. Cover with a second rectangle. Pile the vanilla pudding on this layer. Spread to the edges. Put the last rectangle on top. Frost the top layer with Cherry Glaze.

EACH SERVING CONTAINS: CALORIES: 86 ▲ CARBOHYDRATES: 16 G ▲ EXCHANGE: 1 FRUIT

❖ Cherry Glaze ❖

This can be refrigerated and reheated when needed.

1/4 cup	sugar-free cherry preserves	60 mL
1 teaspoon	Kirsch wine (cherry liqueur)	5 mL

Put the cherry preserves into a small saucepan. Add the cherry liqueur and mix well with a fork or wire whisk. Heat gently, stirring constantly. Cool.

EACH SERVING CONTAINS: CALORIES: 13 ▲ CARBOHYDRATES: 0 G ▲ EXCHANGE: FREE

❖ Mocha Napoleon ❖

YIELD: 1 MOCHA NAPOLEON

3 piles	phyllo dough napoleon rectangles (4 deep)	3 piles
1/4 cup	Mocha Tart Filling (recipe follows)	60 mL
1 teaspoon	seedless, no-sugar-added raspberry jam	5 mL
1/4 cup	frozen, low-fat non-dairy whipped topping	60 mL
1 teaspoon	Mocha Glaze (p. 73)	5 mL

Bake sheets of phyllo according to the instructions on page 7. Cut the pile of four sprayed sheets into 16 rectangles. Bake in a preheated 375°F (190°C) oven for 8 minutes.

Arrange one phllo rectangle on a dessert plate. Spread the Mocha Tart Filling on top of the phyllo. Put a second phyllo rectangle on a flat surface such as a tabletop. Carefully spread the raspberry jam on this rectangle and then place this, jam side up, on the previous layer. Spread the non-dairy whipped topping on top of the jam. Top this layer with the last rectangle. Smooth the Mocha Glaze on the top.

EACH SERVING CONTAINS: CALORIES: 122 ▲ CARBOHYDRATES: 18 G ▲ EXCHANGE: 1 FRUIT, 1/2 HIGH-FAT MEAT

❖ Mocha Tart Filling ❖

YIELD: ENOUGH FOR 6 NAPOLEONS

For a sharper coffee taste, use instant espresso coffee powder.

1 package	(4 servings) sugar-free chocolate pudding mix	1 package
1 1/2 cups	skim milk	375 mL
3 teaspoons	instant coffee powder	15 mL

Combine all the ingredients in a saucepan. Bring to a boil and cook, stirring constantly until pudding has thickened.

THE FILLING FOR EACH NAPOLEON CONTAINS: CALORIES: 24 ▲ CARBOHYDRATES: 4 G ▲ EXCHANGE: 1 VEGETABLE

❖ Mocha Glaze ❖

Drizzle over napoleons for a coffee–chocolate accent.

2 tablespoons	cocoa powder	30 mL
2 teaspoons	instant coffee powder	10 mL
2 tablespoons	hot water	30 mL
2 tablespoons	fat-free cream cheese	30 mL
2 teaspoons	aspartame sweetener	10 mL

Stir together the cocoa powder and instant coffee powder. Add the hot water and mix together until the mixture is smooth and evenly moist. Beat in the cream cheese and sweetener until smooth.

EACH SERVING CONTAINS: CALORIES: 5 ▲ CARBOHYDRATES: 0.9 G ▲ EXCHANGE: FREE

❖ Banana Split Napoleon ❖

YIELD: 1 BANANA SPLIT NAPOLEON

For each napoleon, prepare the following:

3 piles	phyllo dough napoleon rectangles (4 deep)	3 piles
1/2	medium ripe banana, peeled	1/2
1/2 teaspoon	lemon juice	3 mL
2 tablespoons	sugar-free vanilla pudding made with skim milk	30 mL
2 teaspoons	crushed pineapple (packed in juice), drained	10 mL
2 tablespoons	frozen low-fat non-dairy whipped topping, thawed	30 mL
1 teaspoon	Chocolate Glaze (p. 74)	5 mL

Bake sheets of phyllo according to the instructions on page 7. Cut the pile of four sprayed sheets into 16 rectangles. Bake in a preheated 375°F (190°C) oven for 8 minutes.

Arrange one phyllo rectangle on a dessert plate. Slice the banana into a bowl. Toss with the lemon juice and mash with a fork. Spread the banana evenly on the phyllo rectangle. Top with a second phyllo rectangle. Put the vanilla pudding in a small bowl. Add the pineapple and whipped topping. Blend with a fork and spread on top of the phyllo. Put the last rectangle onto a flat surface. Spread with the Chocolate Glaze gently, taking care not to break the phyllo. Top the napoleon with this layer.

EACH SERVING CONTAINS: CALORIES: 132 ▲ CARBOHYDRATES: 26 G ▲ EXCHANGE: 1 FRUIT; 1 STARCH/BREAD

❖ Chocolate Glaze ❖

YIELD: ENOUGH FOR 15 NAPOLEONS

Add a little extra milk to get the right consistency if this is too thick.

2 tablespoons	cocoa powder	30 mL
2 tablespoons	skim milk	30 mL
2 tablespoons	fat-free cream cheese	30 mL
2 teaspoons	aspartame sweetener	10 mL

Combine the cocoa powder and skim milk in a small bowl until the mixture is moistened. Using a fork, beat in the cream cheese. The mixture will be smooth. Add in the aspartame and mix well.

THE FILLING FOR EACH NAPOLEON CONTAINS: CALORIES: 5 ▲ CARBOHYDRATES: 0.9 G ▲ EXCHANGE: FREE

❖ Hot Fudge Napoleon ❖

YIELD: 1 HOT FUDGE NAPOLEON

For each napoleon, prepare the following:

3 piles	phyllo dough napoleon rectangles (4 deep)	3 piles
1/4 cup	sugar-free vanilla low-fat ice cream or frozen yogurt	60 mL
2 tablespoons	sugar-free vanilla pudding made with skim milk	30 mL
2 tablespoons	frozen low-fat non-dairy whipped topping, thawed	30 mL

5 teaspoons	Napoleon Fudge Topping (recipe follows)	25 mL
1	fresh cherry or maraschino cherry	5 mL

Bake sheets of phyllo according to the instructions on page 7. Cut the pile of four sprayed sheets into 16 rectangles. Bake in a preheated 375°F (190°C) oven for 8 minutes.

Arrange one phyllo rectangle on a dessert plate. Put the ice cream onto the rectangle and cover with another phyllo rectangle. In a small bowl, combine the pudding and whipped topping with a fork. Spread this onto the phyllo rectangle. Lay the last rectangle on the top of the pile. Top the napoleon with the hot Napoleon Fudge Topping and the cherry.

EACH NAPOLEON CONTAINS: CALORIES: 160 ▲ CARBOHYDRATES: 18 G ▲ EXCHANGE: 1 STARCH/BREAD, 1 FAT

❖ Napoleon Fudge Topping ❖

YIELD: ENOUGH FOR 2 NAPOLEONS

Rich and creamy, this topping tastes like the kind from the nicest bakeries.

2 tablespoons	cocoa powder, unsweetened	30 mL
1 teaspoon	canola oil	5 mL
2 teaspoons	skim milk	10 mL
2 teaspoons	aspartame sweetener	10 mL
1/2 teaspoon	vanilla extract	3 mL
1/8 teaspoon	butter extract	1 mL

Put the cocoa powder in a small saucepan. Add the canola oil and skim milk. Heat gently over a low flame, stirring constantly, until the mixture is blended and heated. Remove from heat. Stir in the aspartame and extracts and mix well. Spoon while still warm over the top of the napoleon.

THE TOPPING FOR EACH NAPOLEON CONTAINS: CALORIES: 90 ▲ CARBOHYDRATES: 12 G ▲ EXCHANGE: 1 STARCH/BREAD

❖ Vanilla Tart Filling ❖

10 SERVINGS (2 CUPS)

1³/4 cups	skim milk	435mL
2 tablespoons	butter or margarine	30 mL
3 tablespoons	cornstarch	45 mL
2 tablespoons	sugar	30 mL
3 packages	acesulfame-K	3 packages
1	egg or equivalent egg substitute	1
1 tablespoon	vanilla extract	

Heat the milk and butter over simmering water in the top of a double boiler. In a bowl, mix together the cornstarch, sugar and acesulfame-K. Add the egg and then the vanilla, blending well after each addition. Pour the cornstarch mixture into the warm milk. Mix with a wire wisk over simmering water until the mixture is thick. When the whisk leaves patterns, the pudding is finished cooking. Cool before using.

EACH SERVING CONTAINS: CALORIES: 63 ▲ CARBOHYDRATES: 7G ▲ EXCHANGE: 1/2 STARCH/BREAD, 1/2 FAT

❖ Phyllo Strudel ❖

YIELD: 10 SLICES

You won't believe how easy strudel is until you try.

Read the directions for phyllo dough on page 7. Layer four sheets, spraying each from edge to edge with non-stick cooking spray. Don't cut them into napoleon rectangles. Leave 1 inch (2.5 cm) free of filling at each edge. Spoon the filling, leaving 1 inch (2.5 cm) clear from the left edge along the short side. Roll from the right side. The filling will roll up into the inside.

Put the roll on an ungreased cookie sheet with the seam down and tuck the ends under. Brush with melted butter. Bake in a preheated 325°F (165°C) oven for 25 to 30 minutes. Cool before slicing. Best if sliced with an electric knife or a very sharp serrated knife.

EACH SLICE WITHOUT THE FILLING CONTAINS: CALORIES: 33 ▲ CARBOHYDRATES: 4 G ▲ EXCHANGE: 1/2 FAT

❖ Cherry Strudel Filling ❖

YIELD: FILLING FOR 10 SERVINGS

No one will believe this is low-calorie, it's so yummy.

1 pound	sweet cherries, pitted	450 g
1/4 cup	almonds, chopped	60 mL
2 tablespoons	sugar	30 mL

Combine all ingredients. Roll and bake in phyllo sheets as directed on page 76.

EACH SERVING CONTAINS: CALORIES: 63 ▲ CARBOHYDRATES: 11 G ▲ EXCHANGE: 1/2 STARCH/BREAD, 1/2 FAT

❖ Apple Strudel Filling ❖

YIELD: FILLING FOR 10 SERVINGS

The traditional filling you expect.

3	apples, peeled, cored, and sliced	3
1/4 cup	raisins	60 mL
1/4 cup	almonds, chopped	60 mL
2 tablespoons	sugar	30 mL
1/2 teaspoon	cinnamon	3 mL

Put the apples, raisins, and almonds in a mixing bowl. Toss to combine. In a small bowl, mix the sugar and cinnamon together. Toss with the apple mixture.

Roll and bake in phyllo sheets as directed on page 76.

EACH SERVING CONTAINS: CALORIES: 66 ▲ CARBOHYDRATES: 12 G ▲ EXCHANGE: 1/2 FRUIT, 1/2 FAT

❖ Prune Filling for Strudel ❖

YIELD: FILING FOR 10 SERVINGS

1 cup	prunes, pitted	250 mL
1/2 cup	unsweetened apple juice	125 mL
2 teaspoons	lemon peel	10 mL

In a small saucepan, cover the prunes with the juice. Bring to a boil over medium heat. Let stand 10 minutes. Pour off any unabsorbed liquid. Purée in a blender or food processor. Mix in the lemon peel. Roll and bake in phyllo sheets as directed on page 76.

EACH SERVING CONTAINS: CALORIES: 44 ▲ CARBOHYDRATES: 11 G ▲ EXCHANGE: 2/3 FRUIT

❖ Apricot Filling for Strudel ❖

YIELD: FILLING FOR 10 SERVINGS

A little sweet and tangy.

1 cup	dried apricots	250 mL
1/2 cup	orange juice	125 mL
2 teaspoons	orange rind	10 mL

Put the apricots into a small saucepan. Cover with orange juice. Bring to a boil. Let stand 10 minutes. Pour out any unabsorbed liquid. Purée in a food processor or blender. Mix in the orange rind. Roll and bake in phyllo sheets as directed on page 76.

EACH SERVING CONTAINS: CALORIES: 44 ▲ CARBOHYDRATES: 11 G ▲ EXCHANGE: 2/3 FRUIT

Phyllo Tarts

Handle phyllo sheets according to the directions on page 7. Coat a 12-inch (30-cm) quiche or tart pan with non-stick cooking spray.
    Prepare a stack of four sheets of phyllo dough, coating each layer evenly with non-stick cooking spray. Butter flavor is great! Using

your pan as a pattern, cut a circle larger than the pan by enough extra so the dough will cover the sides of the pan.

Place the cut-out circle in the tart pan. Use your fingers to shape the dough to the bottom and sides of the pan. Brush with melted butter or margarine.

Bake the shell in a preheated 325°F (165°C) oven for 8 to 10 minutes. The shell will be lightly browned. Cool before filling. Remove from the pan and put it on a pretty dish or leave in the pan for extra strength.

Choose a filling found on the following pages, make it, and fill the shell.

❖ Strawberry Cream Cheese Tart ❖

YIELD: 10 SERVINGS

Fat-free cream cheese makes this a low-calorie tart. It's very beautiful.

1	phyllo dough tart shell for 12" (30 cm) tart, baked	1
¼ cup	sugar-free strawberry preserves	60 mL
1 tablespoon	water	15 mL
3 ounces	fat-free cream cheese, softened	80 g
2 tablespoons	sugar	15 mL
2 tablespoons	cornstarch	15 mL
1 cup	skim milk	250 mL
1	egg or equivalent egg substitute, lightly beaten	1
2 teaspoons	orange extract	5 mL
1 teaspoon	butter extract	5 mL
1 cup	frozen, low-fat non-dairy whipped topping, thawed	250 mL

Prepare the phyllo tart shell described on page 78. Mix together the strawberry preserves and water and spread carefully over the bottom of the tart shell. In a heavy-bottomed medium-size saucepan, combine the cream cheese, sugar, and cornstarch. Put over low heat and, stirring constantly, heat gently until the sugar is dissolved. Gradually stir in the milk and egg. When the mixture is smooth and combined, bring to a boil. Allow to bubble for one minute, stirring constantly. Cool, stirring occasionally. Stir in the extracts. Fold in the whipped topping. Refrigerate until completely cool. Spread the cream cheese mixture over the strawberry preserves.

EACH SERVING CONTAINS: CALORIES: 88 ▲ CARBOHYDRATES: 14 G ▲ EXCHANGE: 1 STARCH/BREAD

❖ Pistachio Pineapple Tart ❖

YIELD: 10 SERVINGS

A real treat for the eyes and taste buds.

1	phyllo dough tart shell for 12" (30 cm) tart, baked	1
1 package	(4 servings) sugar-free pistachio no-cook pudding mix	1 package
1 3/4 cups	skim milk	435 mL
20 ounces	pineapple slices, packed in juice, drained	565 g
8 teaspoons	fresh cherries, pitted	40 mL

Prepare the phyllo tart shell described on page 78. Put the phyllo shell on a dessert plate. Put the pudding mix into a medium mixing bowl. Add the milk and combine according to the directions on the package. Spoon into the tart shell. Dry the drained pineapple slices on paper towels. Arrange them on the pistachio pudding. Put the cherries in the center.

EACH SERVING CONTAINS: CALORIES: 105 ▲ CARBOHYDRATES: 24 G ▲ EXCHANGE: 1 STARCH/BREAD, 1/2 FRUIT

❖ Chocolate Tart Filling ❖

You might want to use this plain, as an alternative to the chocolate-fruit combination.

1/4 cup	sugar	60 mL
3 packages	acesulfame-K or saccharin	3 packages
2 tablespoons	cocoa powder, unsweetened	30 mL
3 tablespoons	cornstarch	45 mL
1 3/4 cups	skim milk	435 mL
1 teaspoon	vanilla extract	5 mL
1 teaspoon	crème de cacao liqueur (optional)	5 mL

Combine the sugar, sugar substitute, cocoa powder, and cornstarch in a medium saucepan. Add a small amount of the milk. Stir with a wire whisk until the mixture is evenly moistened. Add the remainder of the milk, the vanilla extract, and the crème de cacao, if desired. Cook, stirring constantly until filling is thick and you can see whisk marks as you stir. Cool before pouring into tart shell. Makes 2 cups (500 mL).

EACH SERVING CONTAINS: CALORIES: 56 ▲ CARBOHYDRATES: 11 G ▲ EXCHANGE: 2/3 STARCH/BREAD

PUDDING

❖ Chocolate Mousse Pudding ❖

Light and luscious. Meets a chocoholic's needs.

1 1/2 cups	skim milk	375 mL
1 package	(4 servings) sugar-free, fat-free no-cook chocolate pudding mix	1 package
1 cup	frozen, low-fat non-dairy whipped topping, thawed	250 mL
1 tablespoon	chocolate liqueur (optional) or crème de cacao (optional)	15 mL

Put the skim milk into a large mixing bowl. Add the pudding mix and beat one or two minutes. Add the whipped topping and chocolate liqueur or crème de cacao, if desired. Stir gently, until blended. Spoon into five dessert dishes.

EACH SERVING CONTAINS CALORIES: 37 ▲ CARBOHYDRATES: 4 G ▲ EXCHANGE: 1/2 FAT

❖ Mocha Mousse Pudding ❖

YIELD: 5 SERVINGS

1 3/4 cups	skim milk	435 mL
1/4 cup	very strong brewed coffee	60 mL
1 package	(4 servings) sugar-free, fat-free no-cook chocolate pudding mix	1 package

| 1¼ cups | frozen, low-fat non-dairy whipped topping, thawed | 310 mL |
| 2 tablespoons | coffee liqueur | 30 mL |

Put the skim milk and coffee into a large mixing bowl. Add the pudding mix and beat one to two minutes. Add the whipped topping and coffee liqueur. Stir gently until blended. Spoon into five dessert dishes.

EACH SERVING CONTAINS: CALORIES: 69 ▲ CARBOHYDRATES: 8 G ▲ EXCHANGE: ½ STARCH/BREAD, ½ FAT

❖ Quick (and Foolproof) ❖ Mocha Mousse

YIELD: 4 SERVINGS

1 package	hot chocolate powder, no sugar added	1 package
10 teaspoons	hot coffee	50 mL
2 cups	frozen, low-fat non-dairy whipped topping, thawed	500 mL

Put the hot chocolate powder into a medium mixing bowl. Add the coffee and stir until the powder is dissolved. Gently fold in the whipped topping until evenly mixed.

EACH SERVING CONTAINS: CALORIES: 95 ▲ CARBOHYDRATES: 11 G ▲ EXCHANGE: 1 FRUIT, 1 FAT

❖ Thanksgiving Pumpkin Mousse ❖

YIELD: 6 SERVINGS

A light finish for a turkey dinner.

1¼ cups	skim milk	310 mL
1 cup	pumpkin pie filling	250 mL
¼ teaspoon	cinnamon	2 mL
¼ teaspoon	nutmeg	2 mL

1/4 teaspoon	ginger	2 mL
1 package	(4 servings) sugar-free no-cook butterscotch pudding mix	1 package
1 1/4 cups	water	310 mL
1 cup	frozen, low-fat non-dairy whipped topping	250 mL

In a mixing bowl, combine the milk, pumpkin, cinnamon, nutmeg, and ginger. Add the pudding mix and water and mix with a wire whisk or electric mixer until blended. Add the whipped topping and gently but thoroughly combine. Spoon into individual dessert dishes and chill 2 to 3 hours before serving.

EACH SERVING CONTAINS: CALORIES: 101 ▲ CARBOHYDRATES: 19 G ▲ EXCHANGE: 1 STARCH/BREAD

❖ Ricotta Cheese Pudding ❖

YIELD: 4 SERVINGS

A pudding for grown-ups — rich and very special.

1 pound	fat-free ricotta cheese	450 g
2 tablespoons	frozen low-fat non-dairy whipped topping	30 mL
2 tablespoons	Triple Sec	30 mL
1 teaspoon	aspartame sweetener	5 mL
2 ounces	diabetic chocolate candy bar, coarsely chopped	55 g
1/4 cup	Not-Too-Sweet Chocolate Sauce (p. 85)	60 mL

Process the ricotta in a blender or food processor until smooth. Add the whipped topping, Triple Sec, and aspartame. Blend again. Transfer to a mixing bowl. Fold in the chocolate. Cover the bowl and refrigerate it for one hour before serving. Serve with chocolate sauce.

EACH SERVING CONTAINS: CALORIES: 139 ▲ CARBOHYDRATES: 16 G ▲ EXCHANGE: 1 1/2 MILK

❖ Not-Too-Sweet Chocolate Sauce ❖

YIELD: 24 SERVINGS

Stores well refrigerated, but warm gently before serving.

3 tablespoons	unsweetened cocoa powder	45 mL
1 tablespoon	flour	15 mL
1 1/2 cups	skim milk	375 mL
2 tablespoons	butter or margarine	30 mL
3 teaspoons	sugar substitute	15 mL
1 teaspoon	vanilla extract	5 mL
1/2 teaspoon	butter extract	3 mL

Combine the cocoa powder and flour in the top of a double boiler. Add the milk. Stir until free of lumps. Cook over boiling water, stirring until thick and smooth. Remove from heat. Stir in the butter. Cool for 15 minutes. Stir in the sugar substitute, vanilla extract, and butter extract. Serve over pudding or frozen treats.

EACH SERVING CONTAINS: CALORIES: 18 ▲ CARBOHYDRATES: 2 G ▲ EXCHANGE: FREE

❖ Lemon Sponge Pudding ❖

YIELD: 4 SERVINGS

1 tablespoon	flour	15 mL
2 tablespoons	sugar	30 mL
3 packages	saccharin or acesulfame-K sugar substitute	3 packages
2 tablespoons	lemon juice	30 mL
1 1/2 teaspoons	lemon peel	8 mL
1 cup	skim milk	250 mL
2 large	eggs, separated	2 large

In a mixing bowl, combine flour, sugar, sugar substitute, lemon juice, and lemon peel. Mix in skim milk. In another bowl, beat the egg yolks at high speed until lemon colored. Add the yolks to the flour mixture. Blend well. Beat the egg whites until stiff. Fold them into the custard mixture. Pour the pudding into a casserole coated with non-stick cooking spray. Put the casserole in a pan of hot water in a preheated 350°F (180°C) oven. Bake for 35 to 40 minutes. The top will be lightly browned.

EACH SERVING CONTAINS: CALORIES: 95 ▲ CARBOHYDRATES: 12 G ▲ EXCHANGE: 1 MILK, 1/2 FAT

❖ Quick (Microwave) Custard ❖

YIELD: 4 SERVINGS

1 1/2 cups	milk	375 mL
3	large eggs, or equivalent egg substitute	3
2 tablespoons	sugar	30 mL
3 packages	saccharine	3 packages
1 teaspoon	vanilla	5 mL
1/4 teaspoon	nutmeg	2 mL

Pour the milk into a glass measuring cup and put it in the microwave on high for three minutes. In a mixing bowl, stir together the eggs, sugar, sugar substitute, and vanilla. Gradually stir in the hot milk. Pour into a glass baking dish. Sprinkle nutmeg on top. Cook on "defrost" in the microwave for 10 minutes. The custard will become more firm as it sets.

EACH SERVING CONTAINS: CALORIES: 117 ▲ CARBOHYDRATES: 12 G ▲ EXCHANGE: 1 MILK, 1/2 FAT

❖ Microwave Vanilla Pudding ❖

YIELD: 4 SERVINGS

Perfect for a lazy-day dessert. A spoonful of Not-Too-Sweet Chocolate Sauce makes it extra special.

3 tablespoons	sugar	45 mL
2 tablespoons	cornstarch	30 mL
2 cups	skim milk	500 mL
1	large egg or equivalent egg substitute	1
1 teaspoon	butter or margarine	5 mL

| 2 teaspoons | vanilla | 10 mL |
| 2 packages | sugar substitute | 2 packages |

Put the sugar and cornstarch in a 4-cup (1L) glass mixing bowl. Mix in the skim milk. Cook on HIGH in the microwave for 5 to 7 minutes. Stop a few times to stir during the process. The mixture will be smooth and thick. Beat the egg in a small bowl. Mix in a few spoonfuls of the hot milk mixture. Turn the egg mixture into the thickened milk. Mix well. Return to the microwave and cook on "roast" or medium for a minute or two. Stop and stir during the process. Remove from microwave. Stir in the butter, vanilla, and sugar substitute.

EACH SERVING CONTAINS: CALORIES: 126 ▲ CARBOHYDRATES: 20 G ▲ EXCHANGE: 1 STARCH/BREAD, 1/2 MILK

❖ Banana Pudding ❖

YIELD: 8 SERVINGS

4	large eggs	4
1/4 cup	sugar	60 mL
3 tablespoons	flour	45 mL
2 cups	skim milk	250 mL
1 teaspoon	vanilla	5 mL
18	vanilla wafers	18
4	medium bananas, ripe, peeled and sliced	4
1 tablespoon	sugar	15 mL

Separate 3 eggs. Put the 3 yolks and the remaining whole egg in the top of a double boiler. Add the sugar and mix well. Stir in the flour. Using a wire whisk, stir in the milk. Put the top of the double boiler over boiling water and cook, stirring constantly until the mixture thickens. Stir in the vanilla and cool slightly. Spoon some custard onto the bottom of a 10-cup (1.5-L) casserole. Form a layer on top of the custard using 6 wafers. Cover with layer of banana slices. Repeat layerings, ending with custard. Beat the egg whites and remaining sugar until stiff. Spoon this meringue on top of the pudding. Cover entirely, up to the edges. (If the meringue doesn't attach to the edges it will shrink during baking.) Bake in a preheated 425°F (220°C) oven for about five minutes. The meringue will be delicately browned.

EACH SERVING CONTAINS: CALORIES: 216 ▲ CARBOHYDRATES: 36 G ▲ EXCHANGE: 2 STARCH/BREAD, 1 FAT

❖ Easy German Rice Pudding ❖

1/2 cup	long-grain rice	125 mL
1 cup	boiling water	250 mL
3 cups	skim milk	750 mL
1/4 cup	granulated sugar replacement	125 mL
1/2 teaspoon	salt	2 mL
1 teaspoon	vanilla extract	-5 mL
	ground cinnamon	

Combine rice and boiling water in a 2-quart (2-L) saucepan. Bring to a boil; then reduce heat and cook, uncovered, until all the water is absorbed. Stir occasionally. Stir in the milk. Simmer for 20 minutes, stirring occasionally. Add sweetener and salt. Continue simmering 20 to 25 more minutes or until mixture is creamy and very soft. Stir in vanilla. Serve warm, sprinkled with ground cinnamon.

EACH SERVING CONTAINS: CALORIES: 150 ▲ CARBOHYDRATES: 29 G ▲ EXCHANGE: 1 BREAD, 3/4 SKIM MILK

❖ Baked Apple Pudding ❖

YIELD: 12 SERVINGS

1 cup	granulated sugar replacement	250 mL
2	eggs	2
1 tablespoon	liquid fructose	15 mL
2 teaspoons	vanilla extract	10 mL
1/3 cup	all-purpose flour	90 mL
1 tablespoon	baking powder	15 mL
dash	salt	dash
3 cups	chopped pared apples	750 mL

Combine sweetener, eggs, liquid fructose, and vanilla in a bowl. Beat until thick. Stir in flour, baking powder, and salt. Then stir in apples. Spread batter into a well-greased 9 inch (23-cm) square baking pan. Bake at 325°F (165°C) for 25 to 35 minutes or until done. Serve warm.

EACH SERVING CONTAINS: CALORIES: 52 ▲ CARBOHYDRATES: 12 G ▲ EXCHANGE: 1 FRUIT

❖ Milk–Chocolate Pudding ❖

YIELD: 8 SERVINGS

1 cup	granulated sugar replacement	250 mL
2/3 cup	all-purpose flour	180 mL
1/4 cup	unsweetened baking cocoa	60 mL
2 tablespoons	liquid fructose	30 mL
dash	salt	dash
1 quart	skim milk	1 L
1	egg, beaten	1
1 tablespoon	vanilla extract	15 mL

Combine sweetener of your choice, flour, cocoa, fructose, and salt in a nonstick saucepan. Combine milk and egg in measuring cup or bowl. Stir to blend. Gradually stir milk mixture into cocoa mixture. Cook over medium heat until mixture thickens, stirring constantly. Remove from heat, and stir in vanilla. Spoon into eight decorative dessert dishes. Serve warm or chill until set.

EACH SERVING CONTAINS: CALORIES: 117 ▲ CARBOHYDRATES: 13 G ▲ EXCHANGE: 1/2 BREAD, 1/2 LOW-FAT MILK

❖ Caramel Custard ❖

YIELD: 2 SERVINGS

1 tablespoon	sugar-free maple-flavored syrup	15 mL
1	egg	1
1/2 cup	evaporated skim milk	125 mL
1/3 cup	water	90 mL
1 tablespoon	granulated sugar replacement	15 mL
1 teaspoon	vanilla extract	5 mL
dash	salt	dash

Divide maple syrup evenly between two custard cups. Combine egg, milk, water, sugar replacement, vanilla, and salt in a mixing bowl. Beat to blend. Carefully pour custard mixture over the syrup in the custard cups. Set cups in shallow pan holding 1 inch (2.5 cm) of water. Bake at 350°F (175 °C) for 50 minutes or until knife inserted in middle comes out clean.

Microwave: Water bath not needed. Prepare recipe as above. Place custard cups on a flat microwave-proof plate. Cook on low for 8 to 10 minutes or until edges are set and middle is soft but not runny. Allow to cool for 10 to 15 minutes before serving.

EACH SERVING CONTAINS: CALORIES: 85 ▲ CARBOHYDRATES: 7 G ▲ EXCHANGE: 1 SKIM MILK

❖ Baked Coffee Custard ❖

YIELD: 6 SERVINGS

1 1/4 cups	low fat milk	310 mL
1/4 cup	liquid nondairy creamer	60 mL
4 teaspoons	instant coffee powder	20 mL
2	eggs	2
2	egg yolks	2
2 tablespoons	granulated sugar replacement	30 mL
1 tablespoon	granulated fructose	15 mL
dash	salt	dash
1 tablespoon	vanilla extract	15 mL

Place six custard cups in a large baking pan. Place pan with custard cups in a 325°F (165°C) oven. Meanwhile, heat the milk and nondairy creamer until boiling. Remove from heat and stir in the coffee powder. Set aside. Whisk the eggs and egg yolks together in a bowl. Add sugar replacement, fructose, salt, and vanilla. Whisk to thoroughly blend. Gradually whisk in the hot milk. Remove baking pan and custard cups from oven. Divide the coffee mixture evenly among the custard cups. Pour simmering water into baking pan to come halfway up sides of custard cups. Return to oven. Bake for 35 minutes or until the middle moves only slightly. Remove custard cups from baking pan. Cool.

EACH SERVING CONTAINS: CALORIES: 113 ▲ CARBOHYDRATES: 7 G ▲ EXCHANGE: 1/2 LOW-FAT MILK, 1 FAT

❖ Mocha Mousse ❖

1/3 cup	unsweetened cocoa powder	90 mL
1 teaspoon	instant-coffee powder	5 mL
1/4 cup	granulated sugar replacement	60 mL
2 tablespoons	cornstarch	30 mL
1/4 teaspoon	salt	1 mL
2 cups	skim milk	500 mL
1	beaten egg	1
8 ounce	package light cream cheese, softened	240 g package
1 teaspoon	vanilla extract	5 mL

Combine cocoa powder, coffee powder, sugar replacement, corn-starch, and salt in a saucepan. Stir in milk. Cook and stir over medium heat until thick and bubbling. Reduce heat to low. Cook and stir 4 minutes more. Remove from heat. Pour and stir a small amount of hot cocoa mixture into the beaten egg. Pour egg mixture back into cocoa mixture, stirring until well blended. Return to heat and cook for 2 more minutes. Remove from heat. Pour mixture into a mixing bowl. Add cream cheese and vanilla. Beat until fluffy and mixture is well blended. Pour into a 1-quart (1-L) mould or dish, and cover with waxed paper. Chill until firm. Remove waxed paper and unmould.

EACH SERVING CONTAINS: CALORIES: 128 ▲ CARBOHYDRATES: 13 G ▲ EXCHANGE: 1 WHOLE MILK, 1 FAT

❖ Dark-Fudge Pudding ❖

1/2 cup	granulated sugar replacement	125 mL
3 tablespoons	all-purpose flour	45 mL
1 tablespoon	granulated fructose	15 mL
dash	salt	dash
1 1/2 cups	skim milk	375 mL

1 ounce	unsweetened baking chocolate, in small pieces	28.3 g
1	egg, beaten	1
1 tablespoon	margarine	15 mL
1 teaspoon	vanilla extract	5 mL

Combine sugar replacement, flour, fructose, and salt in a nonstick saucepan. Gradually stir in milk. Blend well. Stir in chocolate and egg. Cook over medium heat until mixture thickens, stirring constantly. Remove from heat, and stir in margarine and vanilla. Spoon into six decorative dessert dishes. Serve warm or chill until set.

EACH SERVING CONTAINS: CALORIES: 108 ▲ CARBOHYDRATES: 14 G ▲ EXCHANGE: 1 BREAD, 1/2 FAT

❖ Fluffy Rice Pudding ❖

YIELD: 12 SERVINGS

1/2 cup	water	125 mL
1/2 cup	granulated sugar replacement	125 mL
2 tablespoons	granulated fructose	30 mL
2 envelopes	unflavored gelatin	2 envelopes
1/2 teaspoon	salt	2 mL
2 cups	skim milk	500 mL
1 1/2 cup	cooked rice	375 mL
1 tablespoon	vanilla extract	15 mL
2 cups	prepared non-dairy whipped topping	500 mL

Combine water, sugar replacement, fructose, gelatin, and salt in a saucepan. Heat, stirring constantly until gelatin is dissolved. Stir in milk, rice, and vanilla. Place saucepan in a bowl of ice water. Stir occasionally. When rice mixture has cooled and drops in mounds from a spoon, fold in nondairy whipped topping. Pour into a 6-cup (1500-mL) decorative mould. Cover with plastic wrap and refrigerate until firm. Loosen edges of mould with a spatula, and dip mould briefly in a pan of warm water. Invert on decorative serving plate.

EACH SERVING CONTAINS: CALORIES: 78 ▲ CARBOHYDRATES: 12 G ▲ EXCHANGE: 1 BREAD

❖ Rhubarb Bread Pudding ❖

1 quart	diced rhubarb	1 L
3 1/2 cups	dry bread cubes	875 mL
1 cup	granulated sugar replacement	250 mL
1/4 cup	margarine, melted	60 mL
2 tablespoons	granulated fructose	30 mL
1/2 teaspoon	ground nutmeg	2 mL
1/2 teaspoon	ground cinnamon	2 mL
1/4 teaspoon	ground allspice 1 mL	

Combine all ingredients in a bowl. Toss to mix. Transfer to a well-greased 2-quart (2-L) casserole dish. Cover and bake at 375°F (190°C) for 45 minutes; then uncover and continue baking another 10 minutes or until set. Serve warm.

EACH SERVING CONTAINS: CALORIES: 148 ▲ CARBOHYDRATES: 21 G ▲ EXCHANGE: 1 1/3 BREAD, 1 FAT

ROLL-UPS

❖ Walnut Roll-Up Cookies ❖

YIELD: 24 COOKIES

Most diabetic diet cookies are pretty inedible, in my opinion. These are the exceptions.

1 package	active dry yeast	1 package
1/4 cup	warm water	60 mL
2 cups	flour	500 mL
1/4 cup+2 table-spoons	fat-free fruit-based butter-and-oil replacement	90 mL
2 tablespoons	oil replacement	30 mL
1 large	egg or equivalent egg substitute, lightly beaten	1 large
3 ounces	fat-free cream cheese	80 g
2 tablespoons	sugar	15 mL
1 teaspoon	orange peel, grated	5 mL
1 teaspoon	orange extract	5 mL
1/2 cup	walnuts, finely ground	125 mL

In a small mixing bowl, combine the yeast and warm water. In a large mixing bowl, combine the flour and butter replacement. Beat in the egg. Add the yeast and mix just until blended. On a lightly floured board, roll out the dough into two 13 x 9" (33 x 22 cm) rectangles. In a mixing bowl, beat the cream cheese until light and fluffy. Add the sugar, orange peel, and the orange extract. Beat well. Spread half the cream cheese mixture on each rectangle. Sprinkle with walnuts. Starting at the long side, roll up the rectangles. Place each roll on a cookie sheet that has been coated with non-stick vegetable cooking spray. Put the seam side down. Bake in a preheated 375°F (190°C) oven for 20 to 25 minutes. Cool. Cut into 1-inch (2.5 cm) slices.

EACH SERVING CONTAINS: CALORIES: 73 ▲ CARBOHYDRATES: 12 ▲ EXCHANGE: 1 STARCH/BREAD

❖ Sweet Crêpe Batter ❖

YIELD: 6 CRÊPES

If the first crêpe doesn't move easily in the pan, blend in a little additional milk.

2	large eggs, or equivalent egg substitute	2
3 tablespoons	canola oil	45 mL
1 teaspoon	butter extract	5 mL
1 cup	skim milk	250 mL
2 tablespoons	fruit-flavored liqueur	30 mL
1/2 cup	flour	125 mL
1 tablespoon	sugar	15 mL

Put the ingredients in the blender or food processor in the order listed. Blend at high speed for a minute or more, until the batter is well blended. Cover and refrigerate for an hour or more. To prepare the crêpes, coat a medium-sized heavy-bottomed frying pan with butter-flavored vegetable cooking spray. Heat the pan until it is hot. Remove the pan from the heat source and pour 1/4 cup (60 mL) of the batter into the center of the pan. Tilt the pan quickly in all directions to coat the bottom. Return the pan to the heat and cook for a minute or so. Shake the pan to loosen the crêpe. Lift one edge of the crêpe. If it's a light, golden color, it's done. Turn the crêpe with a spatula and brown this side for about 30 seconds. This side won't look as good and should become the inside when you wrap the crêpes around the filling.

EACH CRÊPE CONTAINS: CALORIES: 80 ▲ CARBOHYDRATES: 6 G ▲ EXCHANGE: 1/2 STARCH/BREAD, 1 FAT

❖ Blintz Filling for Crêpes ❖

YIELD: FILLING FOR 6 CRÊPES

The butter extract gives this filling a rich flavor.

1 pound	fat-free cottage cheese	450 g
2 packages	sugar substitute	2 packages
1 teaspoon	butter extract	5 mL
2 tablespoons	frozen, low-fat non-dairy whipped topping	30 mL

Put all the ingredients into a blender or food processor. Blend until smooth. To serve, put a spoonful of the mixture on the last-cooked side of the crêpe.

EACH CRÊPE FILLING CONTAINS: CALORIES: 49 ▲ CARBOHYDRATES: 5 G ▲ EXCHANGE: 1 LEAN MEAT

❖ Austrian Raspberry Cream Crêpes ❖

YIELD: 12 SERVINGS

You'll think you're in Vienna.

1 recipe	Sweet Crêpe Batter (p. 95)	1 recipe
1 cup	fruit-only seedless raspberry preserves	250 mL
1/2 cup	water	125 mL
2 tablespoons	raspberry flavored brandy (optional)	30 mL
1 1/2 cups	fat-free sour cream	375 mL
1/3 cup	toasted almonds, finely chopped (optional)	80 mL

Prepare the crêpes according to the directions on page 95. Put waxed paper between them as you prepare them and a towel over the top to keep them warm. In a small saucepan, mix together the preserves, water, and brandy, if you are using it. Heat for 5 minutes or so, stirring constantly. Remove from heat. In a small mixing bowl, mix together the sour cream and almonds, if desired. Spread 2 tablespoons (30 mL) of the raspberry mixture on the back of each crêpe, and roll it with the raspberry inside. Arrange crêpes on dessert plates. Spoon on a dollop of sour cream and garnish with any remaining raspberry mixture.

EACH SERVING CONTAINS: CALORIES: ▲ CARBOHYDRATES: 21 G ▲ EXCHANGE: 1 STARCH/BREAD, 1/2 FRUIT, 1 FAT

❖ Kaiser Schmarren ❖

An old German recipe.

1 recipe	Sweet Crêpe Batter (p. 95)	1 recipe
1/2 cup	orange juice	125 mL
1 teaspoon	orange extract	5 mL
1/2 cup	raisins (golden are prettiest)	125 mL
1 teaspoon	butter or margarine	5 mL
1/2 cup	almonds, sliced	125 mL

Prepare the crêpes according to the directions on page 95. In a small bowl, mix together the orange juice, orange extract, and raisins. Let stand for half an hour or so, until the raisins are plump. Melt the butter in a small frying pan. Add the almonds and toast them until they are golden, stirring constantly. Combine the raisin and almond mixtures. Distribute inside each crêpe before rolling.

EACH SERVING CONTAINS: CALORIES: 68 ▲ CARBOHYDRATES: 8 G ▲ EXCHANGE: 1/2 STARCH/BREAD, 1/2 FAT

❖ Crêpes Marcelles ❖

YIELD: 12 SERVINGS

Roll these just before serving. I've used instant pudding in a pinch in place of the tart filling.

1 recipe	Sweet Crêpe Batter (p. 95)	1 recipe
1 recipe	Vanilla Tart Filling (p. 76)	1 recipe
1 tablespoon	cognac	15 mL
1 teaspoon	orange extract	5 mL
1/4 cup	crushed pineapple in juice, drained	60 mL

Prepare the crêpes according to the directions on page 95. Prepare the Vanilla Tart Filling. Mix in the cognac, orange extract, and crushed pineapple. Spoon this filling into the crepes and roll them just before serving.

EACH SERVING CONTAINS: CALORIES: 64 ▲ CARBOHYDRATES: 7 G ▲ EXCHANGE: 1/2 STARCH/BREAD, 1/2 FAT

❖ Basic Roll-Up Recipe ❖

YIELD: 10 SERVINGS

Use this for all the "jelly roll" style recipes that follow. It's easy to do.

1 cup	cake flour, sifted	250 mL
1 teaspoon	baking powder	5 mL
3 large	eggs	3 large
1/4 cup	sugar	60 mL
3 packages	acesulfame-K	3 packages
1/3 cup	water	80 mL
1 teaspoon	vanilla extract	5 mL

Spray a 15 x 10 x 1" (37 x 25 x 3 cm) jelly-roll pan; line the bottom with waxed paper; spray the paper. Sift the flour and baking powder together. With an electric mixer, beat the eggs in a medium bowl until thick and creamy and light in color. Gradually add the sugar and the acesulfame-K, beating constantly until the mixture is very thick. Stir in the water and vanilla. Fold in the flour mixture. Spread the batter evenly in the prepared pan.

Bake at 375°F (190°C) for 12 minutes or until the center of the cake springs back when lightly pressed. Loosen the cake around the edges with a knife. Invert the pan onto a clear tea towel, and peel off the waxed paper. Starting at the short end, roll up the cake and towel together. Place the roll seam side down on a wire rack and cool completely. When cool unroll carefully and assemble with filling. With a sharp knife, score the places where the slices will be, so they are even.

EACH SERVING CONTAINS: CALORIES: 82 ▲ CARBOHYDRATES: 14 G ▲ EXCHANGE: 1 STARCH/BREAD

❖ Fresh Strawberry Roll-Up ❖

YIELD: 10 SLICES

1 recipe	Basic Roll-Up Recipe (above)	1 recipe
2 cups	frozen, low-fat non-dairy whipped topping	500 mL
2 cups	fresh strawberries, hulled and quartered	500 mL

Prepare the Basic Roll-Up Recipe. Cool and unroll. Stir the non-dairy whipped topping and the strawberries together. Spread this filling evenly on the roll. Starting from the short end, roll up the cake by lifting the cake with the end of the towel. Place the roll seam side down on a serving plate.

EACH SERVING CONTAINS: CALORIES: 124 ▲ CARBOHYDRATES: 19 G ▲ EXCHANGE: 1 STARCH/BREAD, 1 FAT

❖ Chocolate Roll-Up ❖

YIELD: 10 SLICES

If you love chocolate this will be your favorite.

1 recipe	Basic Roll-Up Recipe (p. 98)	1 recipe
1 package	(4 servings) sugar-free, low-fat no-cook chocolate pudding mix	1 package
1 1/2 cups	skim milk	375 mL
2 tablespoons	crème de cacao (optional)	30 mL
1/2 cup	white topping (optional)	125 mL

Prepare the Basic Roll-Up Recipe. Cool and unroll. Put the pudding mix in a mixing bowl. Add the skim milk and crème de cacao, if desired. Whip until thickened. Spread the pudding on the roll. Roll up the cake from the short end. To start rolling, lift the cake with the end of the towel. When rolled, place the roll seam side down on a serving plate. Optional: Top each slice with a dollop of your favorite white topping.

EACH SERVING CONTAINS: CALORIES: 96 ▲ CARBOHYDRATES: 17 G ▲ EXCHANGE: 1 FRUIT, 1/2 LEAN MEAT

❖ Peach Melba Roll-Up ❖

Since there is no fresh fruit, you can make this "off the shelf" any-time.

1 recipe	Basic Roll-Up Recipe (p. 98)	1 recipe
1 recipe	Vanilla Tart Filling (p. 76)	1 recipe
15 ounces	sliced peaches in juice, drained	425 g

Prepare the Basic Roll-Up Recipe. Cool and unroll. Prepare the tart filling and then spread it evenly on the cooled roll. Arrange the peach slices all over the surface and roll up the cake from the short end. To start rolling, lift the cake with the end of the towel. When rolled, place the roll seam side down on a serving plate.

EACH SERVING CONTAINS: CALORIES: 1,164 ▲ CARBOHYDRATES: 26 G ▲ EXCHANGE: 1 1/2 STARCH/BREAD, 1/2 FAT

❖ Banana Walnut Roll-Up ❖

1 recipe	Basic Roll-Up Recipe (p. 98)	1 recipe
1 recipe	Vanilla Tart Filling (p. 76)	1 recipe
3	small ripe bananas, peeled and sliced	3
1/4 cup	chopped walnuts	60 mL

Prepare the Basic Roll-Up Recipe. Cool and unroll. Prepare the tart filling and then stir the bananas and walnuts into it. Spread the filling evenly on the cooked roll and roll up the cake from the short end. To start rolling, lift the cake with the end of the towel. When rolled, place the roll seam side down on a serving plate.

EACH SERVING CONTAINS: CALORIES: 195 ▲ CARBOHYDRATES: 29 ▲ EXCHANGE: 2 STARCH/BREAD, 1 FAT

❖ Mocha Raspberry Roll-Up ❖

A grown-up taste. Very elegant.

1 recipe	Basic Roll-Up Recipe (p. 98)	1 recipe
1 recipe	Mocha Tart Filling (p. 72)	1 recipe
2 cups	fresh raspberries	500 mL

Prepare the Basic Roll-Up Recipe. Cool and unroll. Prepare the tart filling, spread it evenly on the cooled roll, and sprinkle the raspberries all over the surface. Roll up the cake from the short end. To start rolling, lift the cake with the end of the towel. When rolled, place the roll seam side down on a serving plate.

EACH SERVING CONTAINS: CALORIES: 96 ▲ CARBOHYDRATES: 17 G ▲ EXCHANGE: 1 STARCH/BREAD, 1/2 FAT

❖ Pistachio Pineapple Roll-Up ❖

The pineapple adds a lightness to the pistachio pudding mix.

1 recipe	Basic Roll-Up Recipe (p. 98)	1 recipe
1 package	(4 servings) sugar-free instant pistachio pudding mix	1 package
1 3/4 cups	skim milk	435 mL
1 cup	crushed pineapple in juice, drained	250 mL

Prepare the Basic Roll-Up Recipe. Cool and unroll. Put the pudding mix into a mixing bowl. Add the skim milk and mix until the pudding is thick. Beat in the pineapple. Spread this filling evenly on the roll and roll up the cake, starting from the short end. To start the rolling, lift the cake with the end of the towel. Place the roll seam side down on a serving plate.

EACH SERVING CONTAINS: CALORIES: 114 ▲ CARBOHYDRATES: 21 G ▲ EXCHANGE: 1 1/2 FRUIT, 1/2 FAT

❖ Apricot Roll-Up ❖

You don't need to know anything about baking to do a great job with this.

1 recipe	Basic Roll-Up Recipe (p. 98)	1 recipe
1/2 cup	fruit-only apricot preserves	125 mL
1/4 cup	water	60 mL

Prepare the Basic Roll-Up Recipe. Cool and unroll. In a small saucepan, mix together the preserves and water over low heat. The heat will help the blending process. Spread the apricot mixture evenly on the roll and roll up the cake, starting from the short end. To start the rolling, lift the cake with the end of the towel. Place the roll seam side down on a serving plate.

EACH SERVING CONTAINS: CALORIES: 111 ▲ CARBOHYDRATES: 21 ▲ EXCHANGE: 1 STARCH/BREAD, 1/2 FAT

❖ Blueberry Crêpes ❖ with Vanilla-Pudding Sauce

YIELD: 20 SERVINGS

1 quart	fresh blueberries	1 L
8 envelopes	aspartame sweetener	8 envelopes
1 package	(4 serving) sugar-free instant vanilla-pudding mix	1 package
2 1/2 cups	skim milk	625 mL
20	Basic Crêpes (p. 95)	20

Clean and lightly crush blueberries. Stir in aspartame sweetener and set aside. Combine vanilla pudding and milk in a bowl. Blend with a wire whisk or electric beater on low until well blended. Set aside. Divide the blueberry mixture evenly among the crepes. Fold each crepe in half and place in a large decorative dessert dish. Pour vanilla pudding over the crepes. Refrigerate at least 2 hours before serving.

EACH SERVING CONTAINS: CALORIES: 65 ▲ CARBOHYDRATES: 7 G ▲ EXCHANGE: 3/4 BREAD

❖ Mocha-Crème Dessert Crêpes ❖

YIELD: 16 CRÊPES

1 box	Sweet 'n Low brand pancake and crêpe mix, plus water low-calorie whipped-topping mix, to make 2 pints plus water and vanilla	1 box
1 teaspoon	instant-coffee granules	5 mL
2 tablespoons	sifted cocoa, unsweetened	10 mL
4 teaspoons	shaved dietetic chocolate	20 mL

Using entire box of pancake and crêpe mix, prepare 16 crêpes according to directions on package. Mix topping mix, coffee granules, and cocoa in mixing bowl. Add water and vanilla according to topping-mix directions. Set crêpes in muffin cups or roll like cones. Fill each crêpe with 1/4 cup mocha-crème mixture. Garnish each with 1/4 teaspoon shaved chocolate.

EACH CRÊPE CONTAINS: CALORIES: 107

PANCAKES &

WAFFLES

❖ Cinnamon Apple Raisin ❖
Dessert Pancakes

YIELD: 12 SERVINGS

1 1/2 cups	all-purpose flour	375 mL
1/4 cup	granulated sugar replacement	60 mL
or		
2 tablespoons	granulated fructose	30 mL
2 teaspoons	baking powder	10 mL
1/2 teaspoon	salt	2 mL
1/2 teaspoon	ground allspice	2 mL
1/2 teaspoon	ground cinnamon	2 mL
1 1/4 cups	skim milk, room temperature	310 mL
2	eggs	2
3 tablespoons	margarine, melted	45 mL
1/2 teaspoon	vanilla extract	2 mL
1 pound can	unsweetened apple slices	1 can (454 g)
1/2 cup	raisins	125 mL
3/4 teaspoon	ground cinnamon	4 mL
3 envelopes	aspartame sweetener	3 envelopes

Combine flour, sweetener, baking powder, salt, allspice, and the 1/2 teaspoon (2 mL) of cinnamon in a bowl. Whisk together 1 cup (250 mL) of the milk and the eggs, melted margarine, and vanilla. Stir liquid into dry mixture just until blended. Cover and refrigerate at least 1 hour. Combine apple slices, raisins, and the 3/4 teaspoon (4 mL) of cinnamon in a bowl. Stir to blend, To assemble: Stir remaining 1/4 cup (60 mL) of milk into the pancake batter. Heat a griddle or heavy large skillet over medium–high heat; spray with a vegetable oil. Ladle batter onto griddle, using about 1/2 cup (125 mL) of batter. Top with about 2 tablespoons (30 mL) of the apple raisin mixture. Then fry until bubbles appear on the surface. Flip pancake and cook until bottom is golden brown. Transfer to a heated platter. Repeat procedure with remaining batter. To serve: Place pancakes on dessert plates, apple side up. Divide any remaining apple mixture among the pancakes. Sprinkle each pancake with 1/4 envelope of aspartame sweetener.

EACH SERVING WITH GRANULATED SUGAR REPLACEMENT CONTAINS: CALORIES: 123 ▲ CARBOHYDRATES: 21 G ▲ EXCHANGE: 1/2 BREAD, 1 FRUIT, 1/4 FAT

EACH SERVING WITH GRANULATED FRUCTOSE CONTAINS: CALORIES: 128 ▲ CARBOHYDRATES: 21 G ▲ EXCHANGE: 1/2 BREAD, 1 FRUIT, 1/4 FAT 76

❖ Apricot Dessert Cakes ❖ with Apricot Sauce

YIELD: 4 SERVINGS

1 pound	apricots in juice	454 g
1 cup	biscuit mix	250 mL
4 envelopes	aspartame sweetener	4 envelopes
4 tablespoons	prepared nondairy whipped topping	60 mL

Drain apricot juice from apricots into a measuring cup. Add enough water to make 3/4 cup liquid. Combine apricot juice and biscuit mix in a bowl. Beat until well blended. Heat a griddle or nonstick skillet over medium heat; spray with a vegetable oil. Ladle about one-fourth of the batter onto the greased surface. Fry until bubbles begin to appear on surface. Turn over and fry until bottom is golden brown. Transfer to warmed platter. Repeat procedure with remaining batter. Transfer apricots to a food processor or blender. Process to a purée. Pour apricot purée into a small sauce pan. Heat thoroughly. Remove from heat and stir in aspartame sweetener. To serve: Place each apricot pancake on a dessert plate. Divide the warm apricot purée evenly among the pancakes. Top each pancake with 1 tablespoon (15 mL) of the nondairy whipped topping. Serve immediately.

EACH SERVING CONTAINS: CALORIES: 65 ▲ CARBOHYDRATES: 14 G ▲ EXCHANGE: 1/2 BREAD, 1/2 FRUIT

❖ Blueberry Ricotta Sweet Pancakes ❖

YIELD: 20 SERVINGS

4	eggs, separated	4
1 cup	ricotta cheese made from skim milk	250 mL
1/3 cup	nonfat plain yogurt	90 mL
3 tablespoons	granulated sugar replacement	45 mL
or		
1 1/2 tablespoons	granulated fructose	21 mL
2/3 cup	all-purpose flour	180 mL
2 teaspoons	baking powder	10 mL
dash	salt	dash
3/4 cup	skim milk	190 mL
2 cups	fresh blueberries	500 mL
1 cup	prepared non-dairy whipped topping	250 mL

Combine egg yolks, ricotta cheese, yogurt, and sweetener of your choice in a bowl. Beat to blend thoroughly. Sift flour, baking powder, and salt together. Stir into cheese mixture. Stir in milk. Fold in blueberries. Beat egg whites until stiff. Fold into batter. Heat a griddle or heavy nonstick skillet over medium heat; spray with a vegetable oil. Ladle about 3 tablespoons (45 mL) of batter onto greased surface. Fry until bubbles begin to appear on surface. Turn over and fry until bottom is golden brown. Transfer to warmed platter. Repeat procedure with remaining batter. To serve: Roll each pancake into a tube. Pipe nondairy whipped topping over pancakes.

EACH SERVING WITH GRANULATED SUGAR REPLACEMENT CONTAINS: CALORIES: 75 ▲
CARBOHYDRATES: 14 G ▲ EXCHANGE: 1 BREAD

EACH SERVING WITH GRANULATED FRUCTOSE CONTAINS: CALORIES: 76 ▲
CARBOHYDRATES: 14 G ▲ EXCHANGE: 1/2 BREAD

❖ Sweet Cakes with ❖
Warm Maple-Cinnamon Topping

YIELD: 16 SERVINGS

1 2/3 cups	nonfat milk	430 mL
1	egg	1
3 tablespoons	liquid fructose	45 mL
2 tablespoons	vegetable oil	30 mL
1 teaspoon	vanilla extract	5 mL
1 cup	all-purpose flour	250 mL
1/2 cup	whole-wheat flour	125 mL
2 tablespoons	yellow cornmeal	30 mL
1 tablespoons	oat bran	15 mL
1 teaspoon	baking powder	5 mL
1 teaspoon	ground cinnamon	5 mL
1/4 teaspoon	salt	1 mL
1/2 cup	sugar-free maple-flavored syrup	125 mL
1/2 teaspoon	ground cinnamon	2 mL

Combine milk, egg, fructose, vegetable oil, and vanilla in a bowl. Beat to blend. Combine flours, cornmeal, oat bran, baking powder, the 1 teaspoon (5 mL) of cinnamon, and the salt in large bowl. Stir to mix. Gradually pour the milk mixture into the flour mixture, stirring or beating on low constantly until the batter is smooth. Heat a griddle or nonstick skillet over medium heat. Grease lightly with a vegetable spray. Spoon batter, about 2 tablespoons (30 mL) at a time, onto the hot griddle. Fry until golden brown on the bottom; turn and fry on the other side. Transfer to warmed platter. Repeat procedure with remaining batter. Combine maple-flavored syrup and the 1/2 teaspoon (2 mL) of cinnamon in a small saucepan or microwave bowl. Stir over medium heat until warmed. To serve: Place pancakes on decorative warmed platter, passing maple-cinnamon topping separately.

EACH SERVING CONTAINS: CALORIES: 65 ▲ CARBOHYDRATES: 11 G ▲ EXCHANGE: 3/4 BREAD

❖ Kids' Color Cakes ❖

YIELD: 16 SERVINGS

2 cups	biscuit mix	500 mL
2 teaspoons	unsweetened soft-drink mix (flavor and color of your choice)	10 mL
1 1/4 cups	skim milk	310 mL

Combine all ingredients in a bowl. Beat to blend. Fry as directed on biscuit package.

EACH SERVING CONTAINS: CALORIES: 62 ▲ CARBOHYDRATES: 11 G ▲ EXCHANGE: 2/3 BREAD

❖ German Apple Pancake ❖

YIELD: 4 SERVINGS

3 large	eggs	3 large
2/3 cup	whole milk	180 mL
1/2 cup	all-purpose flour	125 mL
1/4 cup	margarine, melted	60 mL
1/4 cup	granulated sugar replacement	60 mL
1 teaspoon	ground cinnamon	5 mL
1 large	green apple (peeled, halved, cored, and cut into very thin slices)	1 large

Place eggs, whole milk, flour, 2 teaspoons (30 mL) of the melted margarine, 1 tablespoons (15 mL) of the sugar replacement, and 1/2 teaspoon (2 mL) of the cinnamon in a bowl or food processor. Beat or process until well blended and smooth. Set aside. Brush remaining melted margarine over bottom and sides of a 10-inch (25-cm) heavy oven-proof skillet or pan. Add apple slices, and sprinkle with remaining sugar replacement and cinnamon. Place on top of stove and cook over medium heat until apple slices are tender. Remove from heat, and arrange apple slices in a single layer in the bottom of the same skillet. Pour batter over apple slices, and bake at 450°F (230°C) for

15 minutes or until golden brown. Remove from oven. Cut around outside edge of pancake, and invert on warmed decorative dessert platter. Cut into four wedges and serve immediately.

EACH SERVING CONTAINS: CALORIES: 155 ▲ CARBOHYDRATES: 17 G ▲ EXCHANGE: 2/3 BREAD, 1/2 FRUIT, 2 FAT

❖ Strawberries and Cream Waffles ❖

YIELD: 6 SERVINGS

2 cups	fresh or frozen unsweetened straw-berries, thawed	500 mL
5 envelopes	aspartame sweetener	5 envelopes
1/4 cup	liquid nondairy creamer	60 mL
1/2 cup	prepared nondairy whipped topping	125 mL
6	frozen waffles, thawed and toasted	6

Place strawberries in a bowl; mash slightly with a fork. Sprinkle with aspartame sweetener and stir. Add nondairy creamer. Mix thorough-ly. Fold in nondairy whipped topping. To serve: Place hot waffles on dessert plates. Divide the strawberry cream evenly among the waf-fles. Serve immediately.

EACH SERVING CONTAINS: CALORIES: 125 ▲ CARBOHYDRATES: 14 G ▲ EXCHANGE: 1 BREAD, 1/2 FAT

❖ Pumpkin Waffles ❖

YIELD: 8 SERVINGS

1 1/2 cups	all-purpose flour	375 mL
2 teaspoons	baking powder	10 mL
3/4 teaspoon	ground cinnamon	4 mL
1/2 teaspoon	baking soda	2 mL
1/4 teaspoon	salt	1 mL
1/4 teaspoon	ground cloves	1 mL
1 1/4 cups	buttermilk	310 mL

3/4 cup	pumpkin purée	190 mL
2	eggs, separated	2
2 tablespoons	sugar-free maple-flavored syrup	30 mL
2 teaspoons	vegetable oil	10 mL
2 cups	low-calorie vanilla ice cream	500 mL

Combine flour, baking powder, cinnamon, baking soda, salt, and cloves in a bowl. Stir to mix. In another bowl, combine buttermilk, pumpkin puree, egg yolks, maple-flavored syrup, and vegetable oil. Beat until well blended. Add pumpkin mixture to flour mixture. Fold and stir until flour mixture is moistened. Beat egg whites until stiff. Carefully fold egg whites into pumpkin batter. Do not overmix. Heat a waffle iron according to manufacturer's directions. Grease the iron lightly with a vegetable spray. Spoon the batter onto the iron, filling the surface to about two-thirds full. (Use amount of batter to make total of four large or eight small waffles.) Close the lid and cook for 5 to 6 minutes or until golden brown. Transfer to heated platter. Repeat procedure with remaining batter. To serve: Slice or break large waffles in half. Place waffle-half on a warmed plate. Divide the ice cream evenly among the eight waffle servings. Swirl ice cream in a circular pattern around the top of the waffle. Serve immediately.

EACH SERVING CONTAINS: CALORIES: 130 ▲ CARBOHYDRATES: 21 G ▲ EXCHANGE: 1 1/2 BREAD

MERINGUES

❖ Basic Meringue ❖

YIELD: 4 SERVINGS

Follow the meringue advice on page 8–9 for best results.

3	large egg whites	3
1/4 teaspoon	cream of tartar	2 mL
1/4 cup	sugar	60 mL

Preheat the oven to 250°F (120°C) or the temperature specified in the specific recipe. Cut a brown paper grocery bag or parchment paper to the same size as your cookie sheet. Place the paper on top of the cookie sheet. Using plates, cups, or saucers and a pencil, trace the shape specified in the recipe onto the paper. In a large glass or metal bowl, beat the egg whites with the cream of tartar using an electric mixer. When soft peaks being to form, keep beating, but slowly add the sugar. Increase the mixer speed until stiff peaks form and the meringue is glossy. Don't beat past this point or the meringue will become too dry!

With a clean spoon or rubber scraper transfer the beaten egg white to the circles drawn on the paper. Bake in a 250°F (120°C) preheated oven for the amount of time specified in the recipe. When the time is up, turn off the oven but don't open the oven door. Leave the meringues in the turned off oven for two more hours. Then carefully remove the cookie sheets from the oven. Use a spatula to loosen the meringue from the paper.

EACH SERVING CONTAINS: CALORIES: 61 ▲ CARBOHYDRATES: 13 G ▲ EXCHANGE: 1 STARCH/BREAD

❖ Tart Orange Meringue Tarts ❖

Thin slices of orange make a festive garnish.

1 recipe	Basic Meringue (p. 111)	1 recipe
2 tablespoons	sugar	30 mL
4 teaspoons	cornstarch	20 mL
1 cup	unsweetened orange juice	250 mL
1 tablespoon	lemon juice (fresh is best)	15 mL
1 teaspoon	aspartame sweetener	5 mL
1/2 cup	white topping (optional)	125 mL

Prepare the Basic Meringue with the following variation: Draw six 4" (10 cm) circles on the brown paper. Spoon the meringue into the circles, building up the edges by 1" (2.5 cm), and form a depression in the middle to make a tart shell. Bake in a preheated 250°F (120°C) oven for 1 hour. Cool in the oven for two hours longer without opening the door.

After the meringues are in the oven, prepare the filling by combining the sugar and cornstarch in a saucepan. Use a whisk to blend in the orange juice. Stirring constantly, cook over a medium heat until mixture thickens. Remove from heat and stir in the lemon juice, and aspartame. Cool and store in the refrigerator until just before serving. Then, spoon the filling into the cooked meringue shells. Top with a dollop of your favorite white topping, if desired.

EACH TART CONTAINS: CALORIES: 84 ▲ CARBOHYDRATES: 19 G ▲ EXCHANGE: 1 STARCH/BREAD

❖ Valentine Tarts ❖

1 recipe	Basic Meringue (p. 111)	1 recipe
1 pound	sweet cherries, pitted	450 g
1 tablespoon	sugar	15 mL
1 tablespoon	brandy or water	15 mL

Prepare the meringue according to the directions for Basic Meringue. Trace eight circles or hearts about 2 1/2" (12 cm) in diameter onto parchment or onto the inside of clean brown paper grocery bags cut to the size of your cookie sheets. Spoon the meringue inside the patterns and smooth to the shapes traced. Place in a preheated 250°F (120°C) oven for 30 minutes. Leave the oven door closed, turn off the heat, and let the meringue remain in the oven for two more hours. Cool on a wire rack.

Using a spatula, carefully remove the meringues from the paper. Place one meringue on each of four desert plates. Prepare the cherry topping by putting the cherries, sugar, and brandy or water in a microwave-safe bowl. Stir. Microwave for a minute or two on "high" until the cherries become juicy and steamy. Alternatively, put the cherries, sugar, and brandy or water into a medium saucepan. Stir constantly and heat until the berries are soft and juicy. Put a spoonful of the sauce on top of each of the four meringues. Top each with a second meringue and then distribute the remaining cherries. Top with a dollop of your favorite white topping, if desired.

EACH SERVING CONTAINS: CALORIES: 164 ▲ CARBOHYDRATES: 35 G ▲ EXCHANGE: 1 STARCH/BREAD, 1 1/2 FRUIT

❖ Tangerine Cream Tarts ❖

YIELD: 6 TANGERINE CREAM TARTS

Great in the winter when tangerines are sweet.

1 recipe	Basic Meringue (p. 111)	1 recipe
1 package	(8 ounces) fat-free cream cheese	1 package (225 g)
3 tablespoons	Triple Sec	45 mL
4 teaspoons	cornstarch	20 mL
1 1/3 cups	orange or tangerine juice, unsweetened (okay from frozen concentrate)	330 mL
3	tangerines, peeled and separated into segments, seeded	3

Prepare the Basic Meringue. To prepare the filling, put the cream cheese in a mixing bowl. Add the liqueur and beat until well mixed. Put the cornstarch into a small saucepan. Stir in the orange juice very gradually. Bring to a boil, stirring constantly. Boil for one minute. Remove from heat. Snip the center of each tangerine segment and remove the seeds. Put the seedless tangerine segments into the saucepan with the thickened juice. Put one-sixth of the cheese filling into the bottom of each meringue shell. Top with one-sixth of the tangerine mixture. Chill 1 to 2 hours before serving.

EACH SERVING CONTAINS: CALORIES: 151 ▲ CARBOHYDRATES: 26 ▲ EXCHANGE: 2 STARCH/BREAD

❖ Traditional Pavlova ❖

YIELD: 10 SERVINGS

This lovely dessert was created for the graceful Anna Pavlova, the Russian ballerina.

1 recipe	Basic Meringue (p. 111)	1 recipe
2 cups	frozen, low-fat non-dairy whipped topping, thawed	500 mL
2 cups	fresh strawberries, hulled	500 mL
4	ripe kiwi fruit, peeled	4

Prepare the Basic Meringue. Trace a 12" (30 cm) circle on the inside of a clean brown paper grocery bag or a piece of parchment paper. Put the paper on an ungreased cookie sheet. Spoon the meringue into the circle. Spread so it is evenly distributed. Bake in a preheated 250°F (120°C) oven for 1 hour. Turn off the oven. Leave the meringue in the oven for an additional 30 minutes without opening the door. Then cool on a wire rack. Carefully remove the brown paper and place the meringue on a serving plate. Just before serving, spread the whipped topping carefully over the top of the meringue. Slice the strawberries lengthwise. Place them, cut-side-down, so the points extend out past the edge of the meringue. Slice the kiwis in thin "coins" and overlap them in a ring. Arrange the remaining strawberries in the center.

EACH SERVING CONTAINS: CALORIES: 84 ▲ CARBOHYDRATES: 15 G ▲ EXCHANGE: 1 STARCH/BREAD

❖ Pavlova Wedges with Kiwis ❖
and Raspberry Sauce

YIELD: 8 SERVINGS

Individual servings of a variation of the traditional Pavlova.

1 recipe	Basic Meringue (p. 111)	1 recipe
4	ripe kiwis	4
1 recipe	Raspberry Sauce (recipe follows)	1 recipe

Prepare the Basic Meringue. Trace a 12" (30 cm) circle on the inside of a clean brown paper grocery bag or a piece of parchment paper. Put the paper on an ungreased cookie sheet. Spoon the meringue into the circle. Spread the meringue so it is evenly distributed. Bake in a preheated 250°F (120°C) oven for 1 hour. Turn off the oven. Leave the meringue in the oven for an additional 30 minutes without opening the door. Carefully cut the meringue into eight wedges. Put each wedge on a dessert plate. Peel the kiwis. Slice thinly. Arrange one-half sliced kiwi on each slice of meringue. Spoon raspberry sauce over the fruit and meringue.

EACH SERVING CONTAINS: CALORIES: 98 ▲ CARBOHYDRATES: 21 G ▲ EXCHANGE: 1 STARCH/BREAD, 1/2 FRUIT

❖ Raspberry Sauce ❖

YIELD: 3/4 CUP (185 ML) OR 8 SERVINGS

Seedless raspberry preserves are the best and are worth the effort to find.

1/2 cup	no-sugar-added, seedless raspberry preserves	125 mL
2 tablespoons	Chambord liqueur or raspberry brandy	30 mL
2 tablespoons	water	30 mL

Put the preserves into a small saucepan. Add the raspberry liqueur and water. Mix well with a wire whisk. Heat gently, stirring constantly.

EACH SERVING CONTAINS: CALORIES: 44 ▲ CARBOHYDRATES: 9 G ▲ EXCHANGE: 1/2 FRUIT

❖ French Raspberry Pavlova ❖

YIELD: 10 SERVINGS

You will be a hit with everyone when you serve this. Don't expect leftovers!

1 recipe	Basic Meringue (p. 111)	1 recipe
1 recipe	Vanilla Tart Filling (p. 76)	1 recipe
2 cups	fresh raspberries	500 mL

Prepare the Basic Meringue. Trace a 12" (30 cm) circle on the inside of a clean brown paper grocery bag or a piece of parchment paper cut to fit your cookie sheet. Put the paper on an ungreased cookie sheet. Spoon the meringue into the circle. Spread so it is evenly distributed. Bake in a preheated 250°F (120°C) oven for 1 hour. Turn off the oven. Don't open the door. Leave the meringue in the oven for an additional 30 minutes. Remove to a wire rack to cool.

Carefully separate the meringue from the paper using a spatula. Place the meringue on a serving plate. Prepare the Vanilla Tart Filling. Spoon on the filling. Smooth it evenly to the edges. Arrange the raspberries in concentric circles, beginning at the outside edge. Serve immediately. Meringue gets soggy in damp weather and as the filling sits on top of it.

EACH SERVING CONTAINS: CALORIES: 100 ▲ CARBOHYDRATES: 15 G ▲ EXCHANGE: 1 STARCH/BREAD, 1/2 FAT

❖ Peach Pavlova ❖

YIELD: 10 SERVINGS

This Pavlova uses ice cream or frozen yogurt along with the meringue. The combination of chewy meringue and ice cream is delightful.

1 recipe	Basic Meringue (p. 111)	1 recipe
2 cups	fat-free vanilla ice cream or frozen yogurt, softened	500 mL
15 ounces	peach slices in juice, drained	420 g

Prepare the Basic Meringue. Trace a 12" (30 cm) circle on the inside of a clean brown paper grocery bag or a piece of parchment paper cut to fit your cookie sheet. Put the paper on an ungreased cookie sheet. Spoon the meringue into the circle. Spread so it is evenly distributed. Bake in a preheated 250°F (120°C) oven for 1 hour. Turn off the oven. Don't open the door. Leave the meringue in the oven for an additional 30 minutes. Remove to a wire rack to cool.

Carefully separate the meringue from the paper using a spatula. Put the meringue on a serving plate. Just before serving, spread the ice cream on the baked meringue and arrange peach slices in a circle at the edge. Put any remaining peach slices in the center in a pretty pattern.

EACH SERVING CONTAINS: CALORIES: 83 ▲ CARBOHYDRATES: 18 G ▲ EXCHANGE: 1 STARCH/BREAD

❖ Lemon Meringue Kisses ❖

YIELD: 5 DOZEN

Use a pastry bag with a 1/2" (13 mm) star tip for an even, professional look for kisses.

1 recipe	Basic Meringue (p. 111)	1 recipe
2 teaspoons	lemon zest, finely grated	10 mL
1/2 teaspoon	lemon extract	3 mL

Prepare the Basic Meringue with the following change: After peaks have formed, quickly beat in the lemon zest and extract. Cut parchment paper or brown paper grocery bags to cover the ungreased cookie sheets. Drop the meringue by teaspoonfuls (5 mL) onto the paper. Bake in a preheated 250°F (120°C) oven for 40 minutes. Turn the oven off and leave the meringues inside the closed oven for an additional 5 minutes. Remove from the oven and cool for a minute or two. Use a spatula to remove the meringues from the paper.

EACH KISS INCLUDES: CALORIES: 4 ▲ CARBOHYDRATES: 0.9 G ▲ EXCHANGE: FREE

❖ Lemon Meringue Torte ❖

YIELD: 8 SERVINGS

This torte has the meringue on the bottom and the top.

1 recipe	Basic Meringue (p. 111)	1 recipe
1 package	(4 servings) sugar-free lemon pudding mix	1 package
1 1/4 cups	water or skim milk	1 1/4 cups
2 teaspoons	lemon juice	10 mL

Prepare the Basic Meringue. Trace two dinner plates on parchment or the inside of a brown paper bag that has been cut the same size as your cookie sheets. Put the paper on ungreased cookie sheets. Distribute the meringue between the two circles and smooth it evenly. Bake in a preheated 250°F (120°C) oven for 1 hour. Turn off the oven but do not open the door. Leave in the oven for an additional 30 minutes. Remove to wire racks to cool.

Use a spatula to remove the torte shells from the paper. Prepare the lemon pudding according to package directions, using water or skim milk. Mix in the lemon juice. Put one of the meringues on a serving plate just before you are ready to serve. Scoop half the lemon mixture on top of the meringue. Top with the second meringue. Decorate the top with dollops of the remaining pudding mix.

EACH SERVING CONTAINS: CALORIES: 33 ▲ CARBOHYDRATES: 7 G ▲ EXCHANGE: 1/2 STARCH/BREAD

❖ Chocolate Dream Torte ❖

YIELD: 8 SERVINGS

A pile of meringues and fillings.

1 recipe	Basic Meringue (p. 111)	1 recipe
1 package	(4 servings) sugar-free chocolate pudding mix	1 package
1 1/4 cups	water or skim milk	310 mL
1 cup	frozen, low-fat non-dairy whipped topping, thawed	250 mL

Prepare the Basic Meringue. Trace an 8" (20 cm) pie pan three times on parchment paper or the inside of a brown paper bag that has been cut the same size as your cookie sheets. Put the paper on ungreased cookie sheets. Distribute the meringue between the three circles and smooth it evenly. Bake in a preheated 250°F (120°C) oven for 40 minutes. Turn off the oven but do not open the door. Leave in the oven for an additional 30 minutes. Remove to wire racks to cool.

When you are ready to assemble the torte, remove one of the meringues carefully from the paper and place it on a serving plate. Prepare the pudding according to package directions, using the water or skim milk. (Cool, if it is a cooking recipe.) Put half the pudding on the first meringue. Smooth to the edges. Put the second meringue (with paper removed) on top and repeat with the last of the pudding and the third meringue. Cut carefully. Top each serving with a dollop of whipped topping.

EACH SERVING CONTAINS: CALORIES: 74 ▲ CARBOHYDRATES: 12 G ▲ EXCHANGE: 1 STARCH/BREAD

❖ Double Meringue Butterscotch Pie ❖

YIELD: 8 SERVINGS

There is meringue on the bottom (chunky), butterscotch in the middle (creamy and smooth), and meringue on top (chewy)— "something for everyone."

1 recipe	Basic Meringue, but use 4 egg whites (p. 111)	1 recipe
1 package	(4 servings) sugar-free butterscotch pudding mix (use the cooked variety, not the instant)	1 package
2 cups	skim milk	500 mL

Prepare the Basic Meringue with four egg whites and smooth two-thirds of the amount onto the inside of a 10" (25 cm) pie pan that has been coated with non-stick cooking spray. Shape the meringue into the shape of the pie pan. Save the remaining meringue in the refrigerator. Bake the pie crust in a preheated 250°F (120°C) oven for 1 hour. Turn off the oven but don't open the door; leave the pie crust in the oven to cool. Meanwhile, prepare the pudding according to package directions, using the skim milk. Just before serving, spoon the pudding into the shell. Cover with remaining uncooked meringue. Make sure the meringue topping covers the crust all the way around. Use a spoon to form peaks. Bake in a preheated 350°F (180°C) oven for 10 to 15 minutes. The topping will be light brown.

EACH SERVING CONTAINS: CALORIES: 54 ▲ CARBOHYDRATES: 10 G ▲ EXCHANGE: 2/3 STARCH/BREAD

❖ Meringue Chantilly ❖

YIELD: 6 SERVINGS

You can put a few drops of food coloring in the whipped topping to match a party color scheme.

| 1 recipe | Basic Meringue (p. 111) | 1 recipe |
| 2 cups | frozen, low-fat non-dairy whipped topping, thawed | 500 mL |

Prepare the Basic Meringue. Line two ungreased cookie sheets with parchment paper or cut-up brown paper bags. Spoon the meringue onto the paper to make 12 mounds. Place the two cookie sheets into a preheated 275°F (135°C) oven. Bake for 30 minutes. Open the oven and reverse the positions of the cookie sheets. Bake for another 30 minutes. Remove the cookie sheets from the oven. Loosen and turn each meringue over. Gently depress the center of each one with the back of a spoon. Return to the oven and bake 30 more minutes. Remove from oven and cool meringues completely. Just before serving, make sandwiches with two meringues, placing the whipped topping in between.

EACH SERVING CONTAINS: CALORIES: 94 ▲ CARBOHYDRATES: 14 G ▲ EXCHANGE: 1 STARCH/BREAD, 1/2 FAT

❖ Schaum Torte ❖

This is a great strawberry shortcake replacement.

1 recipe	Basic Meringue (p. 111)	1 recipe
1 tablespoon	sugar	15 mL
2 1/4 cups	fresh strawberries or frozen whole unsweetened strawberries, sliced	310 m
9	strawberries, hulled	9
1 cup	frozen, low-fat non-dairy whipped topping	250 mL

Prepare the Basic Meringue. Line ungreased cookie sheets with parchment paper or brown paper bags cut to fit cookie sheets. Drop meringue onto the paper, making 9 mounds. Use a tablespoon (15 mL) dipped in cold water to make an indentation in the top of each mound. Bake in a preheated 275°F (135°C) oven for 45 minutes. Cool thoroughly on wire racks. Meanwhile, sprinkle the sugar over the sliced strawberries, mix, and let stand. To assemble, place a meringue on a dessert plate. Scoop strawberries into the indentation. Top with a dollop of whipped topping and garnish with a whole strawberry.

EACH SERVING CONTAINS: CALORIES: 72 ▲ CARBOHYDRATES: 14 G ▲ EXCHANGE: 1 STARCH/BREAD

❖ Strawberry Bombe ❖

In the same class as "Baked Alaska." Prepare this for a crowd.

1 recipe	Basic Meringue (p. 111)	1 recipe
1 quart	fat-free strawberry ice cream	950 mL
1 teaspoon	vanilla extract	5 mL

Prepare basic meringue according to the recipe. Trace a 9" (22 cm) circle on a piece of parchment paper or the inside of a brown paper bag. Cut the paper to the size of an ungreased cookie sheet. Smooth one-third of the meringue inside the circle and place the paper on the cookie sheet in a 275°F (135°C) oven for 30 minutes. Turn off the oven but do not open the door. Let the meringue sit in the oven for an additional 20 minutes. Cool on a wire rack but do not remove the paper. Just before serving time, preheat the oven to 450°F (230°C).

Heap the ice cream carefully in a mound on the meringue. Beat the vanilla extract into the remaining uncooked meringue. Smooth the uncooked meringue evenly over the strawberry ice cream dome, making sure it touches the baked meringue at all points. Bake until the meringue is a delicate brown, about 3 minutes. Serve right away, being careful to cut servings away from the brown paper.

EACH SERVING CONTAINS: CALORIES: 131 CARBOHYDRATES: 27 G EXCHANGE: 1 STARCH/BREAD, 1 FRUIT

❖ Hawaiian Alaska ❖

YIELD: 10 SERVINGS

There is no ice cream in this pineapple baked Alaska. An advantage is that you make individual servings.

Base

1/3 cup + 1 tablespoon	cold water	95 mL
1/4 cup + 2 tablespoons	fat-free butter and oil replacement product	90 mL
2 cups	flour	500 mL

Filling

3 ounces	fat-free cream cheese	80 g
1	large egg	1
1 teaspoon	vanilla extract	5 mL
10	pineapple rings in juice, drained	10 slices

Topping:

1 recipe	Basic Meringue (p. 111)	1 recipe

To prepare the base, put all the base ingredients in a mixing bowl. Mix with an electric mixer at low speed until well blended. Shape into a ball and transfer to a floured board. Roll out to 1/8" (32 mm) thickness. Cut ten 4" (10 cm) circles. Place the circles on cookie sheets that have been coated with non-stick vegetable cooking spray. Prick them all over with a fork. Bake in a preheated 450°F (230°C) oven for 8 to 10 minutes. Cool on a wire rack. Do not remove from cookie sheets.

Prepare the filling by blending all the filling ingredients except the pineapple rings. Place a pineapple ring on each of the bases. Spoon the filling evenly into the center of each ring. Return the cookie sheets to a preheated 400°F (200°C) oven for just 3 minutes. Quickly cover each cookie with the meringue. Return to the 400°F (200°C) oven and bake 8 to 10 minutes more. The meringue will be golden brown.

EACH SERVING CONTAINS: CALORIES: 175 ▲ CARBOHYDRATES: 36 G ▲ EXCHANGE: 2 STARCH/BREAD

CREAM PUFFS

❖ Cream Puff Pastry ❖

YIELD: 12 CREAM PUFFS

You won't believe how easy cream puffs are until you prepare them yourself. This recipe is practically foolproof and needs no exotic kitchen equipment.

1 cup	water	250 mL
1/3 cup	canola oil	80 mL
1 cup	flour	250 mL
4	large eggs or equivalent egg substitute	4
1 teaspoon	butter extract	5 mL
1 teaspoon	vanilla extract	5 mL

Put the water and canola oil in a medium saucepan. Heat to a rolling boil. Lower the heat and add the flour all at once, stirring with a wooden spoon until the mixture forms a ball. Remove from the heat. With an electric mixer, beat in the eggs one at a time. Add the extracts. Using a spoon, drop 12 cream puffs onto an ungreased cookie sheet. Bake in a 400°F (200°C) oven for 10 minutes. Reduce the heat to 350°F (180°C) and bake for 25 minutes longer. Turn off the oven but do not remove cream puffs until they are quite firm to the touch. Cool them away from drafts. To fill, cut the puffs horizontally, using a sharp knife. If any damp dough remains inside, scoop it out before filling.

EACH PUFF CONTAINS: CALORIES: 117 ▲ CARBOHYDRATES: 8 G ▲ EXCHANGE: 1/2 STARCH/BREAD, 1/4 HIGH FAT MEAT; 1 FAT

❖ Light Chocolate Cream Puffs ❖

Very impressive, and easier than pie!

1 recipe	Cream Puff Pastry (p. 124)	1 recipe
1 recipe	Chocolate Mousse Pudding (p. 82)	1 recipe
1 recipe	Chocolate Glaze (p. 74) or Napoleon Fudge Topping recipe (p. 75)	1 recipe

Prepare the cream puffs from the puff pastry, make the Chocolate Mousse Pudding, and the glaze or fudge topping. Assemble the cream puffs by putting the pudding inside the pastry and drizzling the glaze or fudge topping over the top.

EACH PUFF CONTAINS: CALORIES: 139 ▲ CARBOHYDRATES: 11 G ▲ EXCHANGE: 2 VEGETABLE, 3 FAT

❖ Light Mocha Cream Puffs ❖

YIELD: 12 CREAM PUFFS

For those who love that mocha flavor.

1 recipe	Cream Puff Pastry (p. 124)	1 recipe
1 recipe	Mocha Tart Filling (p. 72)	1 recipe
1 recipe	Chocolate Glaze (p. 74) or Napoleon Fudge Topping (p. 75)	1 recipe

Prepare the cream puff pastry and the mocha filling. Bake the cream puffs. Assemble by putting the filling inside the cream puffs. Drizzle chocolate glaze or fudge topping over the top of the cream puffs.

EACH PUFF CONTAINS: CALORIES: 125 ▲ CARBOHYDRATES: 10 G ▲ EXCHANGE: 2 VEGETABLE, 1 1/2 FAT

❖ Traditional Cream Puffs ❖

YIELD: 12 CREAM PUFFS

These look and taste like the cream puffs sold in bakeries.

1 recipe	Cream Puff Pastry (p. 124)	1 recipe
1 recipe	Vanilla Tart Filling (p 76)	1 recipe
1 recipe	Chocolate Glaze (p. 74) or	1 recipe
	Napoleon Fudge	
	Topping (p. 75)	

Prepare the puff pastry, tart filling, and one of the toppings. Bake the cream puffs. Assemble by putting tart filling inside the puffs, covering with the tops, and drizzling with Chocolate Glaze (p. 75) or Napoleon Fudge Topping (p. 75).

EACH PUFF CONTAINS: CALORIES: 176 ▲ CARBOHYDRATES: 15 G ▲ EXCHANGE: 1 STARCH/BREAD, 2 FAT

❖ Mocha Cream Puffs ❖

YIELD: 12 CREAM PUFFS

A more pronounced coffee flavor.

1 recipe	Cream Puff Pastry (p. 124)	1 recipe
1 recipe	Mocha Tart Filling (p. 72)	1 recipe
1 recipe	Mocha Glaze (p. 73)	1 recipe

Prepare the puff pastry, Mocha Tart Filling, and Mocha Glaze. Bake the cream puffs. Assemble by putting the coffee filling inside the puffs, covering with the tops, and drizzling with glaze.

EACH PUFF CONTAINS: CALORIES: 125 ▲ CARBOHYDRATES: 10 ▲ EXCHANGE: 2 VEGETABLE, 1 1/2 FAT

❖ Strawberry Cream Puffs ❖

An easy alternative to strawberry shortcake and very pretty.

1 recipe	Cream Puff Pastry (p. 124)	1 recipe
3 cups	fresh strawberries, or frozen whole straw-berries without sugar	750 mL
1 cup	frozen low-fat non-dairy whipped topping	250 mL

Make and bake the cream puffs. Put 1/4 cup (60 mL) strawberries in each puff. Put the top back on. Add a dollop of whipped topping to the top.

EACH PUFF CONTAINS: CALORIES: 142 ▲ CARBOHYDRATES: 12 G ▲ EXCHANGE: 1 STARCH/BREAD, 1 1/2 FAT

❖ Banana Cream Puffs ❖

If you have bananas, all the rest of the ingredients are "on the shelf."

1 recipe	Cream Puff Pastry (p. 124)	1 recipe
1 recipe	Vanilla Tart Filling (p. 76)	1 recipe
4	medium bananas, peeled and sliced	4
3 teaspoon	lemon juice	15 mL
1 cup	frozen low-fat non-dairy whipped topping	250 mL

Prepare the cream puffs and Vanilla Tart Filling. Bake the cream puffs. Put the banana slices into a medium mixing bowl. Pour the lemon juice over the bananas and toss to distribute the lemon juice evenly. Add the pudding and mix. Spoon this pudding mixture into the cream puffs. Put the cream puff tops on and add a dollop of white topping.

EACH PUFF CONTAINS: CALORIES: 216 ▲ CARBOHYDRATES: 24 ▲ EXCHANGE: 1 1/2 STARCH/BREAD, 2 FAT

❖ Cream Puffs with Raspberry Sauce ❖

YIELD: 12 CREAM PUFFS

The raspberry sauce is striking against the light colors of the puffs and filling and adds a contrasting flavor and texture, too.

1 recipe	Cream Puff Pastry (p. 124)	1 recipe
1 recipe	Vanilla Tart Filling (p. 76)	1 recipe
1 recipe	Raspberry Sauce (p. 225)	1 recipe

Prepare the cream puffs, tart filling, and Raspberry Sauce. Bake the cream puffs. Fill them with the filling and put the tops back on. Spoon the sauce over the puffs.

EACH PUFF CONTAINS: CALORIES: 199 ▲ CARBOHYDRATES: 20 G ▲ EXCHANGE: 1 STARCH/BREAD, 1 VEGETABLE, 2 FAT

❖ New Zealand Cream Puffs ❖

YIELD: 12 CREAM PUFFS

Kiwis are ready to eat when they yield to gentle pressure. Eat them at their sweetest.

1 recipe	Cream Puff Pastry (p.124)	1 recipe
4	kiwi fruit, peeled and chopped	4
2 cups	fresh strawberries, hulled and sliced	500 mL
2 cups	frozen low-fat non-dairy whipped topping, thawed	500 mL

Prepare the cream puffs according to the directions. When ready to assemble, put the chopped kiwis and sliced strawberries in a bowl. Add the whipped topping and fold the mixture together. Spoon the fruit mixture into the cream puffs. Put the tops back on and serve immediately.

EACH PUFF CONTAINS: CALORIES: 167 ▲ CARBOHYDRATES: 16 G ▲ EXCHANGE: 1 STARCH/BREAD, 2 FAT

❖ Icy Peach Cream Puffs ❖

Only the puffs are prepared ahead of time for this. Prepare them in the morning and refrigerate the peaches. Assemble everything after serving dinner.

1 recipe	Cream Puff Pastry (p.124)	1 recipe
3 cups	sugar-free low-fat vanilla icecream or frozen yogurt	750 mL
30 ounces	canned peaches packed in juice, drained, chopped and chilled	850 g

Prepare the basic cream puff recipe. Bake the puffs. When ready to serve, put 1/4 cup (60 mL) ice cream in each puff. Distribute the chopped peaches over the ice cream. Put on the tops and serve immediately.

EACH PUFF CONTAINS: CALORIES: 172 ▲ CARBOHYDRATES: 22 G ▲ EXCHANGE: 1 1/2 STARCH/BREAD, 1 FAT

❖ Frozen Chocolate Cream Puffs ❖

Prepare these ahead of time and freeze them. Move them to the refrigerator just as you're putting dinner on the table. They are perfect for dessert.

1 recipe	Cream Puff Pastry (p. 124)	1 recipe
3 cups	cold skim milk	750 mL
2 packages	(4-servings) sugar- free chocolate pudding mix	2 packages

Prepare the basic cream puffs. Bake them. In a medium mixing bowl, beat together the skim milk and the pudding mix with an electric mixer until thick. Scoop the pudding into the cream puffs. Put the tops on and freeze. When frozen, put them in plastic bags until you are ready to use them.

EACH PUFF CONTAINS: CALORIES: 141 ▲ CARBOHYDRATES: 12 G ▲ EXCHANGE: 1 MILK, 1 1/2 FAT

❖ Frozen Raspberry Cream Puffs ❖

YIELD: 12 CREAM PUFFS

These make-ahead cream puffs are perfect to freeze and eat one at a time.

| 1 recipe | Cream Puff Pastry (p. 124) | 1 recipe |
| 1 recipe | Raspberry Filling for Raspberry Cream Pie, without frozen pie crust (p. 61) | 1 recipe |

Prepare the basic cream puffs and the filling for the raspberry cream pie. Bake the puffs. Spoon the filling into the cream puffs, put on the tops, and freeze them. After they are frozen, put them in plastic freezer bags. Remove from the freezer at the beginning of dinner and they will be ready by dessert time.

EACH PUFF CONTAINS: CALORIES: 156 ▲ CARBOHYDRATES: 15 G ▲ EXCHANGE: 1 STARCH/BREAD, 2 FAT

❖ Frozen Strawberry Cream Puffs ❖

YIELD: 12 CREAM PUFFS

Remove as many as you need from the freezer when you get dinner ready.

| 1 recipe | Cream Puff Pastry (p. 124) | 1 recipe |
| 1 recipe | Strawberry Ice Cream Pie, without pie crust (p. 63) | 1 recipe |

Prepare the basic cream puffs and the strawberry ice cream pie filling from the Strawberry Ice Cream Pie recipe. Spoon the filling inside the baked cream puffs. Put the tops on and freeze. After freezing the puffs, put them in plastic freezer bags.

EACH PUFF CONTAINS: CALORIES: 148 ▲ CARBOHYDRATES: 14 G ▲ EXCHANGE: 1 STARCH/BREAD, 1 1/2 FAT

DRESSED-UP
ANGELS

❖ Snowball Cake ❖

YIELD: 16 SERVINGS

Impressive! Prepare this any time you want to show off. It looks
fabulous on a buffet table.

1 package	(4 servings) sugar- free strawberry gelatin mix	1 package
1 cup	hot water	250 mL
1 cup	cold water	250 mL
1 cup	frozen low-fat non-dairy whipped topping, thawed	250 mL
2 cups	fresh strawberries or frozen, sugar-free, defrosted	500 mL
1	angel food cake, cut into 1" cubes	1 (2.5 cm)

Prepare the gelatin by putting the powder into a mixing bowl. Add
the hot water and stir until the powder is dissolved. Add the cold
water and stir to combine. Refrigerate an hour or so until partially
set. In another bowl, fold together the whipped topping and the
strawberries. Fold into the partially set gelatin. Return to the refrigerator.

Line a deep mixing bowl with long pieces of waxed paper. The
pieces should extend over the edge, travel down the inside of the
bowl and up the other side, extending past the rims. Use several

overlapping strips so the inside of the bowl is totally covered. Alternate layers of the gelatin mixture with cake cubes in the bowl. Refrigerate 8 hours or overnight. Before serving, put a cake plate upside down on top of the bowl. Turn the whole thing over. Peel off the waxed paper carefully.

EACH SERVING CONTAINS: CALORIES: 112 ▲ CARBOHYDRATES: 25 G ▲ EXCHANGE: 1 STARCH/BREAD, 1/2 FRUIT

❖ Gourmet Strawberries and Mint ❖

YIELD: 8 SERVINGS

Not your run-of-the-mill strawberry shortcake. This is a nice treat at a luncheon.

4 cups	fresh strawberries, sliced	1 L
2 tablespoons	powdered sugar	30 mL
1 tablespoon	fresh mint leaves, finely chopped	15 mL
1 cup	fat- free sugar-free lemon yogurt	250 mL
14 cups	fat-free sour cream	60 mL
1	angel food cake, cut in 16 slices	1

Mix the strawberries, powdered sugar, and mint together in a mixing bowl. Set aside for an hour at room temperature. This will cause the strawberries to let out their juice. When you are ready to serve, mix the yogurt and sour cream together in a small bowl. Put one slice of cake on each of 8 dessert plates. Put a spoonful of strawberries on top and then the second slice of cake. Top with the rest of the strawberries and distribute the yogurt–sour cream mixture.

EACH SERVING CONTAINS: CALORIES: 161 ▲ CARBOHYDRATES: 36 G ▲ EXCHANGE: 1 STARCH/BREAD, 1 1/2 FRUIT

❖ Tiramisu ❖

This popular Italian dessert is both rich and beautiful. Try this easy yet impressive version.

1 cup	skim milk	250 mL
1 tablespoon	butter or margarine	15 mL
1 1/2 tablespoons	cornstarch	23 mL
1 tablespoon	sugar	15 mL
3	large egg yolks, mixed lightly	3
2 teaspoon	vanilla extract	10 mL
1 1/2 cups	fat-free ricotta cheese or fat-free cottage cheese	375 mL
2 cups	frozen low-fat non-dairy whipped topping, thawed	500 mL
1/4 cup	strong espresso, cooled	60 mL
1/4 cup	coffee liqueur	60 mL
1	angel food cake	1
2 cups	fresh raspberries, or frozen, thawed	500 mL

Warm the milk and butter in a heavy-bottom medium saucepan or the top of a double boiler, stirring constantly. In a small bowl, mix together the cornstarch, sugar, and egg yolks. Blend well. Add the vanilla and blend. Transfer the egg mixture to the warm milk. Continue to heat and mix with a wire whisk until the mixture is thick. Look for whisk patterns, which indicate that it's done. Cool. Put the cheese into a mixing bowl. Beat at high speed with an electric mixer for 3 to 4 minutes. Add the cooled mixture and beat the two together at a low speed until well mixed. Fold in the whipped topping until thoroughly blended. In a small bowl, stir together the espresso and liqueur.

Using a sharp knife, cut the angel food cake crosswise into three layers. Put one layer into the bottom of a serving bowl. Brush with the espresso liqueur mixture. Turn the layer over and brush the other side. Spoon one-third of the milk-cheese mixture over the cake. Arrange one-third of the raspberries around edges. Brush one side of another angel food cake layer and put it (brushed-side-down) in the bowl. Brush the top and spoon on one third of the milk-cheese mixture and raspberries. Repeat the process for the last layer. Pour any remaining espresso liqueur on top of the third layer. Smooth the top and cover tightly. Refrigerate for at least 6 hours or up to 2 days before serving.

EACH SERVING CONTAINS: CALORIES: 242 ▲ CARBOHYDRATES: 43 G ▲ EXCHANGE: 3 STARCH/BREAD

❖ Strawberry Charlotte ❖

YIELD: 12 SERVINGS

This charlotte is layered angel food cake filled with pudding and strawberry preserves. If the preserves are too rigid to spread, add a little hot water and mix well. This should soften them up.

1	angel food cake	1
1/3 cup	fruit-only strawberry preserves	80 mL
1 recipe	Vanilla Tart Filling (p. 76), or	1 recipe
1 package	(4 servings) sugar-free low-fat strawberry pudding, made with skim milk, according to package directions	1 package

Slice the angel food cake crosswise into three sections. Lay the bottom part cut-side-up, on a serving plate. Spread with one-third of the jam. Prepare the tart filling and then spoon one-third of the vanilla filling or pudding evenly on top of the jam layer. Spread jam on top of the next layer of angel food cake and place it on top of the pudding layer. Repeat, ending with pudding on top. Refrigerate until serving.

EACH SERVING CONTAINS: CALORIES: 196 ▲ CARBOHYDRATES: 39 G ▲ EXCHANGE: 1 1/2 STARCH/BREAD, 1 FRUIT

❖ Peach Charlotte ❖

A taste of Georgia. Use fresh peaches instead of canned, if you have them, for the most authentic charlotte of all.

1	angel food cake	1
1/3 cup	fruit-only peach preserves	80 mL
1 recipe	Vanilla Tart Filling (p. 76) or sugar-free low-fat vanilla pudding from a 4-serving package, made with skim milk according to package directions.	1 recipe
15 ounces	canned peaches, sliced, packed in juice without sugar, drained and chopped	425 g

Slice the angel food cake crosswise into three sections. Place the bottom part, cut-side-up, onto a serving plate. Prepare the tart filling. Spread the cut side of the cake on the plate with one-third of the jam. Mix the vanilla filling with the drained, chopped peaches. Spoon one-third of this mixture onto the first layer of the cake. Spread jam on top of the next layer of the cake and repeat, ending with pudding. Refrigerate until serving time.

EACH SERVING CONTAINS: CALORIES: 211 ▲ CARBOHYDRATES: 43 G ▲ EXCHANGE: 2 STARCH/BREAD, 1 FRUIT, 1/2 FAT

❖ Chocolate Charlotte ❖

YIELD: 12 SERVINGS

1	angel food cake	1
1/3 cup	fruit-only cherry preserves or seedless raspberry fruit-only preserves	80 mL

| 1 recipe | Chocolate Tart Filling (p. 81), or sugar-free low-fat chocolate pudding from a package, made with skim milk according to package directions. | 1 recipe |

Follow the directions for Strawberry Charlotte, page 134.

EACH SERVING CONTAINS: CALORIES: 190 ▲ CARBOHYDRATES: 43 G ▲ EXCHANGE: 1/2 MILK, 2 FRUIT

❖ Jamaican Trifle ❖

YIELD: 12 SERVINGS

Taste this to see if the rum flavor is strong enough for you, and add more if you like. This is a buffet-table favorite.

15 ounces	crushed pineapple, packed in juice, with no sugar added	420 g
1 tablespoon	rum extract	15 mL
1	angel food cake	1
2 cups	frozen low-fat non-dairy whipped topping, thawed	500 mL

Drain the crushed pineapple, reserving the juice. Measure out 1/2 cup (125 mL) of the juice. Put it in a small bowl and mix in the rum extract. Slice the angel food cake into three layers. Brush the bottom of the bottom layer with the juice mixture and place it in a trifle bowl or other glass serving bowl. Brush the top of this layer with the juice. Spoon one-third of the pineapple on top of this layer. Brush the bottom of the next layer. Repeat, using all the juice and the rest of the crushed pineapple. Cover tightly and refrigerate for at least 6 hours. When serving, scoop a dollop of white topping onto each piece.

EACH SERVING CONTAINS: CALORIES: 177 ▲ CARBOHYDRATES: 37 G ▲ EXCHANGE: 1 STARCH/BREAD, 1 1/2 FRUIT

❖ Individual Strawberry Trifles ❖

YIELD: 8 SERVINGS

These look especially elegant in tall, clear glasses.

2 cups	fresh whole strawberries or frozen (no sugar), sliced (reserve 1/2 cup whole for garnish)	500 mL
2 tablespoons	Grand Marnier liqueur	30 mL
1 1/2 cups	skim milk	375 mL
1 cup	egg substitute or 4 eggs, slightly beaten	250 mL
1 teaspoon	vanilla extract	5 mL
4 packages	saccharin or acesulfame-K sugar substitute	4 packages
1/2	angel food cake, cut into 8 pieces	1/2
1 1/4 cups	frozen low-fat non-dairy whipped topping, slightly softened	310 mL

In a small bowl, toss the sliced strawberries with the Grand Marnier. Cover and refrigerate. In the top of a double boiler over boiling water, scald the milk. Put the lightly beaten eggs in a small bowl. Pour about 1/2 C (125 mL) of the hot milk on top of the eggs, stirring constantly. Pour this mixture into the top of a double boiler. With only simmering water, and being sure the top pan does not come into contact with the water, cook, stirring constantly. When the custard is finished, it will easily coat a metal spoon. Remove the custard from over the water. Stir in the extract and sugar substitute.

When ready to assemble, put the custard into a medium mixing bowl and gently but thoroughly fold in the whipped topping. Tear off half of each of the eight pieces of angel food cake and push the half to the bottom of a tall parfait glass. Distribute half the strawberries over the pieces of angel food cake. Distribute half the custard in a similar fashion. Repeat with the other half pieces of angel food cake, strawberries, and custard. Cover tightly with plastic wrap and refrigerate until serving time, at least 2 hours. Garnish with the reserved strawberries.

EACH SERVING CONTAINS: CALORIES: 202 ▲ CARBOHYDRATES: 33 G ▲ EXCHANGE: 2 STARCH/BREAD, 1 FAT

❖ Lemony Angel Food ❖

The perfect solution for leftover angel food cake that is getting stale. The topping revives the cake.

1/2	angel food cake, cut into 6 pieces	
1 package	(4 servings) sugar-free lemon pudding mix (prepared according to package directions)	1 package
1 1/4 cup	water or skim milk	310 mL
1 teaspoon	lemon juice	5 mL
1 recipe	Lemon Sauce (recipe follows)	1 recipe
1/2 cup	frozen low-fat non-dairy whipped topping (optional)	125 mL

Cut each of the six pieces of cake into chunks and arrange them in six serving dishes. Mix the lemon pudding, made with water or skim milk, with the lemon juice and spoon over the angel food cake. Drizzle Lemon Sauce over the mixture. Top with a dollop of white topping, if desired.

EACH SERVING CONTAINS: CALORIES: 149 ▲ CARBOHYDRATES: 35 G ▲ EXCHANGE: 1 STARCH/BREAD, 1 1/2 FRUIT

❖ Lemon Sauce ❖

This lemon sauce is best when used in a day or two. Keep it refrigerated.

1/3 cup	fresh lemon juice	80 mL
6 packages	saccharin or acesulfame-K sugar substitute	6 packages
1	large egg or equivalent egg substitute	1

1 tablespoon	cornstarch	15 mL
1 tablespoon	water	15 mL
1 teaspoon	vanilla extract	5 mL
1 teaspoon	aspartame sweetener	5 mL

Combine the lemon juice and saccharin or acesulfame-K in a saucepan over medium heat. Bring to a simmer. In a medium mixing bowl, beat the egg. Using a fork, blend together the cornstarch and water in a cup. Add this to the egg. Add a small amount of the lemon juice mixture to the egg mixture. Now put this into the saucepan with the remaining lemon mixture. Cook over medium heat, stirring constantly until thickened. Remove from heat. Cool. Stir in the vanilla and aspartame.

EACH SERVING CONTAINS: CALORIES: 27 ▲ CARBOHYDRATES: 4 G ▲ EXCHANGE: FREE

❖ Strawberries Chantilly ❖

YIELD: 4 SERVINGS

Don't forget to let the strawberries stand. That's the secret of getting them juicy.

2 cups	fresh strawberries or frozen (no sugar), thawed	500 mL
1 tablespoon	sugar	15 mL
1 tablespoon	Kirsch or cherry liqueur (optional)	15 mL
1 cup	frozen low-fat non-dairy whipped topping, thawed	250 mL
1/3	angel food cake	1/3

Cut the strawberries in half. In a mixing bowl, combine the strawberries, sugar, and liqueur, if you are using it. Let stand 1/2 hour to 1 hour. Just before serving fold together the strawberries and the whipped topping. Put one slice of angel food cake on each of four dessert plates. Spoon the strawberry mixture on top.

EACH SERVING CONTAINS: CALORIES: 202 ▲ CARBOHYDRATES: 41 G ▲ EXCHANGE: 1 STARCH/BREAD, 2 FRUIT

BAKED

GOODIES

CAKES

❖ Langues de Chat ❖

YIELD: 30 COOKIES

2 tablespoons	butter or margarine	30 mL
2 tablespoons	fat-free cream cheese	30 mL
3 packages	acesulfame-K sugar substitute	3 packages
3 tablespoons	sugar	45 mL
1	large egg or equivalent egg substitute, lightly beaten	1
1 teaspoon	vanilla extract	5 mL
1/4 teaspoon	butter extract	2 mL
1/2 cup	flour, sifted	125 mL

In a medium bowl, beat the butter, cream cheese, acesulfame-K, and sugar until light and fluffy. Slowly beat in the egg and the two extracts. Fold in the flour to make a soft dough. Spoon the dough carefully into a pastry bag fitted with a 3/8" (1 cm) plain tip. Squeeze out 3" (7.5 cm) lengths onto greased baking sheets that have been lined with parchment or waxed paper. Cut off the dough with a sharp knife in between the cookies. Bake in a preheated 425°F (220°C) oven for 8–10 minutes, until the edges are lightly browned. Cool the sheets on a wire rack before removing the cookies.

EACH COOKIE CONTAINS: CALORIES: 23 ▲ CARBOHYDRATES: 3 G ▲ EXCHANGE: FREE

❖ Chocolate Mayonnaise Cake ❖

YIELD: 8 PIECES

This would have been loaded with fat before fat-free mayonnaise. It's a moist, rich chocolate cake.

2 cups	sifted flour	500 mL
1/4 cup	sugar	60 mL
6 packages	saccharin or acesulfame-K sugar substitute	6 packages
1 1/2 teaspoons	baking soda	8 mL
4 tablespoons	unsweetened cocoa powder	60 mL
1 cup	cold water	250 mL
1 cup	fat-free mayonnaise	250 mL

Mix together the dry ingredients in a large mixing bowl. In another bowl, beat together the cold water and mayonnaise. Add the water mixture to the dry ingredients. Mix well to combine. Prepare an 8 x 12" (20 x 30 cm) sheet cake pan, coating it with non-stick cooking spray. Pour the batter into the pan and bake it in a preheated 350°F (180°C) oven for 45 minutes or until a tester comes out clean. Cut into eight sections.

EACH PIECE CONTAINS: CALORIES: 147 ▲ CARBOHYDRATES: 32 ▲ EXCHANGE: 1 STARCH/BREAD, 1 FRUIT

❖ Rich Lemon Shorties ❖

YIELD: 30 SQUARES

For the calories, these are delicious. It's worth using potato flour for its smooth texture.

Base:

1/2 cup	fat-free cream cheese	125 mL
1/2 cup	butter or margarine	125 mL
2 tablespoons	sugar	30 mL
3 packages	acesulfame-K sugar substitute	3 packages
2 cups	flour	500 mL
1/2 cup	potato flour	125 mL

Topping:

2 tablespoons	lemon peel, freshly grated	30 mL
3 tablespoons	sugar	45 mL
3 packages	acesulfame-K sugar substitute	3 packages
3	large eggs or equivalent egg substitute	3
1/2 cup	sifted flour	125 mL
3/4 teaspoon	baking powder	4 mL
3 tablespoons	lemon juice	45 mL
1/2 teaspoon	sugar (optional)	3 mL

Using an electric mixer, cream together the cream cheese, butter, sugar, and acesulfame-K. In another bowl, sift together the two flours. Add the flour mixture to the cream cheese mixture. Mix. With your hands, spread the mixture along the bottom of a 9 x 13" (23 x 33cm) lasagna pan. Refrigerate while you preheat a 350°F (180°C) oven. Bake 15 to 20 minutes. Base will be lightly browned. Cool on a wire rack.

Beat the lemon peel, sugar, acesulfame- K and eggs until smooth and creamy. Sift the flour and baking powder together into a small bowl. Fold the sifted ingredients into the egg mixture. Stir in the lemon juice. Pour the mixture over a cooled base. Bake in a 350°F (180°C) oven for 25 minutes. Cool on a wire rack. Cut into squares. Sprinkle with the remaining sugar, if desired.

EACH SQUARE CONTAINS: CALORIES: 95 ▲ CARBOHYDRATES: 13 G ▲ EXCHANGE: 1 STARCH/BREAD, 1/2 FAT

❖ Cherry Cheese Suzette ❖

Rich and sweet. A brunch favorite.

Batter:

1/4 cup	fat-free butter and oil replacement product	60 mL
2	large eggs or equivalent egg substitute	2
1 1/4 cup	flour	310 mL
1 teaspoon	baking powder	5 mL
3/4 cup	skim milk	185 mL

Filling:

2 cups	fat-free cottage cheese	500 mL
1 teaspoon	butter extract	5 mL
1 package	saccharin or acesulfame-K sugar substitute	1 package
1/2 cup	fruit-only cherry preserves	125 mL

Put the butter replacement in the mixing bowl of an electric mixer. Add the eggs and beat until smooth. In another bowl, combine the flour and baking powder. With mixer running at low speed, add the flour mixture to the egg mixture alternately with the milk. Blend for two minutes at low speed. Coat an 8" (20 cm) pan with non-stick cooking spray. Spoon half the batter into the pan. In a mixing bowl, combine the cottage cheese, butter extract, and sugar substitute. Pour the filling over the batter. Spread so the filling is evenly distributed. Dot with cherry filling. Carefully pour the remaining batter on top. Bake in a preheated 350°F (180°C) oven for 50 to 60 minutes. The top will be lightly browned.

EACH SERVING CONTAINS: CALORIES: 164 ▲ CARBOHYDRATES: 29 G ▲ EXCHANGE: 2 STARCH/BREAD

❖ Carrot Cake ❖
with Cream Cheese Icing

YIELD: 8 SERVINGS

2 cups	flour	500 mL
2 teaspoons	cinnamon	10 mL
1 teaspoon	baking powder	5 mL
1/3 cup	fat-free butter and oil replacement product	80 mL
4 tablespoons	sugar	60 mL
6 packages	saccharin or acesulfame-K sugar substitute	6 packages
3	large eggs or egg substitute	3
3	medium carrots, grated	3
1/2 cup	finely chopped walnuts (optional)	125 mL
1 recipe	Cream Cheese Icing (p. 145)	1 recipe

In a medium mixing bowl, blend together the flour, cinnamon, and baking powder. In another bowl, beat together the butter replacement, sugar, and sugar substitute. Beat in the eggs, one at a time, alternating with the flour mixture. Stir in the carrots and walnuts, if you are using them. Pour the batter into a 9" (14 cm) cake pan coated with non-stick vegetable spray. Bake in a 350°F (180°C) oven for 40 minutes. Cool the cake on a wire rack for 10 minutes before removing it from the pan. Ice with cream cheese frosting.

EACH SERVING CONTAINS: CALORIES: 250 ▲ CARBOHYDRATES: 47 ▲ EXCHANGE: 2 STARCH/BREAD, 1 VEGETABLE, 1 FRUIT

IF CUT INTO 10 SERVINGS, EACH SERVING CONTAINS: CALORIES: 200 ▲ CARBOHYDRATES: 38 G ▲ EXCHANGE: 2 STARCH/BREAD, 1/2 FRUIT

❖ Cream Cheese Icing ❖

Decadent!

1/4 cup	fat- free butter and oil replacement product	60 mL
8 ounces	fat-free cream cheese	225 g
3 packages	aspartame sweetener	3 packages
2 teaspoons	vanilla extract	10 mL

Beat together all the ingredients until they are smoothly blended.

EACH SERVING CONTAINS: CALORIES: 45 ▲ CARBOHYDRATES: 7 G ▲ EXCHANGE: 1/2 STARCH/BREAD

FOR 10 SERVINGS, EACH SERVING CONTAINS CALORIES: 0 ▲ CARBOHYDRATES: 4 G ▲ EXCHANGE: FREE

❖ Orange-Glazed Coffee Cake ❖

YIELD: 12 SERVINGS

Perfect for brunch.

1 package	active dry yeast	1 package
1/4 cup	warm water	60 mL
1/2 cup	warm skim milk, l05–115°F (40–45°C)	125 mL
1/2 cup	fresh orange juice, at room temperature	125 mL
1/2 cup	fat-free ricotta cheese	125 mL
1 tablespoon	orange peel, grated	15 mL
1/2 teaspoon	salt	3 mL
1 large	egg or equivalent egg substitute, lightly beaten	1 large
3 1/2 cups	flour (up to 4 cups)	875 mL
2-3 drops	oil	2–3 drops
1 recipe	Orange Icing (p. 146)	1 recipe

Put the yeast in a large mixing bowl. Add the warm water and stir. Set aside for 5 to 10 minutes. The mixture will become foamy. Add all the remaining ingredients except the flour, oil, and icing, and mix together to blend.

By hand or with a heavy-duty electric mixer, beat in 2 1/2 cups (625 mL) of the flour, a little at a time. The dough will become stiff. Use a handful of the remaining flour to coat a work board. Turn the batter onto the floured board. Adding more flour as the dough becomes sticky, knead the dough until it becomes smooth and elastic. This will take about 10 minutes.

Put a few drops of oil in the bottom of a large mixing bowl. Put the dough in the bowl and turn it over so it is coated with oil. Cover loosely with a damp dishcloth—damp, not wet. Let the dough rise in a warm place for 2 hours or until doubled. Punch down and knead again for a few minutes on the floured board.

Divide the dough into three equal parts. Use your hands to roll the pieces into three 20" (45 cm) strands. Braid. Arrange the braid in a 10" (25 cm) round cheesecake or springform pan. Cover with the damp cloth once again and let rise until doubled.

Bake in a preheated 425°F (220°C) oven for 25 to 30 minutes. Use a sharp knife to loosen the coffee cake from the pan. Remove the cake and cool on a wire rack. Spread Orange Icing on the cake while it is still somewhat warm. This is best served warm.

EACH SERVING CONTAINS: CALORIES: 196 ▲ CARBOHYDRATES: 39 G ▲ EXCHANGE: 2 STARCH/BREAD, 1/2 FRUIT

❖ Orange Icing ❖

YIELD: 3/4 CUP (375 ML), OR 12 SERVINGS

Especially for orange coffee cake or cupcakes.

1/4 cup	fruit-only marmalade preserves	60 mL
1 teaspoon	Triple Sec or orange extract	5 mL
1/2 cup	orange juice	125 mL

Mix all the ingredients together in a small saucepan. Heat gently, stirring constantly until blended.

EACH SERVING CONTAINS: CALORIES: 18 ▲ CARBOHYDRATES: 4 G ▲ EXCHANGE: FREE

❖ Cherry Coffee Cake ❖

YIELD: 22 SERVINGS

1 package	dry yeast	1 package
1/4 cup	warm water	60 mL
3/4 cup	skim milk	190 mL
1 tablespoon	cider vinegar	15 mL
1/2 cup	granulated sugar replacement	125 mL
2 tablespoons	margarine, softened	30 mL
1	egg	1
1 teaspoon	baking powder	5 mL
1/2 teaspoon	salt	2 mL
3 1/4 cups	all-purpose flour	810 mL
1 1/2 cups	fresh or frozen sweet cherries, thawed and drained	375 mL

Dissolve yeast in warm water in a large mixing bowl. Add milk, vinegar, sugar replacement, margarine, egg, baking powder, salt, and 2 cups (500 mL) of the flour. Beat on low until mixture is blended; then mix on medium for 2 minutes. Stir in remaining flour. Transfer to a lightly floured surface, and knead until smooth and elastic (about 5 minutes). Roll dough into a 20 x 6 in. (50 x 15 cm) rectangle. Place on a greased cookie sheet. Cut 2 inch (5cm) slices on each of the 20 inch (5 cm) sides of the dough. Cut cherries in quarters. Place cherries lengthwise down the middle of the rectangles. Crisscross sliced strips over cherries. Cover and allow to rise in a warm place until double in size. Bake at 375°F (190 °C) for 20 to 22 minutes or until golden brown.

EACH SERVING CONTAINS: CALORIES: 63 ▲ CARBOHYDRATES: 13 G ▲ EXCHANGE: 3/4 BREAD

❖ Cherry Chocolate Coffee Cake ❖

YIELD: 18 SERVINGS

2 cups	frozen, unsweetened sweet cherries	500 mL
1 1/2 teaspoons	cornstarch	7 mL

1/4 teaspoon	unsweetened black-cherry powdered soft-drink mix	1 mL
1/4 teaspoon	ground nutmeg	1 mL
1/2 cup	skim milk	125 mL
1 package	dry yeast	1 package
1/4 cup	warm water	1 mL
2/3 cup	granulated sugar replacement	180 mL
1/4 cup	solid shortening	60 mL
1	egg	1
1/2 teaspoon	salt	2 mL
1/3 cup	unsweetened baking cocoa	90 mL
2 1/2 cups	all-purpose flour	625 mL
2 tablespoons	margarine, melted	30 mL

Place frozen cherries in a l-quart (1-L) microwave measuring cup. Heat in microwave on MEDIUM for 2 minutes. Stir and then continue heating on MEDIUM for another 2 minutes. Cherries should be thawed but not hot. Use a scissors to cut cherries into pieces. (If cherries are hot, allow to cool before stirring in cornstarch.) Stir in cornstarch, soft-drink mix powder, and nutmeg. Place back in microwave and cook for 3 to 4 minutes on medium high or until mixture is very thick and clear. Set aside to cool completely. Meanwhile, pour skim milk in small saucepan. Bring to a boil, remove from heat, and allow to cool. Dissolve the yeast in the warm water. Combine skim milk, yeast mixture, sweetener, shortening, egg, and salt in a large mixing bowl. Combine the cocoa with 1 1/4 cup (310 mL) of flour in another bowl. Stir to mix. Add to liquid mixture in bowl. Beat on low until mixture is blended and smooth. Add remaining flour and stir until all the flour is incorporated into the dough. Turn out onto a lightly floured surface; then knead for 4 to 5 minutes until dough is smooth and elastic. Place in a greased bowl, turn dough over, cover, and allow to rise until double in size (about 1 1/2 hours). Punch dough down and roll into a 25 x 12 in. (62 x 30 cm) rectangle. Place dough on a well greased cookie sheet. Make 3 inch (7.5-cm) diagonal cuts at 1 inch (2.5-cm) intervals on the 25 inch (62-cm) side of the rectangle with a scissors. Spread cherry filling down the middle of the coffee-cake dough. Crisscross cut strips at an angle over filling, overlapping the strips so that they are about 1 inch (2.5-cm) apart. Cover coffee cake with plastic wrap, then a towel. Allow to rise until double in size (about 45 to 60 minutes).

Bake at 350°F (175 °C) for 25 to 30 minutes or until done. While warm, brush with melted margarine.

EACH SERVING CONTAINS: CALORIES: 62 ▲ CARBOHYDRATES: 12 G ▲ EXCHANGE: 3/4 BREAD

❖ Easy Apple Coffee Cake ❖

YIELD: 32 SERVINGS

1 pound	frozen bread dough, thawed	500 g loaf
2 tablespoons	margarine, melted	30 mL
1/4 cup	granulated brown-sugar replacement	60 mL
1 tablespoon	all-purpose flour	15 mL
2 teaspoons	ground cinnamon	10 mL
1 teaspoon	ground nutmeg	5 mL
2 cups	grated peeled apple	500 mL

Divide bread dough in half. Roll each half into an 8 inch (20-cm) square. Place each square on a greased cookie sheet. Brush with melted margarine. Combine brown-sugar replacement, flour, cinnamon, and nutmeg in a bowl. Stir to mix. Add grated apple and toss to coat apple. Spoon one half of the apple mixture down the middle of each square. Cut 2 inch (5cm) strips down two of the sides, towards the apple filling, about 1 inch (2.5 cm) apart. Fold strips alternately, overlapping the filling. Cover and allow coffee cake to rise until double in size. Bake at 350°F (175 °C) for 30 to 35 minutes or until golden brown.

EACH SERVING CONTAINS: CALORIES: 57 ▲ CARBOHYDRATES: 12 G ▲ EXCHANGE: 1/2 BREAD, 1/4 FRUIT

❖ Tart Orange Coffee Cake ❖

YIELD: 18 SERVINGS

1 package	dry yeast	1 package
1/4 cup	warm water	60 mL
12 ounce	can frozen orange juice	355 mL can

	concentrate, slightly thawed	
1	egg	1
1/2 teaspoon	salt	2 mL
2 cups	all-purpose flour	500 mL
1 tablespoon	solid shortening, melted	15 mL
1 tablespoon	cornstarch	15 mL
2 tablespoons	cold water	30 mL
1 teaspoon	vanilla extract	5 mL

Dissolve the yeast in warm water. Allow to rest for 5 minutes. Pour into medium-sized mixing bowl. Heat 1/2 cup (125 mL) of the orange juice concentrate just until the chill is off. Pour into yeast mixture. Add egg, salt, and 1 cup (250 mL) of the flour. Beat on low to blend. Then beat on high for 2 minutes. Stir in remaining 1 cup (250 mL) of flour. Beat on low for 1 minute (dough will be soft). Brush about two-thirds of the melted shortening on bottom and sides of a medium-sized bowl. Transfer dough to greased bowl. Brush remaining melted shortening on top of dough. Cover with plastic wrap and then a towel. Allow to rise until double in size. Meanwhile, dissolve cornstarch in cold water. Pour into a saucepan. Add remaining orange juice concentrate. Stir to mix. Cook and stir over medium heat until mixture is very thick. Remove from heat and stir in vanilla. Allow to cool completely. To assemble: Flour your hands and divide dough in half. Press one-half of the dough into the bottom of a greased 9 inch (23 cm) round springform pan, pressing slightly up the sides. Spoon about one-half of the orange juice mixture over the top. Transfer remaining half of dough to a floured surface. Press to flatten dough to a 9 inch (23 cm) round. Place dough round on top of orange juice mixture in pan. Make random indentations in the top of the dough. Spoon remaining orange juice mixture over top. Allow to rise uncovered for 30 to 40 minutes. Place in cold oven. Set oven for 350°F (175 °C). Bake for 25 to 30 minutes or until done. Allow coffee cake to cool in pan 10 minutes; then release sides.

EACH SERVING CONTAINS: CALORIES: 66 ▲ CARBOHYDRATES: 14 G ▲ EXCHANGE: 3/4 BREAD

❖ Pineapple Oatmeal Coffee Cake ❖

YIELD: 16 SERVINGS

1 cup	quick-cooking oatmeal	250 mL
1 cup	unsweetened pineapple juice	250 mL
2 teaspoons	baking powder	10 mL
1/2 teaspoon	baking soda	2 mL
1	egg	1
1 cup	all-purpose flour	250 mL
3 envelopes	aspartame sweetener	3 envelopes

Combine oatmeal and pineapple juice in a mixing bowl. Stir to mix. Allow to rest for 10 to 15 minutes. Add baking powder, baking soda, and egg. Stir vigorously with a spoon. Then stir in flour. Transfer to a greased 9 inch (23-cm) round baking pan. Bake at 350°F (175°C) for 25 to 35 minutes or until pick inserted in middle comes out clean. Remove from oven. Sprinkle top with aspartame sweetener.

EACH SERVING CONTAINS: CALORIES: 66 ▲ CARBOHYDRATES: 12 G ▲ EXCHANGE: 3/4 BREAD

❖ Cupcakes with a Cherry on Top ❖

YIELD: 16 CUPCAKES

Either orange or cream cheese icing can be used, depending on your preference.

1 cup	flour	250 mL
1 package	(4 servings) sugar-free vanilla pudding mix (not instant)	1 package
1 1/4 cups	water or skim milk	310 mL
1 1/2 teaspoons	baking powder	8 mL
3 tablespoons	fat-free butter and oil replacement product	45 mL
2	large eggs or equivalent egg substitute	2
1 teaspoon	vanilla extract	5 mL
1/2 cup	skim milk	125 mL

1 recipe	Orange Icing (p. 146) or Cream Cheese Icing (p. 145)	1 recipe
16 whole	maraschino cherries	16

Combine flour, pudding mix, water or skim milk, and baking powder in a mixing bow. Beat in the butter replacement, eggs, and vanilla extract. Beat for 1 minute. Beat in the milk. Fill muffin tins lined with paper baking cups two-thirds full. Bake in a preheated 350°F (180°C) oven for 15 to 17 minutes. Frost with Orange Icing or Cream Cheese Frosting and a maraschino cherry.

EACH CUPCAKE CONTAINS: CALORIES: 72 ▲ CARBOHYDRATES: 14 G ▲ EXCHANGE: 1 STARCH/BREAD

❖ Blueberry Cupcakes ❖

YIELD: 10 CUPCAKES

1 box	Sweet 'n Low brand white cake mix	
2/3 cup	water	
3/4 cup	blueberries, unsweetened (fresh, canned, or frozen)*	

* Drain canned blueberries, or thaw frozen blueberries.

Mix half the water with cake mix for 3 minutes, using mixer. Add the balance of water and mix 1 minute. Pour batter into 10 muffin cups (paper or foil). Drop a spoon of berries on top of each. Bake at 375°F for 20 minutes.

EACH CUPCAKE CONTAINS: CALORIES: 97

❖ Cream Cheese Pastries ❖

YIELD: 90 (SMALL) PASTRY COOKIES

Without the new fat-free dairy products, this recipe would have too much fat.

4 tablespoons	butter or margarine	60 mL
8 ounces	fat-free cream cheese	225 g

2 tablespoons	sugar	30 mL
4 packages	acesulfame-K sugar substitute	4 packages
1	large egg or equivalent egg substitute, lightly beaten	1
1 1/2 cups	flour	375 mL
1 teaspoon	baking powder	5 mL
1/2 teaspoon	butter extract	3 mL
1/2 cup	fat-free sour cream	125 mL

In a large mixing bowl, cream the butter and cream cheese together until soft and creamy. Blend in the sugar and acesulfame-K. Blend in the egg. In another bowl, sift together the flour and baking powder. In a small bowl, mix together the butter extract and sour cream. In the large mixing bowl containing the butter and cream cheese, alternately add the flour mixture and the sour cream mixture. Blend thoroughly. Make a ball and wrap it in plastic wrap. Refrigerate until chilled. Roll dough on a lightly floured board until it is about 1/8" (3 mm) thick. Use cookie cutters to cut the dough into shapes. Place cookies on a baking sheet that has been coated with non-stick cooking spray. Bake in a preheated 400°F (200°C) oven for 8 to 10 minutes.

EACH COOKIE CONTAINS: CALORIES: 17 ▲ CARBOHYDRATES: 2 G ▲ EXCHANGE: FREE

❖ Cherry Bread Pudding ❖

YIELD: 6 SERVINGS

A good way to use up slightly stale bread.

1 cup	bread crumbs from 3 slices of Italian bread or 6 slices of French bread, toasted and then crumbled	250 mL
1 cup	skim milk	250 mL
1 pound	ripe cherries, pitted	450 g
1/2 cup	fruit-only cherry preserves (no added sugar)	125 mL
1/2 cup	sliced almonds, toasted (optional)	125 mL

| 1 teaspoon | sugar | 5 mL |
| 1 cup | fat-free sour cream | 250 mL |

Crumble the toast into a medium mixing bowl. Add the milk. Stir. Add the cherries and most of the almonds. Reserve a few table-spoons (about 30 mL) of almonds for topping. Coat a six-cup (1.5 L) baking dish with non-stick vegetable cooking spray. Pour the toast mixture into the prepared baking dish and top with the almonds, if you are using them. Sprinkle the teaspoon (5 mL) of sugar on top. Bake in a preheated 350°F (180°C) oven for 35 to 45 minutes. Serve each with a dollop of sour cream.

EACH SERVING CONTAINS: CALORIES: 200 ▲ CARBOHYDRATES: 40 G ▲ EXCHANGE: 2 STARCH/BREAD, 1 FRUIT

❖ Chocolate Cinnamon Rolls ❖

YIELD: 18 SERVINGS

1/2 cup	skim milk	125 mL
1 package	dry yeast	1 package
1/4 cup	warm water	1 mL
2/3 cup	granulated sugar replacement	180 mL
1/4 cup	solid shortening	60 mL
1 tablespoon	granulated fructose	15 mL
1	egg	1
1/2 teaspoon	salt	2 mL
1/3 cup	unsweetened baking cocoa	90 mL
2 1/2 cups	all-purpose flour	625 mL
2 tablespoons	margarine, melted	30 mL
3 tablespoons	granulated sugar replacement	45 mL
2 teaspoons	ground cinnamon	10 mL

Pour skim milk in small saucepan. Bring to a boil, remove from heat, and allow to cool. Dissolve the yeast in the warm water. Combine skim milk, yeast mixture, sweetener, fructose, shortening, egg, and salt in a large mixing bowl. Combine the cocoa with 1 1/4 cups (310 mL) of flour in another bowl. Stir to mix. Add to liquid mixture in bowl. Beat on low until mixture is blended and smooth. Add remaining flour and stir until all the flour is incorporated into the dough. Turn out onto a lightly floured surface; then knead for 4 to 5 minutes until dough is smooth and elastic. Place in a greased bowl, turn dough over, cover, and allow to rise until double in size (about 1 1/2 hours). Punch dough down and roll into a 12 x 9 inch (30 x 23 cm) rectangle. Spread with melted margarine. Combine the 3 tablespoons (45 mL) sugar replacement and cinnamon in a bowl. Stir to mix. Sprinkle over surface of dough. Roll up, beginning at the 12 inch (30-cm) side. Tuck end of dough into the roll to seal. Cut into 18 slices. Place slices slightly apart in a 13 x 9 inch (33 x 23 cm) well-greased pan. Cover, and allow to rise until double in size (about 45 to 60 minutes). Bake at 375°F (190 °C) for 25 to 30 minutes or until done.

EACH SERVING CONTAINS: CALORIES: 60 ▲ CARBOHYDRATES: 11 G ▲ EXCHANGE: 3/4 BREAD

❖ Chocolate Raised Doughnuts ❖

YIELD: 18 SERVINGS

1/2 cup	skim milk	125 mL
1 package	dry yeast	1 package
1/4 cup	warm water	1 mL
2/3 cup	granulated sugar replacement	180 mL
1/4 cup	solid shortening	60 mL
2 tablespoons	granulated fructose	30 mL
1	egg	1
1/2 teaspoon	salt	2 mL
1/3 cup	unsweetened baking cocoa	90 mL
2 1/2 cups	all-purpose flour	625 mL

Pour skim milk in small saucepan. Bring to a boil, remove from heat, and allow to cool. Dissolve the yeast in the warm water. Combine skim milk, yeast mixture, granulated sugar replacement, shortening, fructose, egg, and salt in a large mixing bowl. Combine the cocoa with 1 1/4 cups (310 mL) of flour in another bowl. Stir to mix. Add to liquid mixture in bowl. Beat on low until mixture is blended and smooth. Add remaining flour and stir until all the flour is incorporated into the dough. Turn out onto a lightly floured surface; then knead for 4 to 5 minutes or until dough is smooth and elastic. Place in a greased bowl, turn dough over, cover, and allow to rise until double in size (about 1 1/2 hours). Punch dough down and roll to about 1/2 inch (1.25 cm) thickness. Cut with floured doughnut cutter. Place doughnuts onto a greased cookie sheet or piece of waxed paper. Cover and allow to rise. Heat 2 to 3 inches (5 to 8 cm) of oil in deep fat fryer or heavy saucepan to 375°F (190 °C). Heat a wide spatula in the oil. Gently slide spatula under a doughnut. Place doughnut in the hot oil, and fry about 2 minutes on each side. Remove from oil; drain on paper towels. Repeat with remaining doughnuts.

EACH SERVING CONTAINS: CALORIES: 65 ▲ CARBOHYDRATES: 14 G ▲ EXCHANGE: 3/4 BREAD

❖ Buttermilk Doughnuts ❖

YIELD: 24 SERVINGS

1 package	dry yeast	1 package
1/4 cup	warm water	60 mL
1 cup	buttermilk, warmed	250 mL
1	egg	1
1/2 teaspoon	salt	2 mL
2 tablespoons	margarine, melted	30 mL
1/2 cup	granulated sugar replacement	125 mL
1 tablespoon	granulated fructose	15 mL
3 cups	all-purpose flour	750 mL

Dissolve yeast in warm water. Allow to rest for 5 minutes; then pour into a large mixing bowl. Add buttermilk, egg, salt, margarine, sugar replacement, fructose, and 2 cups (500 mL) of the flour. Beat on low until blended. Then beat on high for 2 minutes. Stir in remaining 1 cup (250 mL) of flour. Transfer dough to a floured surface. Knead until smooth and elastic. Transfer to a greased bowl; turn dough over. Cover with plastic wrap and then a towel. Allow to rise until double in size. Transfer to a lightly floured surface. Pat or roll dough to about 1/3 inch (8-mm) thickness. Cut with floured doughnut cutter. Allow to rest for 10 to 15 minutes. Heat about 3 inches (7.5 cm) of vegetable oil to 375°F (190 °C) in a skillet or deep-fat fryer. Slide doughnuts into hot oil. Fry until golden brown, turning several times. Remove from oil and drain on paper towels.

EACH SERVING CONTAINS:CALORIES: 63 ▲ CARBOHYDRATES: 13 G ▲ EXCHANGE: 3/4 BREAD

❖ Dutch Doughnuts ❖

YIELD: 24 SERVINGS

1 package	dry yeast	1 package
1/4 cup	warm water	60 mL
2	eggs	2
1/2 cup	skim milk	125 mL
1/4 cup	whole milk	60 mL
1 teaspoon	vanilla extract	5 mL
1/3 cup	granulated sugar replacement	90 mL
3 cups	all-purpose flour	750 mL
1 tablespoon	baking powder	15 mL
1 teaspoon	salt	5 mL
1/2 teaspoon	ground cinnamon	2 mL
1/4 teaspoon	ground nutmeg	1 mL

Dissolve yeast in warm water in a large bowl. Add eggs, skim and whole milk, vanilla, and sugar replacement. Beat until light and fluffy. Add 2 cups (500 mL) of the flour and the baking powder, salt, cinnamon, and nutmeg; beat on low until well blended. Stir in remaining flour. Transfer to floured surface. Roll dough to about 1/3-inch (8-mm) thickness. Cut with a floured doughnut cutter. Heat about 3 inches (7.5 cm) of vegetable oil to 375°F (190 °C) in a skillet or deep-fat fryer. Slide doughnuts into hot oil. Fry until golden brown, turning several times. Remove from oil and drain on paper towels.

EACH SERVING CONTAINS: CALORIES: 60 ▲ CARBOHYDRATES: 12 G ▲ EXCHANGE: 3/4 BREAD

❖ Cinnamon Swirl Bread ❖

YIELD: 18 SERVINGS

1 pound	loaf frozen bread dough, thawed	500 g loaf
1 tablespoon	margarine, melted	15 mL
1/3 cup	granulated sugar replacement	90 mL
1 tablespoon	ground cinnamon	15 mL

Roll dough into a 12 x 7 inch (30 x 17 cm) rectangle. Spread dough with melted margarine, mix the sugar replacement with the cinnamon, and sprinkle mixture on top of dough. Roll up jelly roll-style, starting from the short end. Seal edges and end of loaf. Place, seam side down, in a greased loaf pan. Allow to rise. Bake at 375°F (190°C) for 25 to 30 minutes or until done. Remove from oven. Remove loaf from pan. Cool.

EACH SERVING CONTAINS: CALORIES: 58 ▲ CARBOHYDRATES: 15 G ▲ EXCHANGE: 3/4 BREAD

❖ Cinnamon Rolls ❖

YIELD: 18 SERVINGS

Dough mixture:

1/2 cup	skim milk	125 mL
2 teaspoons	cider vinegar	10 mL
1 package	dry yeast	1 package
1/4 cup	warm water	60 mL
1/3 cup	granulated sugar replacement	90 mL
or		
2 teaspoons	granulated fructose	10 mL
3 tablespoons	solid shortening	45 mL
1	egg	1
1/2 teaspoon	salt	2 mL
3 cups	all-purpose flour	750 mL

Cinnamon mixture:

1 tablespoon	margarine, melted	15 mL
1/3 cup	granulated sugar replacement ground cinnamon	90 mL

Dough: Combine skim milk and vinegar in a large mixing bowl. Dissolve the yeast in the warm water. Add to skim-milk mixture. Beat in sweetener of your choice, shortening, egg, and salt. Next, add 2 cups (500 mL) of the flour. Beat on low until the mixture is blended and smooth. Then add remaining flour and stir until all the flour is incorporated into the dough. Turn out onto a lightly floured surface; knead for 4 to 5 minutes until dough is smooth and elastic. Place in a greased bowl, turn dough over, cover, and allow to rise until double in size (about 1 1/2 hours). Punch dough down and roll into a 12 x 9 inch (30 x 23 cm) rectangle.

Cinnamon mixture: Spread dough with melted margarine, mix

the sugar replacement with desired amount of cinnamon, and sprinkle mixture on top of dough.

To assemble: Roll up, beginning at the 12-inch (30-cm) side. Tuck end of dough into the roll to seal. Cut into 18 slices. Place slightly apart in a 13 x 9 inch (33 x 23 cm) well-greased pan. Cover, and allow to rise until double in size (about 45 to 60 minutes). Bake at 375°F (190°C) for 25 to 30 minutes or until done.

EACH SERVING CONTAINS: CALORIES: 73 ▲ CARBOHYDRATES: 13 G ▲ EXCHANGE: 1 BREAD

❖ Pecan Rolls ❖

YIELD: 18 SERVINGS

1 package	dry yeast	1 package
1/4 cup	warm water	60 mL
1/2 cup	whole milk	125 mL
2 tablespoons	margarine, softened	30 mL
1/2 cup	granulated sugar replacement	125 mL
	or	
3 tablespoons	granulated fructose	45 mL
1	egg	1
1/2 teaspoon	salt	2 mL
2 1/2 cups	all-purpose flour	625 mL
1 tablespoon	margarine, melted	15 mL
1/3 cup	granulated sugar replacement	90 mL
	ground cinnamon	
1/2 cup	sugar-free maple-flavored syrup	125 mL
1/3 cup	ground pecans	90 mL

Dissolve the yeast in the warm water. Allow to rest for 2 minutes. Pour into a large mixing bowl. Add milk, softened margarine, the 1/2 cup of sugar replacement or the 3 tablespoons of fructose, egg, salt, and 1/2 cup (375 mL) of the flour. Beat on low to blend, then on high for 2 minutes. Stir in remaining 1 cup (250 mL) of flour. Transfer to a lightly floured surface; knead until smooth and elastic. Place in a greased bowl, turn dough over, and cover with plastic wrap and then a towel. Allow to rise until double in size. Punch dough down and roll into a 12 x 9 inch (30 x 23 cm) rectangle. Spread dough with melted margarine, mix the 1/3 cup (90 mL) of sugar replacement with desired amount of cinnamon, and sprinkle mixture on top of dough. To assemble: Roll up, beginning at the 12 inch (30 cm) side. Tuck end of dough into the roll to seal. Cut into 18 slices. Pour sugar-free maple-flavored syrup in the bottom of a well-greased 13 x 9 inch (33 x 23 cm) pan. Sprinkle pecans over surface of syrup. Place slices of dough on top of the pecans. Then cover, and allow to rise until double in size (about 45 to 60 minutes). Bake at 375°F (190°C) for 25 to 30 minutes or until done.

EACH SERVING CONTAINS: CALORIES: 78 ▲ CARBOHYDRATES: 16 G ▲ EXCHANGE: 1 BREAD

❖ Buttermilk Sticky Rolls ❖

YIELD: 18 SERVINGS

1 package	dry yeast	1 package
1/4 cup	warm water	60 mL
3/4 cup	buttermilk	190 mL
2 tablespoons	margarine, softened	30 mL
1/2 cup	granulated sugar replacement	125 mL
or		
3 tablespoons	granulated fructose	45 mL
1	egg	1
1/2 teaspoon	salt	2 mL
3 cups	all-purpose flour	750 mL
1 tablespoon	margarine, melted	15 mL
1/3 cup	granulated sugar replacement	90 mL
	ground cinnamon	
1/2 cup	sugar-free maple-flavored syrup	125 mL

Dissolve the yeast in the warm water. Allow to rest for 2 minutes. Pour into a large mixing bowl. Add buttermilk, softened margarine, sweetener, egg, salt, and 2 cups (500 mL) of the flour. Beat on low to blend, then on high for 2 minutes. Stir in remaining 1 cup (250 mL) of flour. Transfer to a lightly floured surface, and knead until smooth and elastic. Place in a greased bowl, turn dough over, and cover with plastic wrap and then a towel. Allow to rise until double in size. Punch dough down and roll into a 12 x 9 inch (30 x 23 cm) rectangle. Spread dough with melted margarine, mix the sugar replacement with desired amount of cinnamon, and sprinkle mixture on top of dough. To assemble: Roll up, beginning at the 12 inch (30 cm) side. Tuck end of dough into the roll to seal. Cut into 18 slices. Pour sugar-free maple-flavored syrup in the bottom of a well-greased 13 x 9 inch (33 x 23 cm) pan. Place the cut slices of dough slightly apart on top of the syrup. Cover, and allow to rise until double in size (about 45 to 60 minutes). Bake at 375°F (190°C) for 25 to 30 minutes or until done.

EACH SERVING CONTAINS: CALORIES: 72 ▲ CARBOHYDRATES: 12 G ▲ EXCHANGE: 1 BREAD

❖ Braided Raisin Bread ❖

YIELD: 18 SERVINGS

| 1 pound | frozen bread dough, thawed | 500 g loaf |
| 1 cup | raisins, cut in half | 250 mL |

With your hands, work the raisins into the dough. Divide the dough into three pieces. Cover and allow to rest for 10 minutes. Roll each piece of dough into a ball. Then roll each ball into a rope about 16 inches (40 cm) long. Line up the three dough ropes, about 1 inch (2.5 cm) apart on a greased baking sheet. Very loosely braid the ropes. (Braid by bringing outside ropes alternately over middle rope.) Allow to rise. Bake at 375°F (190°C) for 25 to 30 minutes or until done.

EACH SERVING CONTAINS: CALORIES: 81 ▲ CARBOHYDRATES: 19 G ▲ EXCHANGE: 1 BREAD, 1/3 FRUIT

❖ Orange-Walnut Muffins ❖

YIELD: 12 MUFFINS

Be careful to handle the flour lightly as you measure, so you don't put in too much.

2 cups	flour	500 mL
2 tablespoons	sugar	30 mL
1 tablespoon	baking powder	15 mL
1 cup	water	250 mL

2 teaspoons	orange peel, grated	10 mL
1 teaspoon	orange extract	5 mL
1/2 teaspoon	butter extract	3 mL
2 large	egg whites	2 large
1/4 cup	finely chopped walnuts	60 mL
1 tablespoon	brown sugar	15 mL

In a large bowl, mix together the flour, sugar, and baking powder. Use a wire whisk to mix well. In another bowl, blend the water, orange peel, extracts, and egg whites. Pour on top of the dry ingredients. Stir lightly to moisten. Do not beat or over-stir. In a third bowl mix the walnuts and brown sugar. Spoon the batter into 12 muffin cups that have been coated with non-stick cooking spray. Top the muffins with the nut mixture. Bake in a preheated 400°F (200°C) oven for 14 to 16 minutes or until a tester inserted in the middle comes out clean. Cool the muffins on a wire rack before serving.

EACH MUFFIN CONTAINS: CALORIES: 107 ▲ CARBOHYDRATES: 20 G ▲ EXCHANGE: 1 STARCH/BREAD, 1/2 FAT

❖ Pumpkin Bread ❖

YIELD: 20 SERVINGS

2 cups	all-purpose flour	500 mL
1 cup	granulated brown-sugar replacement	250 mL
1 tablespoon	baking powder	15 mL
2 teaspoons	ground cinnamon	10 mL
1/2 teaspoon	ground nutmeg	2 mL
1/4 teaspoon	salt	1 mL
1/4 teaspoon	baking soda	1 mL
1/8 teaspoon	ground cloves	1/2 mL
1 cup	canned pumpkin	250 mL
1/2 cup	skim milk	125 mL
2	eggs	2
1/3 cup	solid shortening	90 mL

Combine 1 cup (250 mL) of the flour and the brown-sugar replacement, baking powder, cinnamon, nutmeg, salt, baking soda, and cloves in a large mixing bowl. Add the remaining flour, pumpkin, milk, eggs, and shortening. Beat with an electric mixer on low until mixed. Then beat on high for 1 to 2 minutes until well blended. Grease a 9 x 5 x 3 inch (23 x 13 x 8 cm)-loaf pan on the bottom and 1/2 inch (1.25 cm) up the sides. Transfer batter to pan. Bake at 350°F (175°C) for 60 to 65 minutes or until pick inserted in middle comes out clean. Cool in pan for 10 minutes. Carefully slip a knife around the edge of the bread. Transfer to a cooling rack. Allow to cool. Wrap cooled bread in plastic wrap and store at room temperature for a day before slicing.

EACH SERVING CONTAINS: CALORIES: 85 ▲ CARBOHYDRATES: 15 G ▲ EXCHANGE: 1 BREAD

❖ Quick Blueberry Nut Muffins ❖

YIELD: 12 SERVINGS

2 cups	biscuit mix	500 mL
1/4 cup	granulated sugar replacement	60 mL
3/4 cup	skim milk	190 mL
2 tablespoons	margarine, melted	30 mL
1 cup	fresh or frozen blueberries	250 mL
1/3 cup	walnuts, chopped	90 mL

Combine biscuit mix, sugar replacement, milk, and margarine in a medium-sized mixing bowl. Stir to mix. (Batter will be lumpy.) Stir in fresh or frozen blueberries and nuts. Line 12 large muffin cups with paper liners. Divide batter evenly among the muffin cups. Bake at 400°F (200°C) for 20 to 25 minutes or until pick inserted in muffin comes out clean.

EACH SERVING CONTAINS: CALORIES: 112 ▲ CARBOHYDRATES: 20 G

❖ Sweet Corn Cake ❖

YIELD: 12 SERVINGS

1 cup	all-purpose flour	250 mL
3/4 cup	cornmeal	190 mL
1 tablespoon	baking powder	15 mL
1/2 teaspoon	salt	2 mL

1 cup	skim milk	250 mL
1	egg, beaten	1
2 tablespooons	liquid fructose	30 mL
2 tablespoons	margarine, melted	30 mL

Sift together flour, cornmeal, baking powder, and salt into a bowl. In a large mixing bowl, combine milk, egg, fructose, and margarine. Beat with a fork to blend. Stir flour mixture into milk mixture, just enough to moisten. Transfer batter into a greased 8-inch (20-cm) round baking pan. Bake at 400°F (200 °C) for 30 to 35 minutes or until pick inserted in middle comes out clean.

EACH SERVING CONTAINS: CALORIES: 99 ▲ CARBOHYDRATES: 16 G ▲ EXCHANGE: 1 BREAD

❖ Banana Bread ❖

1 3/4 cups	all-purpose flour	440 mL
1 tablespoon	granulated fructose	15 mL
1/2 cup	granulated sugar replacement	125 mL
2 teaspoons	baking powder	10 mL
1/2 teaspoon	baking soda	2 mL
1/4 teaspoon	salt	1 mL
1 cup	mashed banana	250 mL
1/3 cup	solid shortening	90 mL
2 tablespoons	skim milk	30 mL
2	eggs	2

Combine 1 cup (250 mL) of the flour and the fructose, 1/2 cup (125 mL) of granulated sugar replacement, baking powder, baking soda, and salt in a large mixing bowl. Add banana, shortening, and milk. Then add remaining flour. Beat until well blended (at least 2 minutes). Add eggs, one at a time, beating well after each addition. Transfer batter to a well-greased 8 x 4 x 2 inch (20 x 10 x 5 cm)-loaf pan. Bake at 350°F (175°C) for 55 to 65 minutes or until pick inserted in middle comes out clean. Remove from oven, and allow to cool in pan 10 minutes. Transfer to cooling rack. This bread is best the second day.

EACH SERVING CONTAINS: CALORIES: 87 ▲ CARBOHYDRATES: 17 G ▲ EXCHANGE: 1 BREAD

❖ Rhubarb Nut Bread ❖

2 cups	frozen rhubarb	500 mL
2 cups	all-purpose flour	500 mL
1 teaspoon	baking soda	5 mL
1/2 teaspoon	cream of tartar	2 mL
1/2 teaspoon	salt	2 mL
2/3 cup	granulated sugar replacement	180 mL
3 tablespoons	granulated fructose	45 mL
1/3 cup	hot water	90 mL
1	egg	1
2 tablespoons	vegetable oil	30 mL
1/3 cup	walnuts, chopped	90 mL

Chop frozen rhubarb very small, or place frozen rhubarb in food processor and process until chopped. (Rhubarb will have an icy appearance.) Set aside. Combine flour, baking soda, cream of tartar, salt, sweetener, fructose, hot water, egg, and vegetable oil in a mixing bowl. Beat to blend. Add frozen rhubarb. Beat to mix. Beat in nuts. Batter will be very stiff. Allow batter to set for 10 minutes. Beat slightly. Grease two 5 x 3 x 2 inch (13 x 8 x 5 cm)-loaf pans on the bottom and about 1/2 inch (1.25 cm) up the sides. Spoon batter evenly between the two pans. Bake at 350°F (175°C) for 50 to 55 minutes. Allow bread to cool in pans for 10 minutes. Carefully slip a knife around the edge of the bread. Transfer to a cooling rack. Allow to cool. Wrap cooled bread in plastic wrap and store at room temperature for a day before slicing.

EACH SERVING CONTAINS: CALORIES: 48 ▲ CARBOHYDRATES: 12 G ▲ EXCHANGE: 3/4 BREAD

❖ Sweet Zucchini Bread ❖

1 cup	grated, unpeeled zucchini	250 mL
1 cup	granulated sugar replacement	250 mL
1/4 cup	vegetable oil	60 mL
1	egg, slightly beaten	1

1/4 teaspoon	grated lemon peel	1 mL
1 1/2 cups	all-purpose flour	375 mL
2 tablespoons	granulated fructose	30 mL
1 teaspoon	ground cinnamon	5 mL
1 teaspoon	baking soda	5 mL
1/2 teaspoon	cream of tartar	2 mL
1/4 teaspoon	ground nutmeg	1 mL
1/8 teaspoon	ground allspice	1/2 mL

Combine zucchini, sweetener, oil, egg, and lemon peel in a large mixing bowl. Stir to mix. Combine flour, fructose, cinnamon, baking soda, cream of tartar, nutmeg, and allspice in another bowl. Stir to mix. Add flour mixture to zucchini mixture. Stir just enough to blend. Transfer batter to a well-greased 8 x 4 x 2 inch (20 x 10 x 5 cm)-loaf pan. Bake at 350°F (175 °C) for 55 to 65 minutes or until pick inserted in middle comes out clean. Remove from oven, and allow to cool in pan 10 minutes. Transfer to cooling rack. This bread is best the second day.

EACH SERVING CONTAINS: CALORIES: 82 ▲ CARBOHYDRATES: 15 G ▲ EXCHANGE: 1 BREAD

❖ Apricot-Jam Muffins ❖

YIELD: 12 SERVINGS

1 cup	quick-cooking oatmeal	250 mL
1 cup	buttermilk	250 mL
1	egg	1
2 tablespoons	margarine, softened	30 mL
1 cup	all-purpose flour	250 mL
1/3 cup	granulated sugar replacement	90 mL
2 tablespoons	granulated fructose	30 mL
2 teaspoons	baking powder	10 mL
1 teaspoon	baking soda	5 mL
1/2 teaspoon	salt	2 mL
6 teaspoons	all-natural apricot preserves	30 mL

Combine oatmeal and buttermilk in a large mixing bowl. Stir to blend. Allow to rest for 10 minutes. Stir in egg and margarine. Stir in flour, sugar replacement, fructose, baking powder, baking soda, and salt until well blended. Line 12 large muffin cups with paper liners. Divide batter evenly among the muffin cups. Top each muffin with 1/2 teaspoon (2 mL) of the apricot preserves. Bake at 350°F (175°C) for 20 to 25 minutes or until pick inserted in muffin comes out clean.

EACH SERVING CONTAINS: CALORIES: 99 ▲ CARBOHYDRATES: 17 G ▲ EXCHANGE: 1 BREAD

❖ Oatmeal Walnut Muffins ❖

YIELD: 12 SERVINGS

1 cup	quick-cooking oatmeal	250 mL
1 cup	buttermilk	250 mL
1	egg	1
2 tablespoons	margarine, softened	30 mL
1 cup	all-purpose flour	250 mL
1/3 cup	granulated sugar replacement	90 mL
2 tablespoons	granulated fructose	30 mL
2 teaspoons	baking powder	10 mL
1 teaspoon	baking soda	5 mL
1/2 teaspoon	salt	2 mL
1/3 cup	walnuts, chopped fine	90 mL

Combine oatmeal and buttermilk in a large mixing bowl. Stir to blend. Allow to rest for 10 minutes. Stir in egg and margarine. Stir in flour, sugar replacement, fructose, baking powder, baking soda, and salt until well blended. Then stir in the walnuts. Allow batter to rest for 2 minutes. Line 12 large muffin cups with paper liners. Divide batter evenly among the muffin cups. Bake at 375°F (190°C) for 20 to 25 minutes or until pick inserted in muffin comes out clean.

EACH SERVING CONTAINS: CALORIES: 121 ▲ CARBOHYDRATES: 19 G ▲ EXCHANGE: 1 1/3 BREAD

❖ Cranberry Muffins ❖

1 1/4 cups	all-purpose flour	310 mL
1/4 cup	whole-wheat flour	60 mL
1/2 cup	yellow cornmeal	125 mL
1/2 cup	granulated sugar replacement	125 mL
1 tablespoon	granulated fructose	15 mL
1 tablespoon	baking powder	15 mL
1 teaspoon	baking soda	5 mL
1 teaspoon	ground cinnamon	5 mL
dash	salt	dash
1 1/4 cup	buttermilk	310 mL
1 cup	fresh cranberries, chopped	250 mL
1	egg	1
1	egg white	1
3 tablespoons	vegetable oil	45 mL

Combine flours, cornmeal, sugar replacement, fructose, baking powder, baking soda, cinnamon, and salt in a large mixing bowl. Stir to mix. Add buttermilk, cranberries, egg, egg white, and oil. Beat to blend. Line 12 muffin cups with paper cups. Divide the batter evenly among the cups. Bake at 425°F (220°C) for 20 minutes or until muffins are golden brown. Transfer to cooling rack and cool slightly. Serve warm.

EACH SERVING CONTAINS: CALORIES: 110 ▲ CARBOHYDRATES: 20 G ▲ EXCHANGE: 1 1/3 BREAD

❖ Strawberry Banana Muffins ❖

2 cups	biscuit mix	500 mL
1/4 cup	granulated sugar replacement	60 mL
3/4 cup	skim milk	190 mL
2 tablespoons	margarine, melted	30 mL
12	medium fresh strawberries	12
2 small	bananas	2 small

Combine biscuit mix, sugar replacement, milk, and margarine in a medium-sized mixing bowl. Stir to mix. (Batter will be lumpy.) Cut strawberries and bananas into small cube-like pieces. Stir into batter. Line 12 large muffin cups with paper liners. Divide batter evenly among the muffin cups. Bake at 400°F (200°C) for 20 to 25 minutes or until pick inserted in muffin comes out clean.

EACH SERVING CONTAINS: CALORIES: 112 ▲ CARBOHYDRATES: 19 G ▲ EXCHANGE: 1 1/3 BREADS

❖ Big Sweet Biscuits ❖

YIELD: 16 SERVINGS

3 cups	all-purpose flour	750 mL
3 tablespoons	granulated sugar replacement	45 mL
1 tablespoon	granulated fructose	15 mL
4 teaspoons	baking powder	20 mL
3/4 teaspoon	cream of tartar	4 mL
1/2 teaspoon	salt	2 mL
1/4 teaspoon	baking soda	1 mL
3/4 cup	solid shortening, softened	190 mL
1	egg, beaten	1
1 cup	skim milk	250 mL

Combine flour, sugar replacement, fructose, baking powder, cream of tartar, salt, and baking soda in a large mixing bowl. Cut in shortening with a pastry cutter or knives until mixture becomes coarse crumbs. (This part can also be done in a food processor.) Combine egg and milk. Stir into flour mixture just enough to make a soft dough. Transfer dough to a floured surface. Knead lightly 10 to 15 times. Pat or roll out to about 1 inch (2.5-cm) thickness. Cut 16 biscuits with a floured 2 inch (5-cm) doughnut cutter. Place on ungreased cookie sheet. Bake at 450°F (230°C) for 12 to 15 minutes or until golden brown. They are best if served immediately.

EACH SERVING CONTAINS: CALORIES: 163 ▲ CARBOHYDRATES: 28 G ▲ EXCHANGE: 2 BREAD

❖ Cranberry Cake ❖

2 cups	all-purpose flour	500 mL
1/2 cup	granulated sugar replacement	125 mL
1/4 cup	granulated fructose	60 mL
2 teaspoons	baking powder	10 mL
1/2 teaspoon	salt	2 mL
1 cup	skim milk	250 mL
2	eggs	2
2 tablespoons	solid shortening, softened	30 mL
2 teaspoons	vanilla extract	10 mL
1 1/2 cups	fresh cranberries	375 mL

Combine flour, sugar replacement, fructose, baking powder, and salt in a bowl. Add milk, eggs, shortening, and vanilla. Whisk or beat until smooth and creamy. Stir in cranberries. Transfer to a paper-lined or well greased-and-floured 9-in. (23-cm)-square baking pan. Bake at 350°F (175°C) for 35 to 45 minutes or until pick inserted in middle comes out clean.

EACH SERVING CONTAINS: CALORIES: 74 ▲ CARBOHYDRATES: 13 G ▲ EXCHANGE: 1 BREAD

❖ Simple Cake ❖

YIELD: 10 SERVINGS

1 1/3 cups	all-purpose flour	340 mL
1/2 cup	granulated sugar replacement	125 mL
1 tablespoon	granulated fructose	15 mL
2 teaspoons	baking powder	10 mL
2/3 cup	skim milk	180 mL
1	egg	1
2 tablespoons	margarine, softened	30 mL
1 teaspoon	vanilla extract	5 mL

Combine flour, sugar replacement, fructose, and baking powder in a food processor. Process on high for 1 minute. Transfer dry ingredients to a medium-sized bowl. Add milk, egg, margarine, and vanilla. Beat on low for 30 seconds. Then beat on high for 1 to 1 1/2 minutes. Grease the bottom of an 8 inch (20-cm) round baking pan. (Do not grease the sides of the pan.) Line bottom with waxed paper and grease only the waxed paper. Transfer batter to prepared pan. Bake at 350°F (175°C) for 25 to 30 minutes or until pick inserted in middle comes out clean.

EACH SERVING CONTAINS: CALORIES: 72 ▲ CARBOHYDRATES: 13 G ▲ EXCHANGE: 1 BREAD

❖ Buttermilk Cake ❖

YIELD: 10 SERVINGS

1 1/2 cups	sifted cake flours	375 mL
1/2 cup	granulated sugar replacement	125 mL
1 teaspoon	baking powder	5 mL
1/2 teaspoon	salt	2 mL
1/4 teaspoon	baking soda	1 mL
2 tablespoons	solid shortening, softened	30 mL
3/4 cup	buttermilk	190 mL
2	egg whites	2
1 teaspoon	vanilla	5 mL

Sift together flour, sugar replacement, baking powder, salt, and baking soda into a medium-sized bowl. Add shortening and 1/2 cup (125 mL) of the buttermilk. Beat on medium for 2 minutes. Add remaining buttermilk, egg whites, and vanilla. Beat on high for 2 minutes. Transfer batter into an 8 inch (20-cm) round well-greased-and-floured baking pan. Bake at 350°F (175°C) for 22 to 25 minutes or until pick inserted in middle comes out clean. Cool in pan for 5 minutes. Invert onto a cooling rack, and cool completely.

EACH SERVING CONTAINS: CALORIES: 75 ▲ CARBOHYDRATES: 12 G ▲ EXCHANGE: 1 BREAD

❖ Spice Raisin Cake ❖

1 1/3 cups	all-purpose flour	340 mL
1/2 cup	granulated sugar replacement	125 mL
1 tablespoon	granulated fructose	15 mL
2 teaspoons	baking powder	10 mL
1 teaspoon	ground cinnamon	5 mL
1/4 teaspoon	ground nutmeg	1 mL
1/4 teaspoon	ground cloves	1 mL
1/4 teaspoon	ground ginger	1 mL
2/3 cup	skim milk	180 mL
1	egg	1
2 tablespoons	margarine, softened	30 mL
1 teaspoon	vanilla extract	5 mL
1/2 cup	plumped raisins	125 mL

Combine flour, sugar replacement, fructose, baking powder, cinnamon, nutmeg, cloves, and ginger in a medium-sized bowl. Add milk, egg, margarine, and vanilla. Beat on low for 30 seconds. Then beat on high for 1 to 1 1/2 minutes. Fold in raisins. Transfer batter to a well greased and floured 9 inch (23-cm) round baking pan. Bake at 350°F (175°C) for 25 to 30 minutes or until pick inserted in middle comes out clean. (The all-purpose flour makes this cake a little heavy. If you prefer a lighter cake, sift the dry ingredients together several times before adding the liquid ingredients.)

EACH SERVING CONTAINS: CALORIES: 99 ▲ CARBOHYDRATES: 17 G ▲ EXCHANGE: 1 BREAD, 1/3 FRUIT

❖ Fructose Chocolate Cake ❖

1/3 cup	granulated fructose	90 mL
1 cup	all-purpose flour	250 mL
1/4 cup	unsweetened cocoa powder	60 mL
3/4 teaspoon	baking soda	4 mL
1/4 teaspoon	cream of tartar	1 mL
1/4 cup	solid shortening, softened	60 mL
3/4 cup	skim milk	190 mL

| 1 teaspoon | vanilla extract | 5 mL |
| 1 | egg | 1 |

Place fructose in a small blender jar. Blend on high for 20 seconds. (Fructose will powder.) Combine flour, fructose, cocoa, baking soda, and cream of tartar in a medium-sized bowl. Stir to mix. Add shortening, milk, and vanilla. Beat on low until blended. Then beat on high for 1 1/2 minutes. Add egg and continue beating on high for 2 more minutes. Transfer batter to a greased and floured 8- or 9-inch (20- or 23-cm) round baking pan. Bake at 350°F (175°C) for 25 to 30 minutes or until pick inserted in middle comes out clean. Allow cake to cool in pan on cooling rack for 10 minutes. Remove from pan. Cool thoroughly on rack.

EACH SERVING CONTAINS: CALORIES: 141 ▲ CARBOHYDRATES: 16 G ▲ EXCHANGE: 1 BREAD, 1 FAT

❖ Fructose White Cake ❖

YIELD: 10 SERVINGS

1 1/3 cups	all-purpose flour	340 mL
1/4 cup	granulated fructose	60 mL
2 teaspoons	baking powder	10 mL
3 tablespoons	margarine, softened	45 mL
2/3 cup	skim milk	180 mL
1	egg	1
1 teaspoon	vanilla extract	5 mL

Combine flour, fructose, and baking powder in a food processor. Process on high for 30 seconds. Add margarine and process for 30 seconds more. Transfer ingredients to a medium-sized bowl. Add milk, egg, and vanilla. Beat on low for 30 seconds. Then beat on high for 2 minutes. Grease the bottom of an 8 inch (20-cm) round baking pan. (Do not grease the sides of the pan.) Line bottom with waxed paper and grease the waxed paper. Transfer batter to prepared pan. Bake at 350°F (175°C) for 25 to 30 minutes or until pick inserted in middle comes out clean.

EACH SERVING CONTAINS: CALORIES: 109 ▲ CARBOHYDRATES: 14 G ▲ EXCHANGE: 1 BREAD, 1/2 FAT

❖ Perfect Chocolate Cake ❖

YIELD: 10 SERVINGS

1 package	(8 ounces) package fructose-sweetened chocolate cake mix	1 package (227 g)
1/2 cup	water	125 mL
6	egg whites, room temperature	6

Line bottom of a 9 inch (23-cm) cake pan with waxed paper. (Do not grease bottom or sides of pan. Do not use a smaller cake pan; this cake will fill a 9-in. [23-cm] pan.) Combine cake mix and water in a mixing bowl. Beat on low just until mixed. Then beat on high for 2 minutes. Add egg whites, and beat on high for 5 to 7 minutes. Transfer cake batter to pan. Bake at 350°F (175 °C) for 35 to 40 minutes or until pick inserted in middle comes out clean. Do not underbake. Allow cake to cool in pan for 10 minutes. Carefully slip a knife around the outside edge of the cake, invert to a cooling rack, and remove waxed paper. Invert to right-side-up position. Cool completely.

EACH SERVING CONTAINS: CALORIES: 100 ▲ CARBOHYDRATES: 18 G ▲ EXCHANGE: 1 BREAD, 1/2 FAT

❖ Happy Birthday Cake ❖

YIELD: 10 SERVINGS

1	4.5 ounce box sugar-free white frosting mix	128 g
	food coloring	
1	(10 serving) prepared sugar-free cake	1
5	sugar-free hard candies	5
1 teaspoon	sugar-free soft-drink mix powder	5 mL

Prepare frosting mix as directed on package. Set aside one-third of the frosting. Frost sides and top of cake. Tint the reserved frosting with food coloring. Using a small writing tip, pipe Happy Birthday on top of cake. Place hard candies (any color) in a heavy zip-lock plastic bag, and cover plastic bag with a folded washcloth. Using a hammer, pound the candies into small pieces. Sprinkle pieces around edges or over cake. Sprinkle soft-drink powder (any color) over cake.

EACH SERVING CONTAINS: CALORIES: 150 ▲ CARBOHYDRATES: 24 G ▲ EXCHANGE: 1 1/2 BREAD, 1/2 FAT

❖ Basket Cake ❖

YIELD: 10 SERVINGS

2	boxes (4.5 ounce) sugar-free frosting mix	2 boxes (128 g)
1	8 inch prepared round cake	20 cm
3 tablespoons	unsweetened cocoa powder	45 mL
	green food coloring	
10	sugar-free gum drops	10

Prepare one box of frosting mix as directed on package. Frost sides and top of cake. Prepare second box of frosting mix as directed on package. Divide frosting in half and place in separate bowls. Add the cocoa to one of the bowls. Stir and blend completely. Using tip #21, pipe a medium-sized basket shape on top of the cake. Make a woven design or use loops or strips and wavy lines on the sides of the basket shape. Tint the second bowl of frosting green. Using various tips, make stems, leaves, and other designs emerging from the basket and/or around the cake. Cut gum drops lengthwise, fan, and place on stems for flowers.

EACH SERVING CONTAINS: CALORIES: 145 ▲ CARBOHYDRATES: 22 G ▲ EXCHANGE: 1 1/2 BREAD, 1/2 FAT

❖ Smiling Face ❖

YIELD: 10 SERVINGS

1	4.5 ounce box sugar-free white frosting mix yellow food coloring	128 g box
1	8 inch prepared round cake	20 cm
6	sugar-free licorice gum drops	6

Prepare frosting mix as directed on package. Tint a bright yellow. Frost sides and top of cake. Cut licorice gum drops in half lengthwise. Place two halves in the position for an eye. Repeat for other eye. Cut one of the remaining halves in half widthwise. Place these two pieces in the middle for the nose. Place seven halves in the position for a smiling mouth.

EACH SERVING CONTAINS: CALORIES: 148 ▲ CARBOHYDRATES: 23 G ▲ EXCHANGE: 1 1/2 BREAD, 1/2 FAT

❖ Rainbow Cake ❖

YIELD: 10 SERVINGS

| 1 | 8 inch prepared round sugar-free cake | 20 cm |
| 2 cups | prepared non-dairy whipped topping yellow food coloring red food coloring blue food coloring | 500 mL |

Frost the sides and top of the cake with a light coating of the white nondairy whipped topping. Use about one-third of the whipped topping. Transfer about 1/3 cup (90 mL) of white whipped topping to another small bowl. Tint yellow. Place the yellow whipped topping in the middle of the cake. Spread it into a circle to represent the sun. Spoon the remaining whipped topping equally into two small bowls. Tint one red, the other blue. Place and spread the red whipped topping in a semicircle around the "sun." Spread the blue whipped topping in a semicircle around the red whipped topping. The red and blue semicircles represent the rainbow.

EACH SERVING CONTAINS: CALORIES: 136 ▲ CARBOHYDRATES: 20 G ▲ EXCHANGE: 1 BREAD, 1 FAT

❖ Butterfly Cake ❖

YIELD: 10 SERVINGS

1	8 inch prepared round sugar-free cake	20 cm
1 box	(4.5 ounces) sugar-free white frosting mix	1 box (128 g)
	food coloring	
1 teaspoon	sugar-free hot-cocoa mix powder	5 mL
12	sugar-free gum drops	12

Cut cake in half. Cut out a 1 inch (2.5-cm) equilateral triangle in the middle of the straight side of the cake. Place the cake on a decorative plate with the curved sides of the cake facing each other to form the body of the butterfly. Prepare frosting mix as directed on package. Use a very small amount of the white frosting to "stick" the two triangles together. Place it between the two pieces and at the top of the cake to form the head of the butterfly. Frost the head and the inside edges of the butterfly with the white frosting. Tint the remaining frosting a bright color, such as fuchsia, red, green, or aqua. Frost the outside edges of the butterfly with the bright frosting. Using the tips of a fork, draw across the top of the bright frosting into the white frosting to produce stripes. Sprinkle the cocoa powder on the head of the butterfly. Heat one gum drop at a time, either in your hand or in the microwave, for 5 to 6 seconds. Roll the gum drop with your fingers into a long round stripe. Repeat with five more gum drops. Arrange gum drop stripes to radiate out from the middle of the curved edges of the butterfly body to the outside edges of the wings. Use six gum drop stripes per side of butterfly.

EACH SERVING CONTAINS: CALORIES: 148 ▲ CARBOHYDRATES: 23 G ▲ EXCHANGE: 1 1/2 BREAD, 1/2 FAT

❖ Doll Cake ❖

1 package	(8-ounces) sugar-free cake mix	1 package (227 g)
1	3 to 4 inch plastic doll	7.5 to 10 cm
1 box	(4.5-ounces) box sugar-free white frosting mix	1 box (128 g)
	food coloring	

Prepare cake mix as directed on package. Bake in a 1 quart (1–L) half-circle metal gelatin mould or a plum-pudding mould. Baking time will be about 30 to 35 minutes, according to type of mould used. When a pick inserted in middle comes out clean, cake is done. (Middle will rise higher than sides.) Allow cake to cool in pan for 10 minutes; then move to rack to cool completely. Place cake on a decorative plate. Check height of doll to cake; cake should be to doll's waist or higher. Prepare white frosting mix as directed on package. Color, if desired. Place narrow strips of waxed paper around lower edge of cake. Frost the lower edge of the cake. Securely place the doll into the middle of the cake. Frost the top of the doll and then the skirt. Place a few drops of desired food coloring in a small bowl or glass. For lighter shades, add a few drops of water; for deep shades, use the coloring as is. With a small paint brush, color the dress of the doll. Always start with the lighter shades of color; then add deeper and darker color.

EACH SERVING CONTAINS: CALORIES: 147 ▲ CARBOHYDRATES: 22 G ▲ EXCHANGE: 1 1/2 BREAD, 1/2 FAT

❖ Ball Cake ❖

1 box	(4.5-ounces) sugar-free white frosting mix	1 box (128 g)
1	8 inch prepared round sugar-free cake	20 cm
10	sugar-free licorice gum drops	10
	food coloring	

Prepare frosting mix as directed on package. Frost sides and top of cake. Soften gum drops, one at a time, either in your hand or place in the microwave for 5 to 6 seconds. Roll gum drops with your fingers into a 4-inch (10-cm) strip. Place three strips down each side of the cake (in a curved design) to designate the stitching line. Cut remaining licorice strips into small pieces; place at an angle to the stitch line to finish the stitches. Place a few drops of food coloring (any color) in a small glass or bowl. With a small thin brush, write your message, such as the ball player's name, Great Game, or Congratulations.

EACH SERVING CONTAINS: CALORIES: 148 ▲ CARBOHYDRATES: 23 G ▲ EXCHANGE: 1 1/2 BREAD, L/2 FAT

❖ Star Cake ❖

YIELD: 10 SERVINGS

| 1 package | (8-ounces) package sugar-free white cake mix | 1 package (227 g) |
| 1 box | (4.5-ounces) sugar-free white frosting mix blue food coloring red food coloring | 1 box (128 g) |

Prepare cake mix as directed on package. Bake in a prepared 1-quart (1-L) star-shaped gelatin mould. Allow cake to cool 10 minutes in pan before removing. Then cool completely. Prepare frosting mix as directed on package. Transfer one-third of the frosting to another bowl. Tint blue. Frost top third of the cake with the blue frosting. (This is one point and two half-points of the star form.) Transfer about one-third of the remaining white frosting to another bowl. Tint red. Make five stripes down the remaining part of the cake. Starting at the left side of the cake, frost first stripe white, second stripe red, continuing across cake.

EACH SERVING CONTAINS: CALORIES: 148 ▲ CARBOHYDRATES: 23 G ▲ EXCHANGE: 1 1/2 BREAD, 1/2 FAT

❖ Merry Christmas Wreath Cake ❖

YIELD: 10 SERVINGS

1 package	(8 ounces) sugar-free cake mix	1 package (227 g)
1 box	(4.5 ounces) box sugar-free white frosting mix green food coloring	1 box (128 g)
3	sugar-free red gum drops	3

Prepare cake mix as directed on package. Bake in a 1 quart (l-L) shiny metal ring mould. Baking time will be about 20 to 25 minutes, according to type of mould used. When a pick inserted in middle comes out clean, cake is done. Allow cake to cool in pan for 10 minutes; then move to rack to cool completely. Prepare frosting mix as directed on package; tint a bright green. Frost cake. Soften gum drops one at a time, either in your hand or in the microwave for 5 to 6 seconds. Roll two of the gum drops with your fingers into a 4 inch (10-cm) strip. Roll the third gum drop into a 2 inch (5-cm) strip. Form the two 4 inch (10-cm) strips into the bow. Twist the 2 inch (5-cm) strip in the middle of the bow. Place in desired position on frosted cake.

EACH SERVING CONTAINS: CALORIES: 148 ▲ CARBOHYDRATES: 23 G ▲ EXCHANGE: 1 1/2 BREAD, 1/2 FAT

❖ Nutmeg Cake Ring ❖

YIELD: 10 SERVINGS

1 box	Sweet 'n Low brand banana cake mix	1 box
1/8 tablespoon	nutmeg	2 mL
2 tablespoons	finely chopped almonds	30 mL
2/3 cup	water	180 mL

Combine cake mix, nutmeg, and 1 tablespoon chopped almonds in mixing bowl. Add half the water and mix 3 minutes. Add balance of water and mix 1 minute. Lightly grease and wax paper-line a ring mould (1 quart capacity). Sprinkle remaining tablespoon chopped almonds on bottom of pan. Pour batter into pan. Bake at 375°F for 25 to 30 minutes. Cool slightly. Invert onto serving plate.

EACH SERVING CONTAINS: CALORIES: 101

❖ Bell Cake ❖

YIELD: 10 SERVINGS

1 box	(8 ounces) sugar-free	1 box (227 g)
	white cake mix	
1 box	(4.5-ounces) box sugar-free	1 box (128 g)
	white frosting mix	
	food coloring	

Prepare cake mix as directed on package, but bake in a bell-shaped pan. Allow to cool completely. Prepare frosting mix as directed on box. Frost the top and sides of the cake with a very light coating. Tint remaining frosting with color of your choice. Pipe designs on the cake, such as wedding bells or flowers, and messages, like Best Wishes or Happy New Year.

EACH SERVING CONTAINS: CALORIES: 143 ▲ CARBOHYDRATES: 21 G ▲ EXCHANGE: 1 1/2 BREAD, 1/2 FAT

❖ Marble Cake ❖

YIELD: 10 SERVINGS

1 box	Sweet 'n Low brand	1 box
	white cake mix	
2/3 cup	water	180 mL
2 tablespoons	cocoa (unsweetened)	30 mL

Mix half the water with cake mix for 3 minutes, using mixer. Add the balance of water and mix 1 minute. Pour 1 1/3 cups of this white batter into lightly greased and wax paper-lined pen. Use either 8 inch square, 8 inch round, or 8 x 4 inch loaf pan. Sift the cocoa into remaining white batter and mix until well blended. Spoon chocolate batter on top of white batter. Zigzag knife through to marble batter. Bake at 375°F for 25 minutes for round or square cake, and for 35 to 40 minutes for loaf cake. Cool slightly before removing from pan.

EACH SERVING CONTAINS: CALORIES: 95

❖ Mocha Torte ❖

Cake:

1 box	Sweet 'n Low brand chocolate cake mix	1 box
1/4 teaspoon	salt	1 mL
3/4 cup	water	180 mL

Filling and topping:

1 cup	low-calorie whipped topping	250 mL
1/4 teaspoon	instant-coffee granules	1 mL
1 1/2 teaspoons	sifted cocoa, unsweetened	8 mL
1 teaspoon	shaved chocolate, dietetic	5 mL

Cake: Mix cake mix and salt with half the water for 3 minutes in mixer. Add the balance of water and mix 1 minute. Pour batter into lightly greased and wax paper-lined 8 x 4 inch loaf pan. Bake at 375°F 35 to 40 minutes. Cool slightly before removing from pan. Cool thoroughly before slicing horizontally into three layers.

Filling and Topping: Flavor low-calorie whipped topping with coffee granules and cocoa. Spread 1/4 cup topping over each layer (including top layer) and the remaining 1/4 cup on the sides of the loaf after the layers are stacked. Garnish top of torte with 1 teaspoon of shaved chocolate. Refrigerate until serving time.

EACH SERVING CONTAINS: CALORIES: 105

❖ Lemon Cheesecake ❖

Crust:

1 cup	saltine-cracker crumbs	250 mL
1 tablespoon	soft margarine	15 mL
1 teaspoon	grated lemon peel	5 mL

Filling:

1 package	(4 serving) sugar-free lemon gelatin	1 package
2 cups	hot water	500 mL

2 tablespoons	finely grated lemon peel	30 mL
1 package	(8 ounces) light cream cheese	1 package (227 g)
1 cup	prepared non-dairy whipped topping	250 mL

Crust: Mix together the saltine-cracker crumbs, margarine, and 1 teaspoon (5 mL) of the lemon peel. Press into the bottom and slightly up the sides of an 8 inch (20-cm) pie pan. Refrigerate until ready to use.

Filling: Dissolve the lemon gelatin in the hot water. Stir in the 2 remaining tablespoons (30 mL) of lemon peel, and allow to cool until mixture is a thick syrup. Whip cream cheese until light and fluffy. Gradually add lemon-gelatin mixture. Fold in non-dairy whipped topping. Transfer to saltine-cracker crust. Refrigerate at least 2 to 3 hours or until firm.

EACH SERVING CONTAINS: CALORIES: 224 ▲ CARBOHYDRATES: 23 G ▲ EXCHANGE: 1 BREAD, 3/4 LOW-FAT MILK, 1 FAT

❖ Fresh Strawberry Cheesecake ❖

YIELD: 20 SERVINGS

Crust:

1 1/2 cups	graham-cracker crumbs	375 mL
1 tablespoon	soft margarine	15 mL
1/2 teaspoon	ground nutmeg	2 mL
1 tablespoon	water	5 mL

Filling:

1 package	(8 ounces) low-fat cottage cheese	1 package (227 g)
1 package	(8 ounces) light cream cheese	1 package (227 g)
2/3 cup	granulated sugar replacement	180 mL
1 1/2 teaspoons	vanilla extract	7 mL
2 envelopes	unflavored gelatin	2 envelopes
1/2 cup	cold water	125 mL
2 cups	prepared non-dairy whipped topping	500 mL
3	egg whites, beaten stiff	3
2 cups	halved strawberries	500 mL

Crust: Mix the graham-cracker crumbs, margarine, and nutmeg together. Stir in the water until mixture is moist. Press into the bottom and slightly up the sides of a 10 inch (25-cm) springform pan. Refrigerate until ready to use.

Filling: Combine cottage cheese and cream cheese in a food processor or large bowl. Process or beat until cheeses are blended and creamy. Beat in sugar replacement and vanilla. Sprinkle and soften the gelatin in the cold water in a microwave-proof cup or bowl. Heat in the microwave for 1 to 2 minutes. Stir to dissolve the gelatin. Then completely fold the gelatin into the cheese mixture. Fold 1 cup (250 mL) of the prepared whipped topping and the three stiffly beaten egg whites into the cheese mixture. Transfer mixture to prepared crust. Chill thoroughly.

To serve: Remove sides of pan. Place cheesecake on decorative serving plate. Spread remaining 1 cup (250 mL) of non-dairy whipped topping over top of cheesecake. Arrange the halved strawberries in the whipped topping.

EACH SERVING CONTAINS: CALORIES: 140 ▲ CARBOHYDRATES: 9 G ▲ EXCHANGE: 3/4 WHOLE MILK

❖ Semisweet Chocolate Cheesecake ❖

YIELD: 20 SERVINGS

Crust:

1 1/2 cups	vanilla-cookie crumbs	375 mL
1 tablespoon	soft margarine	15 mL
1 tablespoon	water	15 mL

Filling:

1 can	(12 ounces) skim evaporated milk	1 can (354 g)
2 tablespoons	cornstarch	30 mL
1/3 cup	granulated fructose	90 mL
3 ounces	semisweet chocolate	86 g
2 packages	(8 ounces) light cream cheese	2 packages (227 g)
3	eggs	3

2 teaspoons	chocolate extract	10 mL
1 teaspoon	vanilla extract	5 mL
2 teaspoons	all-purpose flour	10 mL

Crust: Combine crumbs, margarine, and water in a bowl or food processor. Blend completely. Press firmly into the bottom of a 9 inch (23-cm) springform pan. Refrigerate or place in freezer until chilled.

Filling: Combine evaporated milk, cornstarch, and granulated fructose in a saucepan. Cook and stir over medium heat until mixture is thick and very creamy. Remove from heat, add chocolate, and stir until chocolate is melted. Cool to room temperature. Beat cream cheese until light and fluffy. Beat in cooled chocolate-milk mixture. Beat in eggs, one at a time. Beat in chocolate and vanilla extracts and flour. Transfer to crumb-lined pan. Bake at 325°F (165 °C) for 45 to 60 minutes or until middle is set. Allow to cool. Remove from pan. Chill thoroughly before serving.

EACH SERVING CONTAINS: CALORIES: 148 ▲ CARBOHYDRATES: 12 G ▲ EXCHANGE: 1 WHOLE MILK

❖ Cherry Cheesecake ❖

YIELD: 20 SERVINGS

Crust:
1 1/2 cups	cornflake crumbs	375 mL
1 tablespoon	soft margarine	15 mL
1 tablespoon	granulated sugar replacement	15 mL
2 teaspoons	water	5 mL

Filling:
1 package	(8 ounces) light cream cheese	1 package (227 g)
1/2 cup	granulated sugar	125 mL
2	eggs, separated	2
1 1/2 tablespoons	all-purpose flour	21 mL
1/8 teaspoon	salt	2 mL
1/2 teaspoon	vanilla extract	2 mL
1/2 cup	evaporated milk, chilled	125 mL
1 1/2 tablespoons	lemon juice	21 mL

Topping:
| 1 1/2 cups | fresh tart red cherries | 375 mL |

1/2 cup	water	125 mL
1/2 cup	granulated sugar replacement	125 mL
1 envelope	unflavored gelatin	1 envelope
2 tablespoons	cold water	30 mL
	red food coloring	

Crust: Mix together cornflake crumbs, margarine, and the 1 table-spoon (15 mL) of granulated sugar replacement. Add the 1 teaspoon (5 mL) of water and thoroughly blend. Press into bottom and slightly up sides of a 9 inch (23-cm) springform pan. Refrigerate until ready to use.

Filling: Whip the cream cheese until soft and fluffy. Beat in 1/2 cup (125 mL) of granulated sugar replacement and egg yolks (one at a time). Beat in the flour, salt, and vanilla extract. Whip the evaporated milk until thick, add the lemon juice, and continue beating until stiff. Gently fold into cream mixture. Beat the egg whites until stiff. Fold into the cream mixture. Transfer to prepared cornflake crust. Bake at 325°F (165 °C) for 1 hour. Turn off heat and allow cheesecake to cool in oven.

Topping: Combine tart cherries, the 1/2 cup (125 mL) of water, and the 1/2 cup (125 mL) of granulated sugar replacement in a saucepan. Mix well and bring to a boil. Reduce heat and simmer for 8 minutes. Dissolve the gelatin in 2 tablespoons (30 mL) of cold water. Stir into cherry mixture. Cook until gelatin is dissolved. Remove from heat. Add a few drops of red food coloring. Cool until thickened. At serving time, spread cherry mixture over cheesecake.

EACH SERVING CONTAINS: CALORIES: 125 ▲ CARBOHYDRATES: 15 G ▲ EXCHANGE: 1 BREAD, 1 FAT

❖ Cinnamon Apple Cheesecake ❖

Crust:

1 cup	graham-cracker crumbs	250 mL
1 tablespoon	soft margarine	15 mL
1 teaspoon	ground cinnamon	5 mL

Filling:

2 cups	cinnamon apple juice	500 mL
1 envelope	unflavored gelatin	1 envelope
1 package	(4 serving) sugar-free vanilla pudding mix (to cook)	1 package
3 inch	cinnamon stick	7.5 cm
1 package	(8 ounces) light cream cheese	1 package (227 g)

Crust: Mix together the graham-cracker crumbs, margarine, and cinnamon. Press into the bottom and slightly up the sides of an 8 inch (20-cm) pie pan. Refrigerate until ready to use.

Filling: Pour cinnamon apple juice in a saucepan. Sprinkle gelatin over top and allow to soften for 3 to 4 minutes. Stir in pudding mix. Add cinnamon stick. Cook and stir over medium heat until mixture is smooth and thickened. Remove from heat and allow to cool to room temperature. Remove cinnamon after mixture is cooled. Whip cream cheese until light and fluffy. Slowly add cooled cinnamon-apple mixture. Beat thoroughly. Pour into 8 inch (20-cm) graham-cracker crust. Refrigerate at least 2 to 3 hours or until firm.

EACH SERVING CONTAINS: CALORIES: 240 ▲ CARBOHYDRATES: 26 G ▲ EXCHANGE: 1 BREAD, 1 LOW-FAT MILK, 1 FAT

PIES

❖ Deep Dish Pie Shell ❖

YIELD: 1 DEEP DISH PIE SHELL, OR 8 SERVINGS

2 cups	flour	500 mL
11 tablespoons	fat-free butter and oil replacement product	165 mL
3–4 tablespoons	ice water	45–60 mL

Put the flour into a bowl. Using two knives or a pastry blender, cut in the butter and oil replacement until the mixture resembles coarse meal. Add about two tablespoons (30 mL) of water and work it in gently with a fork. Gradually add the ice water a little at a time, using fingers or a fork to work the dough into a ball. Don't let the ball become sticky, the result of too much water. Chill the dough for 30 minutes. On a lightly floured surface, flatten the dough into a circle with roundish edges or rectangular edges, depending on your deep dish pie pan.

With a rolling pin, roll the dough slightly larger than the pan, rolling from the center outward, the thinner the better. Fold the dough in half and gently lift it onto a pie pan coated with non-stick vegetable spray, being careful not to stretch it. Unfold the dough and pat it gently into the pan. Using a kitchen knife, cut away any dough that extends more than 3/4 inch (3 cm) beyond the edge of the pan. Fold the outside dough over to make a double thickness around the rim of the pan. Press the edge down with a fork, or use your fingers to make a fluted edge. If the crust will be baked without any filling, prick the crust all over with a fork. Bake in 425°F (220°C) oven for approximately 12 to 15 minutes or until it looks as brown as you would like, or follow the directions of the recipe contained with the filling recipe.

EACH SERVING CONTAINS: CALORIES: 162 ▲ CARBOHYDRATES: 36 G ▲ EXCHANGE: 1 STARCH/BREAD, 1 FRUIT

❖ Sweet Potato Pie ❖

YIELD: 8 SERVINGS

Rich and satisfying, a great dessert for a light meal.

1	frozen pie crust, unbaked, or Deep Dish Pie Shell, unbaked (p. 188)	1
3 large	sweet potatoes, peeled, cooked, well drained and mashed	3
1/4 cup	sugar	60 mL
6 packages	saccharin	6 packages
2 tablespoons	butter or margarine, melted	30 mL
1 teaspoon	cinnamon	5 mL
1 teaspoon	nutmeg	5 mL
1 teaspoon	allspice	5 mL
1 cup	skim milk	250 mL
4	large eggs or equivalent egg substitute, slightly beaten	4
1 teaspoon	vanilla	5 mL

Use a frozen pie crust or freeze a deep dish pie crust for 30 minutes. In a large bowl, combine the sweet potatoes, sugar, sugar substitute, butter, cinnamon, nutmeg, and allspice. Mix well. In another bowl, combine the remaining ingredients. Pour this wet mixture onto the sweet potato mixture. Mix well to combine. Pour this mixture into the pie crust. Put the pie in a 375°F (180°C) oven for 45–50 minutes. Test the pie for doneness by inserting a knife in the center. The pie is done when the knife comes out clean.

EACH SERVING CONTAINS: CALORIES: 236 ▲ CARBOHYDRATES: 29 G ▲ EXCHANGE: 2 STARCH/BREAD 2 FAT

❖ Squash Pie ❖

YIELD: 8 SLICES

This tastes like coconut custard. If the top is brown but the center isn't cooked, cover the pie with aluminum foil and bake for a few minutes more.

2 cups	yellow squash, freshly grated, peeled	500 mL
1/4 cup	sugar	60 mL
6 packages	saccharin or acesulfame-K sugar substitute	6 packages
1 teaspoon	cornstarch	5 mL
1 teaspoon	vanilla	5 mL
2 teaspoons	coconut extract	10 mL
1 tablespoon	flour	15 mL
3	large eggs or equivalent egg substitute, slightly beaten	3
1/4 cup	butter or margarine, melted	60 mL
1	Deep Dish Pie Shell, unbaked (p. 188)	1

In a large mixing bowl, combine all the ingredients except the pie shell, and mix well. Pour into the unbaked pie shell. Put the pie into a preheated 400°F (200°C) oven for 10 to 15 minutes. Reduce the temperature to 350°F (180°C) for 40 to 50 minutes until the top is golden brown.

EACH SLICE CONTAINS: CALORIES: 280 ▲ CARBOHYDRATES: 46 G ▲ EXCHANGE: 2 STARCH/BREAD, 1 FRUIT, 1 FAT

❖ Blueberry Sour Cream Pie ❖

YIELD: 8 SERVINGS

2 cups	fresh or frozen blueberries	500 mL
1	frozen pie crust, unbaked, or Deep Dish Pie Shell, unbaked (p. 188)	1
1 cup	fat-free sour cream	250 mL
2 tablespoons	sugar	30 mL
3 packages	saccharin or acesulfame-K sugar substitute	3 packages
1	large egg yolk, lightly beaten	1
1 teaspoon	vanilla	1 teaspoon

Put the blueberries in the crust. Mix all the other ingredients in a mixing bowl. Pour this mixture over the blueberries. Bake in a pre-heated 375°F (190°C) oven for 45 minutes. The pie top will be lightly browned. Cool and chill before serving.

EACH SERVING CONTAINS: CALORIES: 143 ▲ CARBOHYDRATES: 19 G ▲ EXCHANGE: 1 STARCH/BREAD; 1 FAT

❖ Quick Custard Pie ❖

YIELD: 8 SERVINGS

Cut down the fat by using egg substitute.

4	large eggs or equivalent egg substitute	4
3 tablespoons	sugar	45 mL
6 packages	saccharin or acesulfame-K sugar substitute	6 packages
1/4 teaspoon	nutmeg	2 mL
1 teaspoon	vanilla extract	5 mL
1/2 teaspoon	butter extract	3 mL
1	unbaked pie crust, or Deep-Dish Pie Shell, unbaked (p. 188)	1

Put all the ingredients (except the pie shell!) into a blender or food processor. Process at a low speed until the sugar is dissolved and the mixture is well blended. Pour into the pie shell. Bake in a preheated 350°F (180°C) oven for 30 minutes or until a knife inserted into the center of the pie comes out clean.

EACH SERVING CONTAINS: CALORIES: 160 ▲ CARBOHYDRATES: 16 G ▲ EXCHANGE: 1 STARCH/BREAD, 2 FAT

❖ Sour Cream Pie ❖

Try serving this pie with raspberry or lemon sauce.

2	large eggs or equivalent egg substitute	2
1 cup	fat-free sour cream	250 mL
1/2 cup	raisins	125 mL
2 tablespoons	sugar	30 mL
6 packages	saccharin or acesulfame-K sugar substitute	6 packages
1 1/2 teaspoons	cinnamon	8 mL
1/4 cup	pecans, chopped fine (optional)	60 mL
1	frozen pie crust, unbaked, or Deep Dish Pie Shell, unbaked (p. 188)	1

Put all the ingredients except the pecans and the pie crust in a blender or food processor. Process at medium speed until well mixed. Scrape the sides a few times, if necessary. Add the pecans if you're using them, and pulse a few times to blend. Pour into the pie shell. Bake in a preheated 450°F (230°C) oven for 15 minutes. Reduce heat to 350°F (180°C) and bake an additional 30 minutes.

EACH SERVING CONTAINS: CALORIES: 163 ▲ CARBOHYDRATES: 22 G ▲ EXCHANGE: 1 1/2 STARCH/BREAD, 1 FAT

❖ Pastry Shell (from Mix) ❖

1	pie-crust stick or mix, for a 9 inch (23-cm) shell	1

Prepare dough as directed on package. Form dough into a 9 inch (23-cm) microwave or glass pie pan. Trim and flute edges as desired. Prick bottom and sides of unbaked shell. Microwave on medium high for 4 to 5 minutes. Rotate dish one-fourth turn after 2 minutes, then again in 2 minutes. Cool.

EACH SERVING CONTAINS: CALORIES: 123 ▲ CARBOHYDRATES: 15 G ▲ EXCHANGE: 1
BREAD, 1 FAT

❖ Graham–Cracker Crust ❖

YIELD: 8 SERVINGS

| 1/3 cup | reduced-calorie margarine | 90 mL |
| 1 1/2 cups | graham-cracker crumbs | 375 mL |

Melt margarine in a 9 inch (23-cm) microwave or glass pie dish. Add cracker crumbs. Using a fork, completely blend crumbs and margarine. Press evenly onto bottom and sides of dish. Microwave, uncovered, on high for 2 minutes. Rotate dish one-fourth turn after 1 minute. Allow crust to rest and cool before filling.

EACH SERVING CONTAINS: CALORIES: 120 ▲ CARBOHYDRATES: 16 G ▲ EXCHANGE: 1
BREAD, 1 FAT

❖ Wafer Crust ❖

YIELD: 8 SERVINGS

| 1/3 cup | reduced-calorie margarine | 90 mL |
| 1 1/2 cups | wafer crumbs (vanilla or chocolate) | 375 mL |

Melt margarine in a 9 inch (23-cm) microwave or glass pie dish. Add wafer crumbs. Using a fork, completely blend crumbs and margarine. Press evenly onto bottom and sides of dish. Microwave, uncovered, on high for 2 minutes. Rotate dish one-fourth turn after 1 minute. Allow crust to rest and cool before filling.

EACH SERVING WITH VANILLA CRUMBS CONTAINS: CALORIES: 120 ▲ CARBOHYDRATES: 15 G
▲ EXCHANGE: 1 BREAD, 1 FAT

EACH SERVING WITH CHOCOLATE CRUMBS CONTAINS: CALORIES: 130 ▲ CARBOHYDRATES: 18 G
▲ EXCHANGE: 1 BREAD, 1 FAT

❖ Flaky Pie Crust ❖

(TWO SHELLS) YIELD: 8 SERVINGS/SHELLS

1 1/2 cups	all-purpose flour	375 mL
dash	salt	dash
1/2 cup	solid vegetable shortening	125 mL
1	egg	1
1 teaspoon	white vinegar	5 mL
2 tablespoons	water	30 mL
2 to 3 drops	yellow food coloring	2 to 3 drops

Sift flour, measure, and resift into a bowl or food processor. Add salt and shortening. Using a pastry blender or food processor, cut until mixture becomes coarse crumbs. In a small bowl, combine egg, vinegar, water, and food coloring. Lightly beat to blend. Drizzle into flour mixture, mixing lightly until all the flour is moistened and forms into a ball. Divide the dough in half, roll out each piece on a lightly floured board, and fit into two 9 inch (23-cm) microwave or glass pie dishes. Prick bottom and sides of each shell. Microwave each shell on medium high for 4 to 5 minutes. Rotate dish one-fourth turn after 2 minutes, then again in 2 minutes. Cool.

EACH SERVING CONTAINS: CALORIES: 214 ▲ CARBOHYDRATES: 16 G ▲ EXCHANGE: 1 BREAD, 3 FAT

❖ Meringue Pie Shell ❖

YIELD: 8 SERVINGS

3	egg whites	3
1/2 teaspoon	vanilla extract	2 mL
1/4 teaspoon	cream of tartar	1 mL
dash	salt	dash
1/2 cup	granulated sugar replacement	125 mL

Combine egg whites, vanilla, cream of tartar, and salt in a bowl. Beat to soft peaks. Gradually beat in sugar replacement. Beat to stiff peaks. Spread on the bottom and sides of a 9 inch (23-cm) pie pan. Bake at

300°F (150°C) for 35 to 40 minutes or until crisp and lightly browned. Cool completely before using.

EACH SERVING CONTAINS: CALORIES: NEGLIGIBLE ▲ CARBOHYDRATES: NEGLIGIBLE ▲ EXCHANGE: NEGLIGIBLE

❖ Nut Meringue Pie Shell ❖

YIELD: 8 SERVINGS

3	egg whites	3
1/2 teaspoon	vanilla extract	2 mL
1/4 teaspoon	cream of tartar	1 mL
dash	salt	dash
1/2 cup	granulated sugar replacement	125 mL
1/4 cup	chopped nuts	60 mL

Combine egg whites, vanilla, cream of tartar, and salt in a bowl. Beat to soft peaks. Gradually beat in sugar replacement. Beat to stiff peaks. Spread on the bottom and sides of a 9 inch (23-cm) pie pan. Sprinkle with chopped nuts. Bake at 275°F (135°C) for 1 hour. Cool completely before using.

EACH SERVING CONTAINS: CALORIES: 23 ▲ CARBOHYDRATES: NEGLIGIBLE ▲ EXCHANGE: 1/2 FAT

❖ Chocolate-Chip Pie ❖

YIELD: 8 SERVINGS

1 recipe	Nut Meringue Pie Shell (above)	1 recipe
1/2 cup	semisweet chocolate chips	125 mL
1/4 cup	hot water	60 mL
1 teaspoon	vanilla extract	5 mL
dash	salt	dash
2 cups	prepared non-dairy whipped topping	500 mL

Melt chocolate chips in the top of a double boiler over simmering water. Stir in hot water, vanilla, and salt. Stir and cook until smooth. Cool completely. Fold in non-dairy whipped topping. Transfer to prepared pie shell. Chill at least 5 hours or overnight.

EACH SERVING CONTAINS: CALORIES: 92 ▲ CARBOHYDRATES: 9 G ▲ EXCHANGE: 3/4 BREAD, 3/4 FAT

❖ Sweet Cherry Dessert Pie ❖

YIELD: 8 SERVINGS

10 inch	baked pie shell	25 cm
1 pound	bag frozen, unsweetened sweet cherries, thawed	457 g bag
1 envelope	unflavored gelatin	1 envelope
1/4 cup	cold water	60 mL
2 cups	prepared non-dairy whipped topping	500 mL
1/4 cup	unsweetened, shredded coconut	60 mL
1/4 cup	chopped pecans	60 mL

Drain cherries, reserving liquid. Soften gelatin in the cold water. Add water to the reserved cherry liquid to make 1 cup (250 mL). Pour into a saucepan. Add softened gelatin, and stir to dissolve gelatin. Bring to a boil. Remove from heat and cool to a thick syrup. Beat until fluffy. Fold non-dairy whipped topping into cherry gelatin. Fold in the cherries, coconut, and pecans. Transfer to baked pie shell. Chill for several hours or until set.

EACH SERVING CONTAINS: CALORIES: 226 ▲ CARBOHYDRATES: 19 G ▲ EXCHANGE: 1 1/3 BREAD, 2 1/2 FAT

❖ Raspberry Cheese Pie ❖

YIELD: 8 SERVINGS

1	9 inch baked pie shell	23 cm
1 package	(4 serving) sugar-free raspberry-flavored gelatin mix	1 package
1 tablespoon	granulated fructose	15 mL
1 1/4 cups	hot water	310 mL
1 pound	bag unsweetened, frozen raspberries	457-g bag
3 ounces	light cream cheese	85 g
2 tablespoons	skim milk	30 mL

Dissolve gelatin and fructose in hot water. Add the frozen raspberries, and stir until berries are separated and mixture begins to thicken. Blend cream cheese with the milk. Spread cheese mixture over the bottom of the baked pie shell. Pour slightly thickened gelatin mixture over cheese. Chill until set.

EACH SERVING CONTAINS: CALORIES: 138 ▲ CARBOHYDRATES: 19 G ▲ EXCHANGE: 1 BREAD, 1/2 FAT, 1/4 FRUIT

❖ Meringue Tart–Lemon Pie ❖

YIELD: 8 SERVINGS

1 recipe	Meringue Pie Shell (page 194)	1 recipe
1 cup	skim milk	250 mL
1/2 cup	lemon juice	125 mL
1 tablespoon	cornstarch	15 mL
1/2 tablespoon	vanilla extract	2 mL
dash	salt	dash
3 egg	yolks, slightly beaten	3
3/4 cup	granulated sugar replacement	190 mL
	or	
1/2 cup	granulated fructose	125 mL
1 tablespoon	grated lemon peel	15 mL

Combine milk, lemon juice, cornstarch, vanilla, and salt in a saucepan. (Mixture will appear curdled.) Cook and stir over medium heat until mixture is consistency of heavy cream. Pour a small amount of hot mixture into beaten egg yolks. Stir slightly; then pour egg yolks into hot mixture. Return to heat and cook until mixture is thick. Stir in sweetener of your choice and grated lemon peel. Remove from heat and cover. Cool completely. Pour into prepared pie shell. Chill until serving time.

EACH SERVING WITH GRANULATED SUGAR REPLACEMENT CONTAINS: CALORIES: 40 ▲ CARBOHYDRATES: 4 G ▲ EXCHANGE: 1/3 LOW-FAT MILK

EACH SERVING WITH GRANULATED FRUCTOSE CONTAINS: CALORIES: 87 ▲ CARBOHYDRATES: 14 G ▲ EXCHANGE: 1/3 LOW-FAT MILK, 2/3 FRUIT

❖ Ginger Banana Pie ❖

YIELD: 8 SERVINGS

1	9 inch baked pie shell	23 cm
6	gingersnaps	6
1 envelope	unflavored gelatin	1 envelope
2/3 cup	granulated sugar replacement	180 mL
3/4 cup	water	190 mL
3	bananas	3
3 tablespoons	fresh lemon juice	45 mL
1 teaspoon	grated lemon peel	5 mL
2	egg whites	2
	lemon juice	

Powder gingersnaps in a food processor or blender. Set aside. Combine gelatin, sugar replacement, and water in a small saucepan or microwavesafe bowl. Stir to mix. Heat until gelatin is completely dissolved. Remove from heat. Meanwhile, mash two of the bananas. Stir the 3 tablespoons (45 mL) of lemon juice and the lemon peel into the mashed bananas. Stir banana mixture into gelatin; then allow to cool until mixture is the consistency of thick cream. Add egg whites. Beat with a rotary beater until mixture begins to hold its shape. Chill if necessary. Spoon mixture into the baked pie shell. Chill thoroughly. At serving time, slice remaining banana and dip each slice in lemon juice. Garnish top of pie with banana slices; then sprinkle with powdered gingersnaps.

EACH SERVING CONTAINS: CALORIES: 159 ▲ CARBOHYDRATES: 23 G ▲ EXCHANGE: 1 BREAD, 1/2 FAT, 2/3 FRUIT

❖ Orange-Juice Angel Pie ❖

YIELD: 8 SERVINGS

1 recipe	Meringue Pie Shell (page 194)	1 recipe
4	egg yolks	4
1	egg	1
1/2 cup	granulated sugar replacement	125 mL
	or	
2 tablespoons	granulated fructose	30 mL
1/4 cup	frozen orange-juice concentrate, undiluted	60 mL
1 tablespoon	fresh lemon juice	15 mL
2 cups	prepared non-dairy whipped topping	500 mL

Beat egg yolks and egg until thick and lemon-colored. Beat in sweetener of your choice, orange-juice concentrate, and lemon juice. Pour into a saucepan. Cook and stir until mixture is very thick. Chill thoroughly. Stir slightly to loosen mixture. Fold nondairy whipped topping into cold orange mixture. Transfer to pie shell. Chill thoroughly.

EACH SERVING WITH GRANULATED SUGAR REPLACEMENT CONTAINS: CALORIES: 94 ▲ CARBOHYDRATES: 4 G ▲ EXCHANGE: 1/3 FRUIT, 1 1/2 FAT

EACH SERVING WITH GRANULATED FRUCTOSE CONTAINS: CALORIES: 102 ▲ CARBOHYDRATES: 7 G ▲ EXCHANGE: 1/2 FRUIT, 1 1/2 FAT

❖ Buttermilk Raisin Crustless Pie ❖

1 envelope	unflavored gelatin	1 envelope
1/4 cup	cold water	60 mL
2 cups	buttermilk	500 mL
1 cup	raisins	250 mL
3 tablespoons	all-purpose flour	45 mL
1/4 cup	sugar-free maple-flavored syrup	60 mL
1/2 teaspoon	ground cinnamon	2 mL
1/4 teaspoon	ground nutmeg	1 mL

Lightly grease the bottom and sides of a 9 inch (23-cm) pie pan. Sprinkle unflavored gelatin over cold water. Stir slightly; then allow to soften for 1 minute. Meanwhile, combine buttermilk, raisins, and flour in a saucepan. Whisk until flour is completely blended and mixture is smooth. Cook over medium-low heat until mixture is warm. Pour in softened gelatin, and continue cooking until gelatin is completely dissolved. Remove from heat. Cover and allow to cool for at least 1/2 hour to plump the raisins. Add maple syrup, cinnamon, and nutmeg. Pour into prepared pie pan. Bake at 350°F (175°C) for 45 minutes. Cool to room temperature; then chill.

EACH SERVING CONTAINS: CALORIES: 77 ▲ CARBOHYDRATES: 18 G ▲ EXCHANGE: 1 FRUIT, 1/4 LOW-FAT MILK

❖ Blueberries–in–Milk Crustless Pie ❖

2 cups	unsweetened, frozen blueberries	500 mL
3 tablespoons	granulated fructose	45 mL
3/4 cup	buttermilk	190 mL
1/4 cup	low-fat milk	60 mL
3 tablespoons	all-purpose flour	45 mL

Lightly grease the bottom and sides of a 9 inch (23-cm) pie pan. Place blueberries in pie pan and level. Sprinkle 1 tablespoon (15 mL)

of the granulated fructose over the top of the blueberries. Bake at 375°F (190°C) for 15 minutes. Meanwhile, combine remaining fructose, buttermilk, milk, and flour in a bowl. Beat or whisk until flour is completely blended and mixture is smooth. Pour buttermilk mixture over blueberries. Return to oven and continue baking for 30 minutes more or until middle of pie is just set. Cool to room temperature; then chill.

EACH SERVING CONTAINS: CALORIES: 53 ▲ CARBOHYDRATES: 10 G ▲ EXCHANGE: 1/2 FRUIT, 1/4 LOW-FAT MILK

COOKIES AND BARS

❖ Raisin Oatmeal Cookies ❖

YIELD: 36 COOKIES

1 cup	all-purpose flour	250 mL
1 teaspoon	ground cinnamon	5 mL
1/2 teaspoon	baking powder	2 mL
1/2 teaspoon	baking soda	2 mL
1/4 teaspoon	salt	1 mL
1/2 cup	(1 stick) solid margarine, softened	125 mL (1 stick)
2 tablespoons	granulated fructose	30 mL
1	large egg	1 large
1 teaspoon	vanilla extract	5 mL
1 cup	granulated sugar replacement	250 mL
1 1/4 cup	quick-cooking oatmeal	310 mL
1/2 cup	raisins	125 mL

Combine flour, cinnamon, baking powder, baking soda, and salt in a bowl. Stir to mix. Combine margarine, fructose, egg, and vanilla in a mixing bowl. Beat until thoroughly blended. Beat in sweetener. Gradually add flour mixture. Beat until blended. Meanwhile, combine oatmeal and raisins in a bowl. Work with your fingers or a spoon to separate the raisins and coat them with the oatmeal. Beat into cookie mixture. Drop by tablespoonfuls onto an ungreased cookie sheet. Bake at 375°F (190°C) for 10 to 12 minutes. Cool slightly on cookie sheet; then move to cooling rack.

EACH SERVING CONTAINS: CALORIES: 61 ▲ CARBOHYDRATES: 7 G ▲ EXCHANGE: 1/2 BREAD, 1/4 FAT

❖ Carob Cookies ❖

1 1/4 cups	all-purpose flour	310 mL
1/3 cup	powdered carob	90 mL
1/2 teaspoon	baking soda	2 mL
1/4 teaspoon	salt	1 mL
1/2 cup	margarine, softened	125 mL
1/2 cup	granulated fructose	125 mL
1	egg	1
1 teaspoon	vanilla extract	5 mL

Combine flour, carob, baking soda, and salt in mixing bowl. In another mixing bowl, cream margarine and fructose. Next, beat in egg and vanilla extract. Then gradually beat in flour mixture. Drop onto an ungreased cookie sheet. Bake at 350°F (175°C) for 10 to 12 minutes. Allow to cool on cookie sheet for 2 minutes before removing to a cooling rack.

EACH COOKIE CONTAINS: CALORIES: 45 ▲ CARBOHYDRATES: 4 G ▲ EXCHANGE: 1/4 BREAD, 1/3 FAT

❖ Carob-Chip Cookies ❖

1 1/2 cups	all-purpose flour	375 mL
3/4 teaspoon	baking powder	4 mL
1/2 teaspoon	salt	2 mL
3/4 cup	margarine, softened	190 mL
1/2 cup	granulated fructose	125 mL
1	egg	1
1 teaspoon	vanilla extract	5 mL
1/2 cup	unsweetened carob mini-chips	125 mL

Combine flour, baking powder, and salt in mixing bowl. In another mixing bowl, cream margarine and fructose; then beat in egg and vanilla extract. Gradually beat flour mixture into creamed mixture. Stir in carob chips. Drop onto an ungreased cookie sheet. Bake at

375°F (190°C) for 8 to 10 minutes. Allow to cool on cookie sheet for 2 minutes before removing to a cooling rack.

EACH SERVING CONTAINS: CALORIES: 43 ▲ CARBOHYDRATES: 4 G ▲ EXCHANGE: 1/4 BREAD, 1/3 FAT

❖ Pecan Cookies ❖

YIELD: 48 COOKIES

1 package	(8 ounces) light cream cheese	1 package (227 g)
3 tablespoons	granulated fructose	45 mL
1 teaspoon	vanilla extract	5 mL
1	egg	1
1	egg white	1
1 cup	all-purpose flour	250 mL
1/2 teaspoon	baking soda	2 mL
1/2 teaspoon	baking powder	2 mL
1/3 cup	sugar-free white frosting mix	90 mL
48	pecan halves	48
1/4 cup	sugar-free white frosting mix	60 mL
1 tablespoon	water	15 mL

Combine cream cheese, fructose, and vanilla in a mixing bowl. Beat until fluffy. Beat in egg and egg white. Beat at least 3 minutes. Combine flour, baking soda, baking powder, and the 1/3 cup (90 mL) of white frosting mix in a bowl. Stir to mix. (Break up any lumps in frosting mix.) Gradually beat flour mixture into cream-cheese mixture. Cover with plastic wrap and refrigerate at least 3 hours or until completely chilled. Drop by teaspoonfuls onto an ungreased cookie sheet. Bake at 325°F (165°C) for 15 to 20 minutes. Remove from pan immediately. Press one pecan half into the middle of each cookie. Combine the 1/4 cup (60 mL) of white frosting mix and water in a cup. Stir to blend into a glaze. Add extra water if needed. Lightly brush a glaze on each cookie. Move to cooling rack.

EACH COOKIE CONTAINS: CALORIES: 30 ▲ CARBOHYDRATES: 4 G ▲ EXCHANGE: 1/3 BREAD, 1/4 FAT

❖ Chocolate Softies ❖

1 package	(8 ounces) light cream cheese	1 package (227 g)
2 ounces	semisweet baking chocolate, melted	57 g
3 tablespoons	granulated fructose	45 mL
1 teaspoon	vanilla extract	5 mL
1	egg	1
1	egg white	1
1 1/4 cups	all-purpose flour	310 mL
1/2 teaspoon	baking soda	2 mL
1/2 teaspoon	baking powder	2 mL

Combine cream cheese, melted baking chocolate, fructose, and vanilla in a mixing bowl. Beat until fluffy. Beat in egg and egg white. Beat at least 3 minutes. Combine flour, baking soda, and baking powder in a bowl. Stir to mix. Gradually beat flour mixture into cream-cheese mixture. Cover with plastic wrap and refrigerate at least 3 hours or until completely chilled. Drop by teaspoonfuls onto an ungreased cookie sheet. Bake at 325°F (165°C) for 15 to 20 minutes. Remove from pan and place on cooling rack immediately.

EACH COOKIE CONTAINS: CALORIES: 31 ▲ CARBOHYDRATES: 2 G ▲ EXCHANGE: 1/6 BREAD, 1/3 FAT

❖ Applesauce Spice Cookies ❖

2 cups	cake flour	500 mL
1 teaspoon	baking powder	5 mL
1/2 teaspoon	baking soda	2 mL
1/2 teaspoon	ground cinnamon	2 mL
1/4 teaspoon	ground cloves	1 mL
1/4 teaspoon	ground nutmeg	1 mL
1/4 teaspoon	salt	1 mL
1/2 cup	(1 stick) solid margarine	125 mL (1 stick)
2 tablespoons	granulated fructose	30 mL
1	large egg	1

3/4 cup	granulated sugar replacement	190 mL
1 cup	unsweetened applesauce	250 mL

Sift cake flour, baking powder, baking soda, cinnamon, cloves, nutmeg, and salt into a bowl. Combine margarine and fructose in a mixing bowl. Beat until creamy. Beat in egg and sweetener. Add flour mixture alternately with applesauce to creamed mixture, beginning and ending with flour mixture. Drop on a well-greased cookie sheet. Bake at 375°F (190 °C) for 12 to 15 minutes.

EACH COOKIE CONTAINS: CALORIES: 57 ▲ CARBOHYDRATES: 4 G ▲ EXCHANGE: 1/3 BREAD, 1/2 FAT

❖ Chocolate Thins ❖

YIELD: 30 COOKIES

1/4 cup	solid margarine, softened	60 mL
4 teaspoons	granulated sugar replacement	20 mL
1	egg	1
2 tablespoons	unsweetened cocoa powder	30 mL
1 teaspoon	vanilla extract	5 mL
1 cup	all-purpose flour	250 mL
1 teaspoon	baking powder	5 mL
1/4 teaspoon	baking soda	1 mL
dash	salt	dash
2 tablespoons	water	30 mL

Combine margarine, sugar replacement, egg, cocoa, and vanilla in a mixing bowl or food processor. With an electric mixer or steel blade, process until creamy. Add flour, baking powder, baking soda, salt, and water. Mix well. Shape dough into two balls. Wrap each ball in plastic wrap and refrigerate at least 2 hours or overnight. Roll out dough to 1/8 inch (3-mm) thickness on a lightly floured surface. Cut with a 2 1/2 inch (6.25-cm) round cookie cutter and place on ungreased cookie sheets. Bake at 350°F (175 °C) for 8 to 10 minutes.

EACH SERVING CONTAINS: CALORIES: 22 ▲ CARBOHYDRATES: 2 G ▲ EXCHANGE: 1/5 BREAD, 1/5 FAT

❖ Hazelnut Cookies ❖

1 package	(8 ounces) package light cream cheese	1 package (227 g)
3 tablespoons	granulated fructose	45 mL
1 teaspoon	vanilla extract	5 mL
1	egg	1
1	egg white	1
1 cup	all-purpose flour	250 mL
1/2 teaspoon	baking soda	2 mL
1/2 teaspoon	baking powder	2 mL
1/3 cup	finely ground hazelnuts	90 mL

Combine cream cheese, fructose, and vanilla in a mixing bowl. Beat until fluffy. Beat in egg and egg white. Beat at least 3 minutes. Combine flour, baking soda, and baking powder in a bowl. Stir to mix. Gradually beat flour mixture into cream-cheese mixture. Stir in ground hazelnuts. Cover with plastic wrap and refrigerate at least 3 hours or until completely chilled. Drop by teaspoonfuls onto an ungreased cookie sheet. Bake at 325°F (165 °C) for 15 to 20 minutes. Remove from pan and place on cooling rack immediately.

EACH COOKIE CONTAINS: CALORIES: 34 ▲ CARBOHYDRATES: 2 G ▲ EXCHANGE: 1/6 BREAD, 1/2 FAT

❖ Sweet "Sugar" Cookies ❖

2 cups	all-purpose flour	500 mL
1/2 teaspoon	baking powder	2 mL
1/2 teaspoon	baking soda	2 mL
1/4 teaspoon	salt	1 mL
1/2 cup	solid vegetable shortening	125 mL
3/4 cup	granulated sugar replacement	190 mL
1	large egg	1
3 tablespoons	skim milk	15 mL
1 teaspoon	vanilla extract	5 mL
1 teaspoon	grated orange peel	5 mL
3 envelopes	aspartame sweetener	3 envelopes

Sift the flour, baking powder, baking soda, and salt together into a bowl. Combine the solid shortening and sweetener in a mixing bowl. Beat until creamy. Beat in the egg, milk, vanilla extract, and orange peel. Blend in the flour mixture. Lightly grease two large cookie sheets. Roll dough out on a lightly floured surface to 1/8 inch (8-mm) thickness. Cut with a doughnut cutter. Transfer dough rounds to prepared cookie sheets. Gather and reroll scraps. Cut additional cookies. Bake at 375°F (190°C) for 14 minutes or until edges of cookies are golden brown. Remove from oven. Sprinkle cookies with aspartame sweetener (use one envelope for eight cookies). Move cookies to cooling rack. For a festive holiday touch, sprinkle cookies with a small amount of colored sugar-free gelatin.

EACH COOKIE CONTAINS: CALORIES: 46 ▲ CARBOHYDRATES: 7 G ▲ EXCHANGE: 1/2 BREAD, 1/4 FAT

❖ Vanilla Wafers ❖

YIELD: 30 COOKIES

1/4 cup	solid margarine, softened	60 mL
4 teaspoons	granulated sugar replacement	20 mL
1	egg	1
1 tablespoon	vanilla extract	15 mL
1 cup	all-purpose flour	250 mL
1 teaspoon	baking powder	5 mL
1/4 teaspoon	baking soda	1 mL
dash	salt	dash
2 tablespoons	water	30 mL

Combine margarine, sugar replacement, egg, and vanilla in a mixing bowl or food processor. With an electric mixer or steel blade, process until creamy. Add flour, baking powder, baking soda, salt, and water. Mix well. Shape dough into two balls. Wrap each ball in plastic wrap and refrigerate at least 2 hours or overnight. Roll out dough to 1/8 inch (3-mm) thickness on a lightly floured surface. Cut with a 2 1/2-inch (6.25-cm) round cookie cutter and place on ungreased cookie sheets. Bake at 350°F (175 °C) for 8 to 10 minutes.

EACH COOKIE CONTAINS: CALORIES: 21 ▲ CARBOHYDRATES: 2 G ▲ EXCHANGE: 1/5 BREAD, 1/5 FAT

❖ Lemon–Sandwich Cookies ❖

Cookie:

1/2 cup	solid margarine	125 mL
1/2 cup	granulated sugar replacement	125 mL
2	eggs	2
1 tablespoon	lemon juice	15 mL
1 teaspoon	vanilla extract	5 mL
1 1/2 cups	all-purpose flour	375 mL
1/4 teaspoon	baking soda	1 mL
dash	salt	dash

Combine margarine, sweetener, eggs, lemon juice, and vanilla in a mixing bowl. Beat to blend. Stir in flour, baking soda, and salt. Work into a soft, smooth dough. Divide dough in half. Shape each half into a 7 x 1 1/2 inch (17.5 x 3.75 cm) roll. Wrap in plastic wrap and chill for 8 hours or overnight. Cut each roll into approximately 1/8 inch (3-mm) slices, or cut 48 slices from each roll. Place on ungreased cookie sheet. Bake at 400°F (200 °C) for 5 to 6 minutes or until edges begin to brown. Cool completely before filling.

Filling:

1/3 cup	sugar-free white frosting-mix powder	90 mL
1 teaspoon	grated lemon peel	5 mL
1 tablespoon	hot lemon juice	15 mL
	yellow food coloring	

Combine frosting-mix powder, lemon peel, hot lemon juice, and yellow food coloring in a small bowl. Beat with a small wire whisk or fork until smooth. Put cookies together in pairs with filling.

EACH COOKIE CONTAINS: CALORIES: 41 ▲ CARBOHYDRATES: 4 G ▲ EXCHANGE: 1/3 BREAD, 1/3 FAT

❖ Fancies ❖

3	eggs	3
1 cup	granulated sugar replacement	250 mL
3 tablespoons	granulated fructose	45 mL
1/2 teaspoon	salt	2 mL
3 tablespoons	melted shortening	45 mL
1 tablespoon	vanilla extract	15 mL
3 cup	quick-cooking oatmeal	750 mL

Beat eggs until lemon-colored. Gradually beat in sugar replacement and fructose. Beat in salt, melted shortening, and vanilla. Beat well. Beat in oatmeal. Drop teaspoonfuls onto a greased cookie sheet. Bake at 325°F (165 °C) for 17 to 20 minutes or until done. Move from pan to cooling rack while still warm.

EACH COOKIE CONTAINS: CALORIES: 13 ▲ CARBOHYDRATES: 2 G ▲ EXCHANGE: 1/6 BREAD

❖ Crisscross Peanut–Butter Cookies ❖

YIELD: 60 COOKIES

1 1/2 cups	all-purpose flour	375 mL
1/2 teaspoon	baking powder	2 mL
1 cup	low-sugar creamy peanut butter	250 mL
1/2 cup	(1 stick) solid margarine	125 mL (1 stick)
2 tablespoons	granulated fructose	30 mL
1 large	egg	1 large
1 teaspoon	vanilla extract	5 mL
1 cup	granulated sugar replacement	250 mL

Combine flour and baking powder in a bowl. Stir to mix. Combine peanut butter, margarine, and fructose in a mixing bowl. Beat until creamy. Beat in egg, vanilla, and sweetener. Gradually add the flour mixture. (If you are using a hand mixer, you may have to stir the last part of the flour into the cookie dough.) Roll teaspoons of dough into a ball. Place on ungreased cookie sheets. Flatten with a fork in a crisscross design. Bake at 375°F (190°C) for 10 to 12 minutes or until cookies are golden brown. Cool slightly on cookie sheet. Then move to cooling rack.

EACH COOKIE CONTAINS: CALORIES: 62 ▲ CARBOHYDRATES: 2 G ▲ EXCHANGE: 1/5 BREAD, 1 FAT

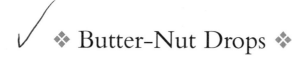

❖ Butter-Nut Drops ❖

YIELD: 25 COOKIES

1/2 cup	solid margarine	125 mL
2 tablespoons	granulated fructose	30 mL
1	egg, separated	1
1/2 teaspoon	vanilla extract	2 mL
1/4 teaspoon	salt	1 mL
1 cup	cake flour	250 mL
1 tablespoon	lemon juice	15 mL
2 tablespoons	grated orange peel	30 mL
1 tablespoon	grated lemon peel	15 mL
1/2 cup	Brazil nuts, finely ground	125 mL

Cream margarine and fructose together. Beat in egg yolk and vanilla. Beat in salt, cake flour, and lemon juice. Add grated orange and lemon peels. Form into a ball and wrap in plastic wrap. Chill thoroughly (at least 2 to 3 hours). Roll dough into tiny balls (about 1/2 teaspoon [2 mL] of dough per ball). Dip each ball into the slightly beaten egg white. Roll in the ground nuts, Place on lightly greased cookie sheets about 1 inch (2.5 cm) apart. Press top slightly with your finger. Bake at 350°F (175°C) for 20 to 25 minutes.

EACH COOKIE CONTAINS: CALORIES: 50 ▲ CARBOHYDRATES: 2 G ▲ EXCHANGE: 1/5 BREAD, 1/2 FAT

❖ Date Crumb Bars ❖

YIELD: 36 BARS

1 package	(8 ounces) chopped dates	1 package (227 g)
2/3 cup	water	180 mL

2 teaspoons	vanilla extract	10 mL
1 1/2 cups	all-purpose flour	375 mL
1 1/2 cups	quick-cooking oatmeal	375 mL
3/4 cup	granulated sugar replacement	190 mL
3/4 teaspoon	baking soda	4 mL
1/4 teaspoon	salt	1 mL
3/4 cup	solid margarine	190 mL

Combine dates and water in a saucepan. Bring to a boil, reduce heat, and simmer until mixture is thick and dates are very soft. Remove from heat and stir in the vanilla. Cool. Combine flour, oatmeal, sugar replacement, baking soda, and salt in a mixing bowl. Add margarine and work with your fingers or a spoon until mixture becomes coarse crumbs. Transfer about two-thirds of the crumb mixture to a greased 9 x 13 inch (23 x 33 cm) baking pan. Reserve remaining crumbs. Firmly press crumb mixture on bottom of pan. Spoon date mixture in large dots around pressed-crumb surface. Using the back of a dampened wooden spoon or a dampened pastry brush, spread date filling over crumb crust. (Occasionally redampening spoon or brush will aid in spreading the filling over the entire surface.) Sprinkle the remaining crumbs over the date filling. Press crumbs lightly into filling. Bake at 350°F (175°C) for 25 to 25 minutes or until top is golden brown. Cool in pan.

EACH BAR CONTAINS: CALORIES: 78 ▲ CARBOHYDRATES: 7 G ▲ EXCHANGE: 1/2 BREAD, 3/4 FAT

❖ Fudgy Bars ❖

YIELD: 36 BARS

1 1/2 cups	all-purpose flour	375 mL
2 teaspoons	baking powder	10 mL
1/2 teaspoon	salt	2 mL
1 cup	(2 sticks) solid margarine	250 mL (2 sticks)
4 ounces	unsweetened baking chocolate	113 g
1 cup	granulated sugar replacement	250 mL
2 tablespoons	granulated fructose	21 mL
3	large eggs	3

| 2 | egg whites | 2 |
| 2 teaspoons | vanilla extract | 10 mL |

Combine flour, baking powder, and salt in a bowl, and mix slightly. Set aside. Combine margarine and baking chocolate either in a large microwave-safe bowl or a saucepan. Heat until chocolate is melted. Stir until smooth. Beat in granulated sugar replacement and fructose. Combine eggs and egg whites in a smaller bowl. Beat with a fork or wire whisk until blended. Gradually pour eggs into chocolate mixture, beating after each addition. Add vanilla. Beat in the flour mixture. Continue beating until smooth. Transfer to a greased 9 x 13 inch (23 x 33 cm) baking pan. Bake at 350°F (175°C) for 20 to 25 minutes or until toothpick inserted in middle comes out with moist crumbs. Cool in pan.

Optional: 1 cup (250 mL) chopped walnuts. Stir walnuts into batter before baking.

Optional: 4.5-ounce (128-g) package of sugar-free chocolate frosting mix. Prepare as directed on package. Frost after bars have cooled.

EACH BAR CONTAINS: CALORIES: 47 ▲ CARBOHYDRATES: 4 G ▲ EXCHANGE: 1/4 BREAD, 1/2 FAT

EACH BAR WITH WALNUTS CONTAINS: CALORIES: 66 ▲ CARBOHYDRATES: 4 G ▲ EXCHANGE: 1/4 BREAD, 1 FAT

EACH BAR WITH CHOCOLATE FROSTING CONTAINS: CALORIES: 61 ▲ CARBOHYDRATES: 7 G ▲ EXCHANGE: 1/2 BREAD, 1/2 FAT

❖ Banana Date Nut Bars ❖

YIELD: 24 BARS

1	small ripe banana (1/3 cup) mashed	1
1 box	Sweet 'n Low brand banana cake mix	1 box
3/4 cup	water	180 mL
1/2 cup	chopped dates (16 dates)	125 mL
1/4 cup	chopped pecans	60 mL

Mash small banana in mixing bowl. Add cake mix and 1/4 cup water. Mix 3 minutes. Add balance of water and mix 1 minute. Pour batter into lightly greased 10-inch square baking pan. (One 8-inch square and one 8 x 4 inch pan can be used instead.) Sprinkle batter with 1/2 cup chopped dates and 1/4 cup chopped pecans. Bake at 375°F for 30 minutes or until done. Cut bars in pan.

EACH BAR CONTAINS: CALORIES: 58

❖ Prune Walnut Bars ❖

YIELD: 24 BARS

1 box	Sweet 'n Low brand lemon cake mix	1 box
1 cup	water	250 mL
1/2 cup	chopped, dried, pitted prunes (10 prunes)	125 mL
1/4 cup	chopped walnuts	60 mL

Mix cake mix and 1/4 cup water in mixer for 3 minutes. Gradually add remaining water and mix 1 minute. Pour batter into lightly greased 10-inch square pan. (One 8-inch square and one 8 x 4 inch pan can be used instead.) Sprinkle chopped prunes and chopped walnuts over the batter. Bake at 375°F for 30 minutes. Cut bars in pan. Cool thoroughly before storing or serving.

EACH BAR CONTAINS: CALORIES: 45

❖ Brownies ❖

YIELD: 24 BROWNIES

1 box	Sweet 'n Low brand chocolate cake mix	1 box
1/4 teaspoon	salt (omit if sodium-restricted)	1 mL
1 cup	water	250 mL
1 teaspoon	vanilla extract	5 mL
1/4 cup	chopped almonds	60 mL

Mix cake mix, salt, 1/4 cup water, and vanilla extract in mixer for 3 minutes. Gradually add balance of water and mix 1 minute. Pour batter into lightly greased 10 inch square baking pan. (One 8-inch square and one 8 x 4-inch pan can be used instead.) Sprinkle batter with chopped almonds. Bake at 375°F for 25 minutes. Cut bars in pan.

EACH BROWNIE CONTAINS: CALORIES: 45

❖ Bells for Christmas ❖

YIELD: 60 COOKIES

1/4 cup	(1/2 stick) solid margarine	60 mL (1/2 stick)
1/4 cup	solid vegetable shortening	60 mL
1/2 cup	granulated sugar replacement	125 mL
1	egg	1
1 teaspoon	vanilla extract	5 mL
1 1/2 cups	all-purpose flour	375 mL
1/4 teaspoon	baking soda	1 mL
dash	salt	dash
	red or green food coloring	

Combine margarine, shortening, sweetener of your choice, egg, and vanilla in a mixing bowl. Beat to blend. Stir in flour, baking soda, and salt. Transfer about two-thirds of the dough to another bowl, and color with several drops of food coloring. (The dough will be stiff. Work dough with a spoon or fork; then knead dough to incorporate the coloring completely.) Shape colored dough into a 10 x 1 1/2 inch (25 x 3.75 cm) roll. Knead remaining uncolored dough until soft. Roll out on a lightly floured surface into a 11 x 6 inch (27.5 x 15 cm) rectangle. Lightly brush surface with water. Wrap uncolored dough around the colored dough roll. Do not wrap the ends of the roll. Cut away any excess dough from seam edge and side edges. Reserve cut-away dough. Dampen edge of dough along 10 inch (25-cm) side of roll. Press edges of dough together to tighten. Carefully roll entire cookie roll to secure the doughs together. Wrap in plastic wrap. With the handle of a wooden spoon or your hands, carefully form the dough into a bell by pressing the top of the roll together slightly and leaving the lower half flared and curved like the bottom of a bell. Refrigerate at least 8 hours or overnight. Cut roll into about 1/8 inch (3-mm) slices. Place cookies on ungreased cookie sheets. Form a very small amount of the reserved dough into a ball to make the clapper for the bell. Place clapper on the bottom edge of bell. Bake at 375°F (190°C) for 7 to 8 minutes or until edges are lightly browned. Move cookies to cooling rack.

EACH COOKIE CONTAINS: CALORIES: 29 ▲ CARBOHYDRATES: 2 G ▲ EXCHANGE: 1/6 BREAD, 1/2 FAT

❖ Anise Cookies ❖

YIELD: 72 COOKIES

1 box	Sweet 'n Low brand lemon cake mix	1 box
3 tablespoons	water	45 mL
1/4 to 1/2 teaspoon	anise extract (depending on flavor intensity desired)	1 to 2 mL
1/4 cup	finely chopped almonds	60 mL

Combine all ingredients in mixing bowl. Mix 3 minutes. Drop by level teaspoons onto lightly greased or foil-lined baking sheet. Bake at 350°F for 10 to 12 minutes.

EACH COOKIE CONTAINS: CALORIES: 1S

CANDY

❖ Coconut Candy ❖

YIELD: 16 CANDIES

1 1/4 cups	unsweetened coconut, grated	310 mL
1/2 cup	milk	125 mL
2 teaspoons	unflavored gelatin	10 mL
1 teaspoon	cornstarch	5 mL
1 teaspoon	white vanilla extract	5 mL
1 recipe	Semisweet Dipping Chocolate (p. 218)	1 recipe

Combine 1/4 cup (60 mL) of the coconut and the milk, gelatin, and cornstarch in a blender, and blend until smooth. Pour into small saucepan; cook and stir over medium heat until slightly thickened. Remove from heat and stir in vanilla and remaining coconut. Form into 16 patties, and allow to cool completely. Dip into chocolate.

EACH CANDY CONTAINS: CALORIES: 66 ▲ CARBOHYDRATES: 4 G ▲ EXCHANGE: 1/3 WHOLE MILK, 1/2 FAT

❖ Crunch Candy ❖

YIELD: 32 CANDIES

6	large shredded-wheat biscuits	6
1 teaspoon	unflavored gelatin	5 mL
3/4 cup	cold milk	190 mL
1/2 cup	creamy peanut butter	125 mL
1 recipe	Semisweet Dipping Chocolate (p. 218)	1 recipe

Break shredded-wheat biscuits into small pieces. Set aside. Soak gelatin in 1/4 cup (60 mL) of the cold milk; set aside. Combine peanut butter and remaining milk in top of a double boiler and place over hot (not boiling) water. Cook and stir until smooth. Add soaked gelatin; then cook and stir until gelatin is completely dissolved and smooth. Fold reserved shredded-wheat pieces into peanut-butter mixture. Drop by teaspoonfuls onto lightly greased waxed paper. Allow to firm and cool; then dip in chocolate.

EACH CANDY CONTAINS: CALORIES: 44 ▲ CARBOHYDRATES: 4 G ▲ EXCHANGE: 1/3 WHOLE MILK

❖ Semisweet Dipping Chocolate ❖ (for Candy)

YIELD: 1 CUP (250 ML)

1 cup	nonfat dry-milk powder	250 mL
1/3 cup	unsweetened cocoa	90 mL
2 tablespoons	grated paraffin wax	30 mL
1/2 cup	water	250 mL
1 tablespoon	vegetable oil	15 mL
1 tablespoon	liquid fructose	15 mL

Combine milk powder, cocoa, and wax in a food processor or blender; process or blend to a soft powder. Transfer into the top of a double boiler and add the water, stirring to blend. Add vegetable oil. Place over hot (not boiling) water. Cook and stir until wax pieces are completely melted and mixture is thick, smooth, and creamy. Remove double boiler from heat. Stir in liquid fructose. Allow to cool slightly. Dip candies according to recipe in cookbook or your recipe. Shake off excess chocolate. Place on very lightly greased waxed paper, and allow candies to cool completely. (If candies cannot be removed easily, slightly warm a cookie sheet in the oven, lay the waxed paper with candies on warmed cookie sheet, and remove them. Store in cool place.)

FULL RECIPE CONTAINS: CALORIES: 427 ▲ CARBOHYDRATES: 30 G ▲ EXCHANGE: 3 LOW-FAT MILK

❖ Chocolate Crunch Candy ❖

YIELD: 30 PIECES

1 cup	nonfat dry-milk powder	250 mL
1/2 cup	unsweetened cocoa powder	125 mL
2 tablespoons	liquid fructose	30 mL
3 tablespoons	water	45 mL
1 1/2 cups	chow mein noodles	375 mL

Combine milk powder and cocoa in a food processor or blender. Process or blend to a fine powder. Stir in liquid fructose and water. Beat until smooth and creamy. Sightly crush the chow mein noodles, and fold them into the chocolate mixture. Drop by teaspoonfuls onto waxed paper. Cool to room temperature.

EACH PIECE CONTAINS: CALORIES: 11 ▲ CARBOHYDRATES: 3 G ▲ EXCHANGE: 1/5 BREAD

❖ Fudge Candy ❖

YIELD: 64 CANDIES

1 can	(13-ounces) evaporated skim milk	1 can (385 mL)
3 tablespoons	unsweetened cocoa powder	45 mL
1/4 cup	butter	60 mL
1 tablespoon	granulated fructose	15 mL
dash	salt	dash
1 teaspoon	vanilla extract	5 mL
2 1/2 cups	unsweetened cereal crumbs	625 mL
1/4 cup	nuts, chopped very fine	60 mL

Combine milk and cocoa in a saucepan. Cook and beat over low heat until cocoa is dissolved. Add butter, fructose, salt, and vanilla. Bring to a boil. Reduce heat and cook for 2 minutes. Remove from heat; add cereal crumbs and work in with a wooden spoon. Cool 15 minutes. Divide dough in half; roll each half into an 8-inch (20-cm) long tube. Roll each tube in the finely chopped nuts. Wrap in waxed paper, and chill overnight. Cut into 1/4 inch (8-mm) slices.

EACH CANDY CONTAINS: CALORIES: 30 ▲ CARBOHYDRATES: 4 G ▲ EXCHANGE: 1/4 BREAD, 1/4 FAT

❖ Fruit Candy Bars ❖

YIELD: 24 BARS

1 envelope	unflavored gelatin	1 envelope
1/4 cup	cold water	60 mL
1 cup	dried apricots	250 mL
1 cup	raisins	250 mL
1 cup	pecans	250 mL
1 tablespoon	all-purpose flour	15 mL
2 tablespoons	grated orange peel	30 mL
1 teaspoon	rum extract	5 mL

Sprinkle gelatin over water in a saucepan; allow to soften for 5 minutes. Heat and stir until gelatin is completely dissolved. Meanwhile, combine apricots, raisins, pecans, flour, and orange peel in a blender or food processor. Blend or process until finely chopped. Add fruit mixture to dissolved gelatin. Add rum extract and stir to completely blend. Line an 8-inch (20-cm) square pan with plastic wrap or waxed paper. Spread fruit mixture evenly in the bottom of the pan. Set aside to cool completely so that candy is firm. Turn out onto a cutting board; then cut into 24 bars and wrap individually.

EACH SERVING CONTAINS: CALORIES: 68 ▲ CARBOHYDRATES: 17 G ▲ EXCHANGE: 1 FRUIT, 1/2 FAT

❖ Coconut Macaroons ❖

YIELD: 48 CANDIES

1 cup	evaporated skim milk	250 mL
2 teaspoons	granulated fructose	10 mL
3 cups	unsweetened shredded coconut	750 mL

Combine milk and fructose in large bowl. Stir until fructose is dissolved. Add coconut and stir until coconut is completely moistened. Drop by teaspoonfuls onto greased cookie sheets, 2 to 3 inches (5 to 7 cm) apart. Bake at 350°F (175 °C) for 15 minutes or until tops are lightly browned. Remove from pan immediately.

EACH CANDY CONTAINS: CALORIES: 31 ▲ CARBOHYDRATES: 2 G ▲ EXCHANGE: 1/5 FRUIT, 1/2 FAT

❖ Butter Rum Candy ❖

YIELD: 20 CANDIES

5 cups	unsweetened puffed rice	1,250 mL
3 tablespoons	granulated fructose	45 mL
2	egg whites	2
2 teaspoons	butter rum flavoring	10 mL
1 teaspoon	vanilla extract	5 mL

Pour rice into blender and work into a powder. Pour into a large bowl or food processor. Add remaining ingredients. Work with wooden spoon or steel blade until mixture is completely blended (mixture will be sticky). Form into 20 patties. Place patties on an ungreased cookie sheet. Bake at 300°F (150 °C) for 20 minutes or until surface of patties feels dry.

EACH CANDY CONTAINS: CALORIES: 23 ▲ CARBOHYDRATES: 3 G ▲ EXCHANGE: 1/5 BREAD

❖ Marshmallow Crème ❖

YIELD: 4 CUPS (1 L)

3 envelopes	unflavored gelatin	3 envelopes
1/4 cup	cold water	60 mL
3/4 cup	boiling water	190 mL
3 tablespoons	granulated fructose	45 mL
1 teaspoon	white vanilla extract	5 mL
3	egg whites	3

Sprinkle gelatin over cold water in a mixing bowl; set aside for 5 minutes to allow gelatin to soften. Add to boiling water in a saucepan; cook and stir until gelatin is dissolved. Remove from heat. Cool to consistency of thick syrup. Stir in fructose and vanilla. Beat egg whites into soft peaks. Very slowly trickle a small stream of gelatin mixture into egg whites, beating until all gelatin mixture is blended. Continue beating until light and fluffy. Pour into prepared pan.

For marshmallows: Fill a 13 x 9 x 2" (33 x 23 x 5 cm) pan with flour or cornstarch to desired depth. Form "moulds" with a small glass on inside of dough cutter, or object of desired size by pressing form into flour to the bottom of the pan. Spoon marshmallow crème into mould and refrigerate until set. Dust or roll tops of marshmallows in flour; shake off excess. Keep refrigerated.

Optional marshmallows: Lightly grease and flour 13 x 9" (33 x 23 cm) baking pan. Pour marshmallow creme in pan, spreading out evenly. Refrigerate until set and cut to desired size.

EACH CUP CONTAINS: CALORIES: NEGLIGIBLE ▲ CARBOHYDRATES: NEGLIGIBLE ▲ EXCHANGE: NEGLIGIBLE

❖ Sweetened Citrus Peel ❖

YIELD: 2 TABLESPOONS (30 ML)

1 cup	water	250 mL
1 1/4 cups	granulated sugar replacement	310 mL
1/3 cup	thin peel of any citrus fruit (cut in matchstick-sized strips)	90 mL

Combine water and granulated sugar replacement in a saucepan. Stir to dissolve powder. Cook over medium heat until just boiling. Reduce heat, add citrus peel, and simmer for 15 minutes. Let cool to room temperature. Cover and refrigerate at least 6 to 8 hours or overnight. Drain peel thoroughly and mince. Use as garnish on desserts.

EACH SERVING CONTAINS: CALORIES: NEGLIGIBLE ▲ CARBOHYDRATES: NEGLIGIBLE ▲ EXCHANGE: NEGLIGIBLE

SAUCES

❖ Rhubarb Sauce ❖

1 pound	fresh or frozen rhubarb	454 g
3/4 cup	water	190 mL
1 teaspoon	cornstarch	5 mL
1/4 cup	cold water	60 mL
3/4 cup	granulated sugar replacement	190 mL
dash	salt (optional)	dash

Combine rhubarb and the 3/4 cup (190 mL) of water in a saucepan or microwavable bowl. Cook until rhubarb is tender, stirring occasionally. Or, microwave on high for 2 minutes; then reduce to medium until rhubarb is tender (about 6 to 7 minutes). Dissolve cornstarch in the 1/4 cup (60 mL) of cold water. Stir into rhubarb mixture. Stir in the sweetener. If desired, add the dash of salt. Cook and stir until mixture has lost its cloudy look. Serve warm or chilled.

EACH SERVING CONTAINS: CALORIES: NEGLIGIBLE ▲ CARBOHYDRATES: NEGLIGIBLE ▲ EXCHANGE: NEGLIGIBLE

❖ Orange Cranberry Sauce ❖

YIELD: 6 SERVINGS, WITH GRANULATED FRUCTOSE

1 package	(12 ounce) fresh cranberries, cleaned	1 package (340 g)
1/2 cup	granulated fructose	125 mL
1/2 cup	orange-juice concentrate, undiluted	125 mL

Combine all ingredients in a saucepan. Cook until mixture comes to a boil, stirring occasionally. Reduce heat and boil gently until all cranberries have "popped." Serve warm or chilled.

EACH SERVING CONTAINS: CALORIES: 64 ▲ CARBOHYDRATES: 16 G ▲ EXCHANGE: 1 FRUIT

❖ Blackberry Sauce ❖

YIELD: 4 SERVINGS

1 package	(1 pound) frozen, unsweetened blackberries, thawed	1 package (453 g)
1 tablespoon	all-natural orange marmalade	15 mL
1 teaspoon	fresh lemon juice	5 mL
2 envelopes	aspartame sweetener	2 envelopes

Combine all ingredients in a food processor or blender. Process or blend into a purée. Strain sauce through a fine sieve to remove seeds. Transfer to a serving bowl. Cover and refrigerate.

EACH SERVING CONTAINS: CALORIES: 54 ▲ CARBOHYDRATES: 15 G ▲ EXCHANGE: 1 FRUIT

❖ Strawberry Sauce ❖

YIELD: 4 SERVINGS

1 quart	fresh or unsweetened frozen strawberries, thawed	1 L
3 envelopes	aspartame sweetener	3 envelope
1 teaspoon	orange juice	5 mL
1	fresh lemon juice	5 mL

Combine all ingredients in a food processor or blender. Process or blend into a puree. Transfer to a serving bowl. Cover and refrigerate.

EACH SERVING CONTAINS: CALORIES: 52 ▲ CARBOHYDRATES: 13 G ▲ EXCHANGE: 1 FRUIT

❖ Raspberry Sauce ❖

1 package	(12 ounces) frozen, unsweetened red raspberries	1 package (340 g)
1/2 teaspoon	cornstarch	2 mL
5 envelopes	aspartame sweetener	5 envelopes

Thaw raspberries. Transfer raspberries and their juice to a saucepan. Stir in the cornstarch. Cook over medium heat until mixture comes to a full boil and the mixture is clear. Remove from heat. Cool until you can place your hand comfortably on the bottom of the pan. Stir in the aspartame sweetener. Serve warm or chilled.

EACH SERVING CONTAINS: CALORIES: 43 ▲ CARBOHYDRATES: 9 G ▲ EXCHANGE: 2/3 FRUIT

❖ Brandy Sauce ❖

YIELD, 1 CUP (250 ML)

1 cup	cool water	250 mL
2 teaspoons	cornstarch	10 mL
2 tablespoons	granulated sugar replacement	30 mL
	or	
6 envelopes	aspartame sweetener	6 envelopes
3/4 teaspoon	brandy extract	4 mL

In a saucepan, dissolve the cornstarch in the cool water. Bring to a boil. Reduce heat and boil gently for 5 minutes. Remove from heat, and cool slightly. Stir in sweetener and the brandy extract. If desired, tint a light shade of brown with food coloring. This is a good sauce to use on top of the Cinnamon Apple Cheesecake.

EACH CUP CONTAINS: CALORIES: NEGLIGIBLE ▲ CARBOHYDRATES: NEGLIGIBLE ▲ EXCHANGE: NEGLIGIBLE

❖ Apricot Lemon Sauce ❖

YIELD: 4 SERVINGS

1 cup	apricot nectar	250 mL
1 tablespoon	cornstarch	15 mL
3 tablespoons	fresh lemon juice	45 mL
1 teaspoon	grated lemon peel	5 mL
2 envelopes	aspartame sweetener	2 envelopes

Combine apricot nectar and cornstarch in a small saucepan. Stir to dissolve cornstarch. Bring to a boil. Cook and stir until mixture is smooth and thick. Stir in lemon juice and lemon peel. Remove from heat. Allow to cool until pan can be set comfortably on the palm of your hand. Stir in aspartame sweetener. This sauce is especially good for fresh berries or on plain cake.

EACH SERVING CONTAINS: CALORIES: 59 ▲ CARBOHYDRATES: 14 G ▲ EXCHANGE: 1 FRUIT

❖ Custard Sauce ❖

YIELD: 8 SERVINGS

3	egg yolks	3
2 tablespoons	granulated sugar replacement	30 mL
dash	salt	dash
1 cup	skim milk	250 mL
1/2 teaspoon	vanilla extract	2 mL
1 cup	prepared non-dairy whipped topping	250 mL

Slightly beat egg yolks. Combine the beaten egg yolks with the sugar replacement and salt in a saucepan. Gradually stir in the skim milk. Cook and stir over low heat until mixture thickens and coats the spoon. Remove from heat and pour into a bowl. Stir in the vanilla. Chill thoroughly. Fold in the nondairy whipped topping.

EACH SERVING CONTAINS: CALORIES: 57 ▲ CARBOHYDRATES: 3 G ▲ EXCHANGE: 1/2 LOW-FAT MILK

❖ Toasted-Coconut Sauce ❖

YIELD: 4 SERVINGS

1/2 cup	unsweetened, grated coconut	125 mL
1 cup	skim milk	250 mL
2 teaspoons	cornstarch	10 mL
1/2 teaspoon	vanilla extract	2 mL
1/2 teaspoon	coconut flavoring	2 mL
3 envelopes	aspartame sweetener	3 envelopes

Place coconut in a small, nonstick saucepan over medium heat. Cook and stir until all the coconut is a dark tan. Combine milk and cornstarch in a measuring cup or bowl. Stir to dissolve cornstarch. Pour into toasted coconut. Continue cooking over medium heat until mixture just begins to thicken. Pour mixture through a fine sieve into a bowl to remove coconut. Return coconut liquid to the saucepan. Cook and stir until mixture is thickened to a light syrup. Remove from heat. Stir in vanilla and coconut flavoring. Cool until pan can comfortably be placed in the palm of your hand. Stir in aspartame sweetener.

EACH SERVING CONTAINS: CALORIES: 63 ▲ CARBOHYDRATES: 6 G ▲ EXCHANGE: 1/2 LOW-FAT MILK

Glazes and Frostings

❖ Egg-White Sweet Wash ❖

YIELD: ENOUGH FOR LARGE COFFEE CAKE OR 12 TO 18 ROLLS

1	egg white	1
1/3 cup	granulated sugar replacement	90 mL

Beat egg white to very soft peaks, beat in sugar replacement, and then brush on desired surface.

EACH SERVING CONTAINS: CALORIES: NEGLIGIBLE ▲ CARBOHYDRATES: NEGLIGIBLE ▲ EXCHANGE: NEGLIGIBLE

❖ Frosting Glaze ❖

YIELD: ENOUGH FOR LARGE COFFEE CAKE OR 12 TO 18 ROLLS

1/4 cup	sugar-free white frosting mix	60 mL
7 teaspoons	boiling water	35 mL

Combine the frosting mix and boiling water in a small narrow bowl or cup. Beat with a small wire whisk or fork until mixture is smooth. Dampen a pastry brush, and brush glaze over desired surface.

EACH SERVING CONTAINS: CALORIES: NEGLIGIBLE ▲ CARBOHYDRATES: NEGLIGIBLE ▲ EXCHANGE: NEGLIGIBLE

❖ Egg-Yolk Glaze ❖

YIELD: ENOUGH FOR LARGE COFFEE CAKE OR 12 TO 18 ROLLS

1	egg yolk	1
2 tablespoons	water	30 mL

Beat egg yolk and water until light and fluffy. Brush on desired surface.

EACH SERVING CONTAINS: CALORIES: NEGLIGIBLE ▲ CARBOHYDRATES: NEGLIGIBLE
▲ EXCHANGE: NEGLIGIBLE

❖ Frosting Drizzle ❖

YIELD: ENOUGH FOR LARGE COFFEE CAKE OR 12 TO 18 ROLLS

2 teaspoons	skim milk	30 mL
1/2 cup	sugar-free white frosting mix	152 mL

Pour milk into a small bowl, cup, or custard cup. Heat in microwave until boiling. Gradually add the frosting mix, 1 tablespoon (15 mL) at a time, while constantly whipping with a fork or small wire whisk. Place in refrigerator and chill thoroughly. Drizzle on desired surface.

EACH SERVING CONTAINS: CALORIES: NEGLIGIBLE ▲ CARBOHYDRATES: NEGLIGIBLE
▲ EXCHANGE: NEGLIGIBLE

❖ Powdered-Fructose Icing or Filling ❖

YIELD: 10 SERVINGS

8 tablespoons	Powdered Fructose (p.230)	20 mL
1/2 teaspoon	vanilla extract	2 mL
1 tablespoon	plain low-fat yogurt	15 mL
1	egg white	1

Combine powdered fructose, vanilla, and yogurt in a small bowl.

Beat to blend. Beat egg white to firm peaks. Very slowly add fructose mixture to beaten egg white.

EACH SERVING CONTAINS: CALORIES: 53 ▲ CARBOHYDRATES: 7 G ▲ EXCHANGE: 1 FRUIT

❖ Powdered–Sugar Replacement ❖

YIELD: 1 CUP (250 ML), 4 SERVINGS

1/2 cup	nonfat dry-milk powder	125 mL
1/2 cup	cornstarch	125 mL
1/4 cup	granulated sugar replacement	60 mL

Combine all ingredients in a blender. Process on high until powdered.

EACH SERVING CONTAINS: CALORIES: 81 ▲ CARBOHYDRATES: 13 G ▲ EXCHANGE: 1/2 SKIM MILK, 1/2 BREAD

❖ Powdered Fructose ❖

YIELD: 24 TABLESPOONS (360 ML)

1 cup	granulated fructose	250 ml
1/3 cup	cornstarch	90 mL

Combine fructose and cornstarch in a blender container. Process on high for 30 to 45 seconds or until mixture appears like powdered sugar. Do not overprocess or mixture will become liquid and sticky.

EACH TABLESPOON CONTAINS: CALORIES: 62 ▲ CARBOHYDRATES: 8 G ▲ EXCHANGE: 1 FRUIT

❖ Sweetened Whipped Topping ❖

YIELD: 1 CUP (250 ML) OR 16 SERVINGS

1 cup	prepared non-dairy whipped topping	250 mL
1 tablespoon	Powdered Fructose (p. 230)	15 mL

Stir fructose into nondairy whipped topping. Refrigerate until ready to use.

EACH SERVING CONTAINS: CALORIES: NEGLIGIBLE ▲ CARBOHYDRATES: NEGLIGIBLE ▲ EXCHANGE: NEGLIGIBLE

❖ Chocolate-Flavored Nondairy ❖ Whipped Topping

YIELD: 2 CUPS (500 ML) OR 10 SERVINGS

1 envelope	nondairy whipped-topping powder (to yield 2 cups)	1 envelope (500 mL)
1 1/2 tablespoons	granulated sugar replacement	21 mL
	or	
2 teaspoons	granulated fructose	10 mL
2 tablespoons	unsweetened cocoa powder	30 mL
1/2 cup	cold skim milk	125 mL

Combine all ingredients in a narrow bowl. Beat until thick and fluffy.

EACH SERVING USED AS FROSTING ON CAKE CONTAINS:
CALORIES: 36 ▲ CARBOHYDRATES: NEGLIGIBLE ▲ EXCHANGE: 1/2 FAT

EACH SERVING OF 1 TABLESPOON USED AS FREE-FOOD GARNISH CONTAINS (YIELD 20 SERVINGS): CALORIES: NEGLIGIBLE ▲ CARBOHYDRATES: NEGLIGIBLE ▲ EXCHANGE: NEGLIGIBLE

❖ Strawberry Kiwi Glaze ❖

25 SERVINGS (1/2 CUP EACH)

Glaze Hawaiian Napoleons with this

1/4 cup	lemon juice	60 mL
1/4 cup	water	60 mL
1 tablespoon	cornstarch	15 mL
2 teaspoons	strawberry-kiwi Crystal Light mix	10 mL

In a small saucepan, mix together the lemon juice, water, and corn-starch. Stir until smooth. Heat over medium heat until the mixture begins to boil. Stirring constantly, lower heat and cook until mixture turns from milky to opaque and thickens. Set aside to cool. Stir in strawberry-kiwi mix. Blend well. Add a few drops of water if the mixture becomes too thick to spread evenly.

EACH SERVING CONTAINS: CALORIES: 2 ▲ CARBOHYDRATES: 1 G ▲ DIABETIC EXCHANGE: FREE

FOOD
EXCHANGE
LISTS

One starch exchange equals
15 grams carbohydrate, 3 grams protein, 0–1 grams fat, and 80 calories.

Bread

Bagel	1/2 (1 oz)
Bread, reduced-calorie	2 slices (1 1/2 oz)
Bread, white, whole-wheat, pumpernickel, rye	1 slice (1 oz)
Bread sticks, crisp, 4 in. long x 1/2 in.	2 (2/3 oz)
English muffin	1/2
Hot dog or hamburger bun	1/2 (1 oz)
Pita, 6 in. across	1/2
Roll, plain, small	1 (1 oz)
Raisin bread, unfrosted	1 slice (1 oz)
Tortilla, corn, 6 in. across	1
Tortilla, flour, 6 in. across	1
Waffle, 4 1/2 in. square, reduced-fat	1

Cereals And Grains

Bran cereals	1/2 cup
Bulgur	1/2 cup
Cereals	1/2 cup
Cereals, unsweetened, ready-to-eat	3/4 cup
Cornmeal (dry)	3 Tbsp
Couscous	1/3 cup
Flour (dry)	3 Tbsp
Granola, low-fat	1/4 cup
Grape-Nuts	1/4 cup
Grits	1/2 cup
Kasha	1/2 cup
Millet	1/4 cup
Muesli	1/4 cup
Oats	1/2 cup
Pasta	1/2 cup
Puffed cereal	1 1/2 cups
Rice milk	1/2 cup
Rice, white or brown	1/3 cup
Shredded Wheat	1/2 cup
Sugar-frosted cereal	1/2 cup
Wheat germ	3 Tbsp

One starch exchange equals
15 grams carbohydrate,
3 grams protein,
0–1 grams fat, and
80 calories.

Starchy Vegetables

Baked beans	1/3 cup
Corn	1/2 cup
Corn on cob, medium	1 (5 oz)
Mixed vegetables with corn, peas, or pasta	1 cup
Peas, green	1/2 cup
Plantain	1/2 cup
Potato, baked or boiled	1 small (3 oz)
Potato, mashed	1/2 cup
Squash, winter (acorn, butternut, pumpkin)	1 cup
Yam, sweet potato, plain	1/2 cup

Crackers And Snacks

Animal crackers	8
Graham crackers, 2 1/2 in. square	3
Matzoh	3/4 oz
Melba toast	4 slices
Oyster crackers	24
Popcorn (popped, no fat added or low-fat microwave)	3 cups
Pretzels	3/4 oz
Rice cakes, 4 in. across	2
Saltine-type crackers	6
Snack chips, fat-free (tortilla, potato)	15–20 (3/4 oz)
Whole-wheat crackers, no fat added	2–5 (3/4 oz)

Beans, Peas, And Lentils
(Count as 1 starch exchange, plus 1 very lean meat exchange.)

Beans and peas (garbanzo, pinto, kidney, white, split, black-eyed)	1/2 cup
Lima beans	2/3 cup
Lentils	1/2 cup
Miso ◢	3 Tbsp

◢ = 400 mg or more sodium per exchange.

One starch exchange equals
15 grams carbohydrate,
3 grams protein,
0–1 grams fat, and
80 calories.

Starchy Foods Prepared With Fat
(Count as 1 starch exchange, plus 1 fat exchange.)

Biscuit, 2 1/2 in. across	1
Chow mein noodles	1/2 cup
Corn bread, 2 in. cube	1 (2 oz)
Crackers, round butter type	6
Croutons	1 cup
French-fried potatoes	16–25 (3 oz)
Granola	1/4 cup
Muffin, small	1 (1 1/2 oz)
Pancake, 4 in. across	2
Popcorn, microwave	3 cups
Sandwich crackers, cheese or peanut butter filling	3
Stuffing, bread (prepared)	1/3 cup
Taco shell, 6 in. across	2
Waffle, 4 1/2 in. square	1
Whole-wheat crackers, fat added	4–6 (1 oz)

Starches often swell in cooking, so a small amount of uncooked starch will become a much larger amount of cooked food. The following table shows some of the changes.

Food (Starch Group)	Uncooked	Cooked
Oatmeal	3 Tbsp	1/2 cup
Cream of Wheat	2 Tbsp	1/2 cup
Grits	3 Tbsp	1/2 cup
Rice	2 Tbsp	1/3 cup
Spaghetti	1/4 cup	1/2 cup
Noodles	1/3 cup	1/2 cup
Macaroni	1/4 cup	1/2 cup
Dried beans	1/4 cup	1/2 cup
Dried peas	1/4 cup	1/2 cup
Lentils	3 Tbsp	1/2 cup

Common Measurements

3 tsp = 1 Tbsp	4 ounces = 1/2 cup
4 Tbsp = 1/4 cup	8 ounces = 1 cup
5 1/3 Tbsp = 1/3 cup	1 cup = 1/2 pint

One fruit exchange equals
15 grams carbohydrate and
60 calories.
The weight includes skin, core, seeds, and rind.

Fruit

Apple, unpeeled, small	1 (4 oz)
Applesauce, unsweetened	1/2 cup
Apples, dried	4 rings
Apricots, fresh	4 whole (5 1/2 oz)
Apricots, dried	8 halves
Apricots, canned	1/2 cup
Banana, small	1 (4 oz)
Blackberries	3/4 cup
Blueberries	3/4 cup
Cantaloupe, small	1/3 melon (11 oz) or 1 cup cubes
Cherries, sweet, fresh	12 (3 oz)
Cherries, sweet, canned	1/2 cup
Dates	3
Figs, fresh	1 1/2 large or 2 medium (3 1/2 oz)
Figs, dried	1 1/2
Fruit cocktail	1/2 cup
Grapefruit, large	1/2 (11 oz)
Grapefruit sections, canned	3/4 cup
Grapes, small	17 (3 oz)
Honeydew melon	1 slice (10 oz) or 1 cup cubes
Kiwi	1 (3 1/2 oz)
Mandarin oranges, canned	3/4 cup
Mango, small	1/2 fruit (5 1/2 oz) or 1/2 cup
Nectarine, small	1 (5 oz)
Orange, small	1 (6 1/2 oz)
Papaya	1/2 fruit (8 oz) or 1 cup cubes
Peach, medium, fresh	1 (6 oz)
Peaches, canned	1/2 cup
Pear, large, fresh	1/2 (4 oz)
Pears, canned	1/2 cup
Pineapple, fresh	3/4 cup
Pineapple, canned	1/2 cup
Plums, small	2 (5 oz)
Plums, canned	1/2 cup
Prunes, dried	3
Raisins	2 Tbsp
Raspberries	1 cup
Strawberries	1 1/4 cup whole berries
Tangerines, small	2 (8 oz)
Watermelon	1 slice (13 1/2 oz) or 1 1/4 cup cubes

Fruit Juice

Apple juice/cider	1/2 cup
Cranberry juice cocktail	1/3 cup
Cranberry juice cocktail, reduced-calorie	1 cup
Fruit juice blends, 100% juice	1/3 cup
Grape juice	1/3 cup
Grapefruit juice	1/2 cup
Orange juice	1/2 cup
Pineapple juice	1/2 cup
Prune juice	1/3 cup

One milk exchange equals
12 grams carbohydrate and
8 grams protein.

Whole Milk
(8 grams fat per serving)

Whole milk . . . . 1 cup
Evaporated whole milk . . . . 1/2 cup
Goat's milk . . . . 1 cup
Kefir . . . . 1 cup

Fat-free And Low-fat Milk
(0–3 grams fat per serving)

Fat-free milk . . . . 1 cup
1/2% milk . . . . 1 cup
1% milk . . . . 1 cup
Fat-free or low-fat buttermilk . . . . 1 cup
Evaporated fat-free milk . . . . 1/2 cup
Fat-free dry milk . . . . 1/3 cup dry
Plain nonfat yogurt . . . . 3/4 cup
Nonfat or low-fat fruit-flavored yogurt sweetened
with aspartame or with a nonnutritive sweetener . . . . 1 cup

Reduced-fat
(5 grams fat per serving)

2% milk . . . . 1 cup
Plain low-fat yogurt . . . . 3/4 cup
Sweet acidophilus milk . . . . 1 cup

Other Carbohydrates List

You can substitute food choices from this list for a starch, fruit, or milk choice on your meal plan. Some choices will also count as one or more fat choices.

Nutrition Tips

1. These foods can be substituted in your meal plan, even though they contain added sugars or fat. However, they do not contain as many important vitamins and minerals as the choices on the Starch, Fruit, or Milk list.
2. When planning to include these foods in your meal, be sure to include foods from all the lists to eat a balanced meal.

Selection Tips

1. Because many of these foods are concentrated sources of carbohydrate and fat, the portion sizes are often very small.
2. Always check Nutrition Facts on the food label. It will be your most accurate source of information.
3. Many fat-free or reduced-fat products made with fat replacers contain carbohydrate. When eaten in large amounts, they may need to be counted. Talk with your dietitian to determine how to count these in your meal plan.
4. Look for fat-free salad dressings in smaller amounts on the Free Foods list.

One exchange equals
15 grams carbohydrate, or 1 starch, or 1 fruit, or 1 milk.

Food	Serving Size	Exchanges Per Serving
Angel food cake, unfrosted	1/12th cake	2 carbohydrates
Brownie, small, unfrosted	2 in. square	1 carbohydrate, 1 fat
Cake, unfrosted	2 in. square	1 carbohydrate, 1 fat
Cake, frosted	2 in. square	2 carbohydrates, 1 fat
Cookie, fat-free	2 small	1 carbohydrate
Cookie or sandwich cookie with creme filling	2 small	1 carbohydrate, 1 fat
Cranberry sauce, jellied	1/4 cup	1 1/2 carbohydrates
Cupcake, frosted	1 small	2 carbohydrates, 1 fat
Doughnut, plain cake	1 medium (1 1/2 oz)	1 1/2 carbohydrates, 2 fats
Doughnut, glazed	3 3/4 in. across (2 oz)	2 carbohydrates, 2 fats
Fruit juice bars, frozen, 100% juice	1 bar (3 oz)	1 carbohydrate
Fruit snacks, chewy (pureed fruit concentrate)	1 roll (3/4 oz)	1 carbohydrate
Fruit spreads, 100% fruit	1 Tbsp	1 carbohydrate
Gelatin, regular	1/2 cup	1 carbohydrate
Gingersnaps	3	1 carbohydrate
Granola bar	1 bar	1 carbohydrate, 1 fat
Granola bar, fat-free	1 bar	2 carbohydrates

One exchange equals

15 grams carbohydrate, or 1 starch, or 1 fruit, or 1 milk.

Food	Serving Size	Exchanges Per Serving
Honey	1 Tbsp	1 carbohydrate
Hummus	1/3 cup	1 carbohydrate, 1 fat
Ice cream	1/2 cup	1 carbohydrate, 2 fats
Ice cream, light	1/2 cup	1 carbohydrate, 1 fat
Ice cream, fat-free, no sugar added	1/2 cup	1 carbohydrate
Jam or jelly, regular	1 Tbsp	1 carbohydrate
Milk, chocolate, whole	1 cup	2 carbohydrates, 1 fat
Pie, fruit, 2 crusts	1/6 pie	3 carbohydrates, 2 fats
Pie, pumpkin or custard	1/8 pie	2 carbohydrates, 2 fats
Potato chips	12–18 (1 oz)	1 carbohydrate, 2 fats
Pudding, regular (made with low-fat milk)	1/2 cup	2 carbohydrates
Pudding, sugar-free (made with low-fat milk)	1/2 cup	1 carbohydrate
Salad dressing, fat-free ◢	1/4 cup	1 carbohydrate
Sherbet, sorbet	1/2 cup	2 carbohydrates
Spaghetti or pasta sauce, canned ◢	1/2 cup	1 carbohydrate, 1 fat
Sugar	1 Tbsp	1 carbohydrate
Sweet roll or Danish	1 (2 1/2 oz)	2 1/2 carbohydrates, 2 fats
Syrup, light	2 Tbsp	1 carbohydrate
Syrup, regular	1 Tbsp	1 carbohydrate
Syrup, regular	1/4 cup	4 carbohydrates
Tortilla chips	6–12 (1 oz)	1 carbohydrate, 2 fats
Vanilla wafers	5	1 carbohydrate, 1 fat
Yogurt, frozen, low-fat, fat-free	1/3 cup	1 carbohydrate, 0–1 fat
Yogurt, frozen, fat-free, no sugar added	1/2 cup	1 carbohydrate
Yogurt, low-fat with fruit	1 cup	3 carbohydrates, 0–1 fat

◢ = 400 mg or more of sodium per exchange.

240

One vegetable exchange equals

5 grams carbohydrate,
2 grams protein,
0 grams fat, and
25 calories.

Artichoke
Artichoke hearts
Asparagus
Beans (green, wax, Italian)
Bean sprouts
Beets
Broccoli
Brussels sprouts
Cabbage
Carrots
Cauliflower
Celery
Cucumber
Eggplant
Green onions or scallions
Greens (collard, kale, mustard, turnip)
Kohlrabi
Leeks
Mixed vegetables (without corn, peas, or pasta)
Mushrooms
Okra
Onions

Pea pods
Peppers (all varieties)
Radishes
Salad greens (endive, escarole, lettuce, romaine, spinach)
Sauerkraut ⬛
Spinach
Summer squash
Tomato
Tomatoes, canned
Tomato sauce ⬛
Tomato/vegetable juice ⬛
Turnips
Water chestnuts
Watercress
Zucchini

⬛ = 400 mg or more sodium per exchange.

Very Lean Meat And Substitutes List
One exchange equals 0 grams carbohydrate, 7 grams protein, 0–1 grams fat, and 35 calories.

● One very lean meat exchange is equal to any one of the following items.

Poultry: Chicken or turkey (white meat, no skin), Cornish hen (no skin) . . . . 1 oz

Fish: Fresh or frozen cod, flounder, haddock, halibut, trout; tuna fresh or canned in water . . . . . 1 oz

Shellfish: Clams, crab, lobster, scallops, shrimp, imitation shellfish . . . . 1 oz

Game: Duck or pheasant (no skin), venison, buffalo, ostrich . . . . 1 oz

Cheese with 1 gram or less fat per ounce:
Nonfat or low-fat cottage cheese . . . . 1/4 cup
Fat-free cheese . . . . 1 oz

Other: Processed sandwich meats with 1 gram or less fat per ounce, such as deli thin, shaved meats, chipped beef🖦, turkey ham. . . . . 1 oz
Egg whites. 2
Egg substitutes, plain . . . . 1/4 cup
Hot dogs with 1 gram or less fat per ounce🖦 . . . 1 oz
Kidney (high in cholesterol) . . . . 1 oz
Sausage with 1 gram or less fat per ounce . . . . . 1 oz

● Count as one very lean meat and one starch exchange.

Beans, peas, lentils (cooked) . . . . 1/2 cup

🖦 = 400 mg or more sodium per exchange.

Lean Meat And Substitutes List
One exchange equals 0 grams carbohydrate, 7 grams protein, 3 grams fat, and 55 calories.

● One lean meat exchange is equal to any one of the following items.

Beef: USDA Select or Choice grades of lean beef trimmed of fat, such as round, sirloin, and flank steak; tenderloin; roast (rib, chuck, rump); steak (T-bone, porterhouse, cubed); ground round . . . . 1 oz

Pork: Lean pork, such as fresh ham; canned, cured, or boiled ham; Canadian bacon🖦; tenderloin, center loin chop . . . . 1 oz

Lamb: Roast, chop, leg . . . . 1 oz

Veal: Lean chop, roast . . . . 1 oz

Poultry: Chicken, turkey (dark meat, no skin), chicken (white meat, with skin), domestic duck or goose (well-drained of fat, no skin) . . . . 1 oz

Fish:
Herring (uncreamed or smoked) . . . . 1 oz
Oysters . . . . 6 medium
Salmon (fresh or canned), catfish. . . . . 1 oz
Sardines (canned) . . . . 2 medium
Tuna (canned in oil, drained) . . . . 1 oz

Game: Goose (no skin), rabbit . . . . 1 oz

Cheese:
4.5%-fat cottage cheese. . . . . 1/4 cup
Grated Parmesan . . . . 2 Tbsp
Cheeses with 3 grams or less fat per ounce . . . . . 1 oz

Other:
Hot dogs with 3 grams or less fat per ounce🖦 . . . 1 1/2 oz
Processed sandwich meat with 3 grams or less fat per ounce, such as turkey pastrami or kielbasa. . . . . . . 1 oz
Liver, heart (high in cholesterol) . . . . 1 oz

Medium-Fat Meat And Substitutes List
One exchange equals 0 grams carbohydrate, 7 grams protein, 5 grams fat, and 75 calories.

- One medium-fat meat exchange is equal to any one of the following items.

Beef: Most beef products fall into this category (ground beef, meatloaf, corned beef, short ribs, Prime grades of meat trimmed of fat, such as prime rib) . . . . 1 oz

Pork: Top loin, chop, Boston butt, cutlet. . . . . 1 oz

Lamb: Rib roast, ground . . . . 1 oz

Veal: Cutlet (ground or cubed, unbreaded) . . . . 1 oz

Poultry: Chicken (dark meat, with skin), ground turkey or ground chicken, fried chicken (with skin) . . . . 1 oz

Fish: Any fried fish product. . . . . 1 oz

Cheese: With 5 grams or less fat per ounce
Feta. . . . . 1 oz
Mozzarella . . . . 1 oz
Ricotta. . . . . 1/4 cup (2 oz)

Other:
Egg (high in cholesterol, limit to 3 per week) 1
Sausage with 5 grams or less fat per ounce . . . . 1 oz
Soy milk. . . . . 1 cup
Tempeh . . . . 1/4 cup
Tofu. . . . . 4 oz or 1/2 cup

🔺 = 400 mg or more sodium per exchange.

High-Fat Meat And Substitutes List
One exchange equals 0 grams carbohydrate, 7 grams protein, 8 grams fat, and 100 calories.

Remember these items are high in saturated fat, cholesterol, and calories and may raise blood cholesterol levels if eaten on a regular basis.

- One high-fat meat exchange is equal to any one of the following items.

Pork: Spareribs, ground pork, pork sausage . . . . 1 oz

Cheese: All regular cheeses, such as American🔺, cheddar, Monterey Jack, Swiss . . . . 1 oz

Other: Processed sandwich meats with 8 grams or less fat per ounce, such as bologna, pimento loaf, salami. . . . . 1 oz
Sausage, such as bratwurst, Italian, knockwurst, Polish, smoked. . . . . 1 oz
Hot dog (turkey or chicken)🔺 1 (10/lb)
Bacon. . . . . 3 slices (20 slices/lb)

- Count as one high-fat meat plus one fat exchange.

Hot dog (beef, pork, or combination)🔺 1 (10/lb)

- Count as one high-fat meat plus two fat exchanges.

Peanut butter (contains unsaturated fat). . . . . 2 Tbsp

Monounsaturated Fats List

One fat exchange equals 5 grams fat and 45 calories.

Avocado, medium	1/8 (1 oz)
Oil (canola, olive, peanut)	1 tsp
Olives: ripe (black)	8 large
green, stuffed ◢	10 large
Nuts	
almonds, cashews	6 nuts
mixed (50% peanuts)	6 nuts
peanuts	10 nuts
pecans	4 halves
Peanut butter, smooth or crunchy	2 tsp
Sesame seeds	1 Tbsp
Tahini paste	2 tsp

Polyunsaturated Fats List

One fat exchange equals 5 grams fat and 45 calories.

Margarine: stick, tub, or squeeze	1 tsp
lower-fat (30% to 50% vegetable oil)	1 Tbsp
Mayonnaise: regular	1 tsp
reduced-fat	1 Tbsp
Nuts, walnuts, English	4 halves
Oil (corn, safflower, soybean)	1 tsp
Salad dressing: regular ◢	1 Tbsp
reduced-fat	2 Tbsp
Miracle Whip Salad Dressing®: regular	2 tsp
reduced-fat	1 Tbsp
Seeds: pumpkin, sunflower	1 Tbsp

Saturated Fats List*

One fat exchange equals 5 grams of fat and 45 calories.

Bacon, cooked	1 slice (20 slices/lb)
Bacon, grease	1 tsp
Butter: stick	1 tsp
whipped	2 tsp
reduced-fat	1 Tbsp
Chitterlings, boiled	2 Tbsp (1/2 oz)
Coconut, sweetened, shredded	2 Tbsp
Cream, half and half	2 Tbsp
Cream cheese: regular	1 Tbsp (1/2 oz)
reduced-fat	2 Tbsp (1 oz)
Fatback or salt pork, see below†	
Shortening or lard	1 tsp
Sour cream: regular	2 Tbsp
reduced-fat	3 Tbsp

†Use a piece 1 in. x 1 in. x 1/4 in. if you plan to eat the fatback cooked with vegetables. Use a piece 2 in. x 1 in. x 1/2 in. when eating only the vegetables with the fatback removed.

*Saturated fats can raise blood cholesterol levels.

◢ = 400 mg or more sodium per exchange.

Free Foods List

A *free food* is any food or drink that contains less than 20 calories or less than 5 grams of carbohydrate per serving. Foods with a serving size listed should be limited to three servings per day. Be sure to spread them out throughout the day. If you eat all three servings at one time, it could affect your blood glucose level. Foods listed without a serving size can be eaten as often as you like.

Fat-free Or Reduced-fat Foods

Cream cheese, fat-free	1 Tbsp
Creamers, nondairy, liquid	1 Tbsp
Creamers, nondairy, powdered	2 tsp
Mayonnaise, fat-free	1 Tbsp
Mayonnaise, reduced-fat	1 tsp
Margarine, fat-free	4 Tbsp
Margarine, reduced-fat	1 tsp
Miracle Whip®, nonfat	1 Tbsp
Miracle Whip®, reduced-fat	1 tsp
Nonstick cooking spray	
Salad dressing, fat-free	1 Tbsp
Salad dressing, fat-free, Italian	2 Tbsp
Salsa	1/4 cup
Sour cream, fat-free, reduced-fat	1 Tbsp
Whipped topping, regular or light	2 Tbsp

Sugar-free Or Low-sugar Foods

Candy, hard, sugar-free	1 candy
Gelatin dessert, sugar-free	
Gelatin, unflavored	
Gum, sugar-free	
Jam or jelly, low-sugar or light	2 tsp
Sugar substitutes†	
Syrup, sugar-free	2 Tbsp

†Sugar substitutes, alternatives, or replacements that are approved by the Food and Drug Administration (FDA) are safe to use. Common brand names include:

Equal® (aspartame)
Sprinkle Sweet® (saccharin)
Sweet One® (acesulfame K)
Sweet-10® (saccharin)
Sugar Twin® (saccharin)
Sweet 'n Low® (saccharin)

Drinks

Bouillon, broth, consommé 🧂
Bouillon or broth, low-sodium
Carbonated or mineral water
Club soda
Cocoa powder, unsweetened .... 1 Tbsp
Coffee
Diet soft drinks, sugar-free
Drink mixes, sugar-free
Tea
Tonic water, sugar-free

Condiments

Catsup .... 1 Tbsp
Horseradish
Lemon juice
Lime juice
Mustard
Pickles, dill .... 1 1/2 large
Soy sauce, regular or light 🧂
Taco sauce .... 1 Tbsp
Vinegar

Seasonings

Be careful with seasonings that contain sodium or are salts, such
garlic or celery salt, and lemon pepper.

Flavoring extracts
Garlic
Herbs, fresh or dried
Pimento
Spices
Tabasco® or hot pepper sauce
Wine, used in cooking
Worcestershire sauce

🧂 = 400 mg or more of sodium per exchange.

Combination Foods List

Many of the foods we eat are mixed together in various combinations. These combination foods do not fit into any one exchange list. Often it is hard to tell what is in a casserole dish or prepared food item. This is a list of exchanges for some typical combination foods. This list will help you fit these foods into your meal plan. Ask your dietitian for information about any other combination foods you would like to eat.

Food	Serving Size	Exchanges Per Serving
Entrees		
Tuna noodle casserole, lasagna, spaghetti with meatballs, chili with beans, macaroni and cheese🔺	1 cup (8 oz)	2 carbohydrates, 2 medium-fat meats
Chow mein (without noodles or rice)🔺	2 cups (16 oz)	1 carbohydrate, 2 lean meats
Pizza, cheese, thin crust🔺	1/4 of 10 in. (5 oz)	2 carbohydrates, 2 medium-fat meats, 1 fat
Pizza, meat topping, thin crust🔺	1/4 of 10 in. (5 oz)	2 carbohydrates, 2 medium-fat meats, 2 fats
Pot pie🔺	1 (7 oz)	2 carbohydrates, 1 medium-fat meat, 4 fats
Frozen entrees		
Salisbury steak with gravy, mashed potato🔺	1 (11 oz)	2 carbohydrates, 3 medium-fat meats, 3–4 fats
Turkey with gravy, mashed potato, dressing🔺	1 (11 oz)	2 carbohydrates, 2 medium-fat meats, 2 fats
Entree with less than 300 calories🔺	1 (8 oz)	2 carbohydrates, 3 lean meats
Soups		
Bean🔺	1 cup	1 carbohydrate, 1 very lean meat
Cream (made with water)🔺	1 cup (8 oz)	1 carbohydrate, 1 fat
Split pea (made with water)🔺	1/2 cup (4 oz)	1 carbohydrate
Tomato (made with water)🔺	1 cup (8 oz)	1 carbohydrate
Vegetable beef, chicken noodle, or other broth-type🔺	1 cup (8 oz)	1 carbohydrate

🔺 = 400 mg or more sodium per exchange.

247

Index

A

Almond flavor, 12
Anise, 216
Anise Cookies, 216
Apple Strudel Filling, 77
Applesauce Spice Cookies, 205
Apricot Cream Pie, 58
Apricot Dessert Cakes with Apricot Sauce, 105
Apricot Filling for Strudel, 78
Apricot Lemon Sauce, 226
Apricot Roll-Up, 102
Apricot-Jam Muffins, 166
Austrian Raspberry Cream Crêpes, 96

B

Baked Apple Pudding, 88
Baked Coffee Custard, 90
Ball Cake, 178
Banana Bread, 164
Banana Cream and Strawberry Pie, 64
Banana Cream Puffs, 127
Banana Date Nut Bars, 213
Banana Pudding, 87
Banana Split Napoleon, 73
Banana Tofu Cream, 11
Banana Walnut Roll-Up, 100
Banana Yogurt Nog, 11
Bananas and Yogurt, 25
Bars,
    banana date nut, 213
    date crumb, 211
    fruit candy, 220
    fudgy, 212
    prune walnut, 214
Basic Meringue, 111
Basic Roll-Up Recipe, 98
Basket Cake, 175
Bell Cake, 181
Bells for Christmas, 215
Big Sweet Biscuits, 169
Biscuits, big sweet, 169
Blackberry Buttermilk Sherbet, 34
Blackberry Lemon Parfait, 35
Blackberry Sauce, 224
Black-Raspberry Tofu Cream, 12
Blintz Filling for Crêpes, 95
Blueberries-in-Milk Crustless Pie, 200
Blueberry Crêpes with Vanilla Pudding
    Sauce, 102
Blueberry Cupcakes, 152
Blueberry Mountain Dessert, 35
Blueberry Ricotta Sweet Pancakes, 106
Blueberry Sour Cream Pie, 190
Blueberry Tofu Cream, 36
Blueberry Yogurt Pie, 56
Braided Raisin Bread, 161
Brandy, 225
Brandy Sauce, 225
Bread
    banana, 164
    braided raisin, 161
    cinnamon swirl, 157
    pumpkin, 162
    rhubarb nut, 165
    sweet zucchini, 165
Brownies, 214
Butter Rum Candy, 221
Butter-Almond Frappé, 12
Butterfly Cake, 177
Buttermilk, 34, 156, 160, 171, 200
Buttermilk Cake, 171
Buttermilk Doughnuts, 156
Buttermilk Raisin Crustless Pie, 200
Buttermilk Sticky Rolls, 160
Butter-Nut Drops, 211
Butterscotch, 67, 119
Butterscotch Pie, 67

C

Cake
    ball, 178
    basket, 175
    bell, 181
    butterfly, 177
    buttermilk, 171
    carrot with cream cheese icing, 144
    chocolate ice-cream, 38
    chocolate mayonnaise, 140
    coffee, cherry, 147
    coffee, cherry chocolate, 148
    coffee, easy apple, 149
    coffee, orange glazed, 145
    coffee, pineapple oatmeal, 151
    coffee, tart orange, 150
    cranberry, 170
    doll, 178
    fructose chocolate, 172
    fructose white, 173
    marble, 181
    merry Christmas wreath, 180
    nutmeg ring, 180
    perfect chocolate, 174
    rainbow, 176

simple, 170
snowball, 131
spice raisin, 172
star, 179
sweet corn, 163
Candy
butter rum, 221
chocolate crunch, 219
coconut, 217
coconut macaroons, 220
crunch, 217
fudge, 219
Caramel, 89
Caramel Custard, 89
Carob, 203
Carob Cookies, 203
Carob, chips, 203
Carob-Chip Cookies, 203
Carrot Cake with Cream Cheese Icing, 144
Charlotte
chocolate, 135
peach, 135
strawberry, 134
Cheese
cottage, 143
cream, 62, 64, 79, 145, 152, 197
ricotta, 84, 106
Cheesecake
cherry, 185
cinnamon apple, 187
fresh strawberry, 183
lemon, 182
semisweet chocolate, 184
Cherry Bread Pudding, 153
Cherry Cheese Suzette, 143
Cherry Cheesecake, 185
Cherry Chocolate Coffee Cake, 148
Cherry Coffee Cake, 147
Cherry Glaze, 71
Cherry Strudel Filling, 77
Chocolate, 13, 37, 68, 69, 74, 81, 82, 85, 89,
91, 99, 118, 125, 129, 135, 140, 154, 172,
174, 205, 206, 219
Chocolate Charlotte, 135
Chocolate chips, 53
Chocolate Chocolate Pie, 68
Chocolate Cinnamon Rolls, 154
Chocolate Crunch Candy, 219
Chocolate Dream Torte, 118
Chocolate Frappé, 13
Chocolate Glaze, 74
Chocolate Graham Cracker Ice-Cream Pie, 37
Chocolate Ice-Cream Cake, 38
Chocolate Mayonnaise Cake, 140
Chocolate Mint Dessert Drink, 13

Chocolate Mousse Pudding, 82
Chocolate Raised Doughnuts, 154
Chocolate Roll-Up, 99
Chocolate Softies, 205
Chocolate Tart Filling, 81
Chocolate Thins, 206
Chocolate, semisweet, 184, 218
Chocolate, semisweet chips, 195
Chocolate-Chip Pie, 195
Chocolate-Flavored Nondairy Whipped
Topping, 231
Chutney, fruit, 30
Cider, hot, 15
Cinnamon, 33, 104, 107, 154, 157, 158, 187
Cinnamon Apple Cheesecake, 187
Cinnamon Apple Raisin Dessert Pancakes, 104
Cinnamon Rolls, 158
Cinnamon Swirl Bread, 157
Clafouti, peach, 25
Cocoa Chiffon Pie, 69
Coconut Candy, 217
Coconut Macaroons, 220
Coffee, 13, 21, 68, 90
Coffee and Cream, 14
Coffee-and-Cream Pie, 68
Cookies
anise, 216
applesauce spice, 205
bells for Christmas, 215
butter-nut drops, 211
carob, 203
carob-chip, 203
chocolate softies, 205
chocolate thins, 206
crisscross peanut butter, 210
fancies, 210
hazelnut, 207
lemon-sandwich, 209
pecan, 204
raisin oatmeal, 202
sweet "sugar", 207
vanilla wafers, 208
Cooler
cranberry grapefruit, 14
double-raspberry, 15
mango, 16
Corn, 163
Cranberry and Raspberry Fool, 32
Cranberry Cake, 170
Cranberry Grapefruit Cooler, 14
Cranberry Muffins, 168
Cream Cheese Icing, 145
Cream Cheese Pastry, 152
Cream Puff Pastry, 124
Cream Puffs with Raspberry Sauce, 128

Cream puffs
    banana, 127
    frozen chocolate, 129
    frozen raspberry, 130
    frozen strawberry, 130
    icy peach, 129
    light chocolate, 125
    light mocha, 125
    mocha, 126
    New Zealand, 128
    strawberry, 127
    traditional, 126
Cream
    banana tofu, 11
    black-raspberry, 12
    blueberry tofu, 37
    coffee and, 14
Crème Fraîche, 26
Crêpes Marcelles, 97
Crêpes
    Austrian raspberry cream, 96
    batter, sweet, 95
    blintz filling for, 95
    blueberry with vanilla pudding sauce, 102
    marcelles, 97
    mocha-crème dessert, 103
Crisscross Peanut-Butter Cookies, 210
Crunch Candy, 217
Cupcakes with a Cherry on Top, 151
Cupcakes
    blueberry, 152
    with a cherry on top, 151
Custard Sauce, 226
Custard
    baked coffee, 90
    caramel, 89
    quick (microwave), 86

D

Dark-Fudge Pudding, 91
Date Crumb Bars, 211
Deep Dish Pie Shell, 188
Doll Cake, 178
Double Blueberry Pie, 51
Double Meringue Butterscotch Pie, 119
Double-Decker Mocha Ice-Cream Pie, 38
Double-Raspberry Cooler, 15
Dough, phyllo, 7
Doughnuts
    buttermilk, 156
    chocolate raised, 154
    dutch, 157
Dutch Doughnuts, 157

E

Easy Apple Coffee Cake, 149
Easy German Rice Pudding, 88
Eggnog, icy, 16
Egg-White Sweet Wash, 228
Egg-Yolk Glaze, 229

F

Fancies, 210
Flaky Pie Crust, 194
Fluffy Rice Pudding, 92
Frappé
    butter-almond, 12
    chocolate, 13
    mocha, 17
    raspberry, 21
French Raspberry Pavlova, 116
Fresh Apple Cinnamon Ice Cream, 39
Fresh Raspberry Ice Cream, 39
Fresh Strawberry Cheesecake, 183
Fresh Strawberry Roll-Up, 98
Fried Spiced Apples, 28
Frosting Drizzle, 229
Frozen Bananas, 28
Frozen Chocolate Cream Puffs, 129
Frozen Pumpkin Pie, 66
Frozen Raspberry Cream Puffs, 130
Frozen Raspberry Mousse with Black-
    Raspberry Sauce, 40
Frozen Strawberry Cream Puffs, 130
Frozen Strawberry Mousse, 40
Frozen Watermelon Pops, 41
Frozen Yogurt, strawberry banana, 52
Fructose, 172, 173
Fructose Chocolate Cake, 172
Fructose White Cake, 173
Fructose, powdered, 229
Fruit Candy Bars, 220
Fruit Chutney, 30
Fruit Platter with Mango Sauce, 30
Fruits
    apple, 39, 149, 77, 88, 104, 108, 187
    apple juice, 32
    apple, spiced, 28
    applesauce, 205
    apricots, 31, 58, 78, 102, 105, 166, 226
    bananas, 11, 17, 25, 27, 28, 32, 52, 64, 73,
        87, 100, 127, 165, 168, 198, 213
    black raspberries, 40
    blackberries, 34, 35, 224
    blueberries, 29, 35, 36, 51, 56, 102, 106,
        163, 190, 200
    cherries, 52, 71, 77, 143, 147, 148, 151,
        153, 185, 196

citrus, 222
coconut, 217, 220, 227
cranberries, 14, 32, 168, 170, 223
dates, 211, 213
grapefruit, 14
grapes, 29, 42
honeydew, 43
kiwis, 115
lemons, 35, 44, 45, 50, 59, 85, 117, 118, 138, 142, 182, 197, 209, 226
limes, 58
mango, 30
oranges, 17, 18, 27, 29, 43, 46, 47, 49, 112, 145, 150, 161, 199, 223
peach, 19, 25, 26, 62, 100, 116, 129, 135
pineapple, 18, 20, 48, 62, 80, 101, 151
prunes, 78, 213
raisins, 104, 161, 172, 200, 202
raspberries, 15, 21, 32, 39, 40, 43, 59, 60, 61, 96, 101, 115, 116, 128, 130, 197, 225
black, 12
rhubarb, 93, 165, 223
strawberries, 22, 23, 33, 40, 48, 50, 51, 52, 63, 64, 64, 65, 79, 98, 109, 121, 127, 130, 132, 134, 137, 139, 168, 183, 224
tangerine, 113
watermelon, 41, 54
Fudge, 212, 219
Fudge Candy, 219
Fudgy Bars, 212

G

German Apple Pancake, 108
Ginger, 198
Ginger Banana Pie, 198
Glazed Apricots, 31
Glazes
cherry, 71
chocolate, 74
egg-white sweet wash, 228
egg-yolk, 229
mocha, 73
Gourmet Strawberries and Mint, 132
Graham cracker, 37
Graham-Cracker Crust, 193
Grand Marnier, 42
Grand Marnier Ice Cream, 42
Grape Sherbet, 42

H

Happy Birthday Cake, 174
Hawaiian Alaska, 122
Hawaiian Napoleon, 70
Hawaiian Pineapple Pie, 62

Hazelnut Cookies, 207
Honeydew Sherbet, 43
Hot Cider, 15
Hot Fudge Napoleon, 74

I

Ice Cream
fresh apple cinnamon, 39
fresh raspberry, 39
grand Marnier, 42
lemon, 44
pumpkin, 66
strawberry, 63
tart cherry, 52
toasted-walnut chocolate-chip, 53
Ice-Cream Loaf with Raspberry Orange Sauce, 43
Icing
cream cheese, 145
frosting drizzles, 229
orange, 146
powdered-fructose, 229
Icy Eggnog, 16
Icy Peach Cream Puffs, 129
Individual Banana Soufflés, 27
Individual Strawberry Trifles, 137

J

Jamaican Trifle, 136

K

Kaiser Schmarren, 97
Kids' Color Cakes, 108

L

Langues de Chat, 140
Lemon Cheesecake, 182
Lemon Chiffon Pie, 59
Lemon Ice Cream, 44
Lemon Meringue Kisses, 117
Lemon Meringue Torte, 118
Lemon Sauce, 138
Lemon Sponge Pudding, 85
Lemon-Sandwich Cookies, 209
Lemony Angel Food, 138
Light Chocolate Cream Puffs, 125
Light Mocha Cream Puffs, 125
Lime Chiffon Pie, 58
Luscious Lemon Ice-Cream Pie, 45

M

Mango Cooler, 16
Maple, 45, 107
Maple Ice Cream Tart, 45
Marble Cake, 181

Marinated Blueberries, 29
Marshmallow Crème, 221
Mayonnaise, 140
Meringue Chantilly, 120
Meringue Pie Shell, 194
Meringue Tart-Lemon Pie, 197
Meringues
    general instructions, 8
    basic, 111
    lemon kisses, 117
    tart orange, 112
Merry Christmas Wreath Cake, 180
Microwave Vanilla Pudding, 86
Milk, 200
Milk-Chocolate Pudding, 89
Mint, 14, 20, 132
Mixed-Fruit Sherbet, 46
Mocha, 17, 38, 72, 82, 83, 91, 101, 103, 125,
    126, 182
Mocha Cream Puffs, 126
Mocha Frappé, 17
Mocha Glaze, 73
Mocha Mousse, 91
Mocha Mousse Pudding, 82
Mocha Napoleon, 72
Mocha Raspberry Roll-Up, 101
Mocha Tart Filling, 72
Mocha Torte, 182
Mocha-Crème Dessert Crêpes, 103
Mousse
    frozen raspberry with black-raspberry
        sauce, 40
    frozen strawberry, 40
    mocha, 91
    (quick and foolproof) mocha, 83
    Thanksgiving pumpkin, 83
Muffins
    apricot jam, 166
    cranberry, 168
    oatmeal walnut, 167
    orange walnut, 161
    quick blueberry nut, 163
    strawberry banana, 168

N
Napoleon Fudge Topping, 75
Napoleons
    banana split, 73
    Hawaiian, 70
    hot fudge, 74
    mocha, 72
    Washington's birthday, 71
New Zealand Cream Puffs, 128
Not-too-Sweet Chocolate Sauce, 85
Nut Meringue Pie Shell, 195

Nutmeg, 180
Nutmeg Cake Ring, 180
Nuts
    Brazil, 211
    hazelnuts, 207
    pecans, 159, 204, 213
    pistachio, 80, 101
    walnuts, 53, 94, 100, 161, 163, 165, 167, 214

O
Oatmeal, 151, 167, 202
Oatmeal Walnut Muffins, 167
Orange Banana Smoothie, 17
Orange Cranberry Sauce, 223
Orange Frost, 46
Orange Icing, 146
Orange Sherbet, 47
Orange Sipper, 18
Orange Walnut Muffins, 161
Orange-Glazed Coffee Cake, 145
Orange-Juice Angel Pie, 199
Oranges and Grapes, 29

P
Pancakes
    apricot dessert with apricot sauce, 105
    blueberry ricotta sweet, 106
    cinnamon apple raisin dessert, 104
    German apple, 108
    with warm maple-cinnamon topping, 107
Parfait, blackberry lemon, 35
Party Pineapple Punch, 18
Pastry Shell (from Mix), 192
Pavlova
    French raspberry, 116
    peach, 116
    tradtional, 114
    wedges with kiwis and raspberry sauce, 115
Peach Charlotte, 135
Peach Clafouti, 25
Peach Cream Cheese Pie, 62
Peach Crème Fraîche, 26
Peach Melba Roll-Up, 100
Peach Pavlova, 116
Peach Slush, 19
Peach Smoothie, 19
Peanut butter, 210
Pecan Cookies, 204
Pecan Rolls, 159
Perfect Chocolate Cake, 174
Phyllo Dough, 7
Phyllo Studel, 76
Phyllo Tarts, 78
Pie
    apricot cream, 58

banana cream and strawberry, 64
blueberry sour cream, 190
blueberry yogurt, 56
blueberries-in-milk crustless, 200
buttermilk raisin crustless, 200
butterscotch, 67
chocolate chip, 195
chocolate chocolate, 68
chocolate graham cracker ice-cream, 37
cocoa chiffon, 69
coffee and cream, 68
deep dish shell, 188
double blueberry, 51
double-decker mocha ice-cream, 38
double meringue butterscotch, 119
flaky crust, 194
frozen pumpkin, 66
ginger banana, 198
graham-cracker crust, 193
Hawaiian pineapple, 62
lemon chiffon, 59
lime chiffon, 58
luscious lemon ice cream, 45
meringue shell, 194
meringue tart-lemon, 197
nut meringue shell, 195
orange-juice angel, 199
pastry shell (from mix), 192
peach cream cheese, 62
pumpkin ice cream, 66
quick custard, 191
raspberry cheese, 197
raspberry cream, 61
raspberry ribbon, 60
raspberry shimmer, 59
sour cream, 192
squash, 189
strawberry cream cheese, 64
strawberry ice cream, 63
strawberry meringue, 65
sweet cherry dessert, 196
sweet potato, 189
wafer crust, 193
Piña Colada Sherbet, 47
Pineapple Oatmeal Coffee Cake, 151
Pineapple Sherbet, 48
Pineapple-Mint Drink, 20
Pink 'n' Pretty Strawberry Frozen Dessert, 48
Pistachio Pineapple Roll-Up, 101
Pistachio Pineapple Tart, 80
Poached Bananas in Apple Juice, 32
Powdered Fructose, 230
Powdered sugar, 230
Powdered Sugar Replacement, 230
Powdered-Fructose Icing or Filling, 229

Prince Alex After-Dinner Drink, 20
Prune Filling for Studel, 78
Prune Walnut Bars, 214
Pudding
    baked apple, 88
    banana, 87
    cherry bread, 153
    chocolate mousse, 82
    dark-fudge, 91
    easy German rice, 88
    fluffy rice, 92
    lemon sponge, 85
    microwave vanilla, 86
    milk-chocolate, 89
    mocha mousse, 82
    rhubarb bread, 93
    ricotta cheese, 84
Pumpkin, 66, 83, 109
Pumpkin Bread, 162
Pumpkin Ice Cream Pie, 66
Pumpkin Waffles, 109
Punch
    party pineapple, 18
    tropical, 23

Q

Quick (and Foolproof) Mocha Mousse, 83
Quick (Microwave) Custard, 86
Quick Blueberry Nut Muffins, 163
Quick Cappuccino, 21
Quick Custard Pie, 191
Quick Orange-Yogurt Pops, 49

R

Rainbow Cake, 176
Raisin Oatmeal Cookies, 202
Raspberry Cheese Pie, 197
Raspberry Cream Pie, 61
Raspberry Frappé, 21
Raspberry Ribbon Pie, 60
Raspberry Sauce, 115, 225
Raspberry Shimmer Pie, 59
Real Lemon Sherbet, 50
Rhubarb Bread Pudding, 93
Rhubarb Nut Bread, 165
Rhubarb Sauce, 223
Rice, 88, 92
Rich Lemon Shorties, 142
Ricotta Cheese Pudding, 84
Roll-ups
    apricot, 102
    banana walnut, 100
    basic recipe, 98
    chocolate, 99
    fresh strawberry, 98

mocha raspberry, 101
peach melba, 100
pistachio pineapple, 101
walnut, 94
Rum, 221

S

Sauces
apricot, 105
apricot lemon, 226
blackberry, 224
black-raspberry, 40
brandy, 225
cinnamon, 33
custard, 226
lemon, 138
mango, 30
not-too-sweet chocolate, 85
orange cranberry, 223
raspberry, 115, 128, 225
raspberry orange, 43
rhubarb, 223
semisweet dipping chocolate, 218
strawberry, 224
toasted coconut, 227
vanilla pudding, 102
Schaum Torte, 120
Semisweet Chocolate Cheesecake, 184
Semisweet Dipping Chocolate (for Candy), 218
Shake, vanilla, 24
Sherbet
blackberry buttermilk, 34
grape, 42
honeydew, 43
mixed fruit, 46
orange, 47
piña colada, 47
pineapple, 48
real lemon, 50
Simple Cake, 170
Slush
peach, 19
strawberry, 22
Smiling Face, 175
Smoothie
orange banana, 17
peach, 19
strawberry, 22
Snowball Cake, 131
Sorbet
strawberry, 51
watermelon, 54
Soufflé, individual banana, 27
Sour Cream, 190

Sour Cream Pie, 192
Spice Raisin Cake, 172
Squash, 189
Squash Pie, 189
Star Cake, 179
Strawberries and Cream Waffles, 109
Strawberries Chantilly, 139
Strawberries with Cinnamon Sauce, 33
Strawberry Banana Muffins, 168
Strawberry Bombe, 121
Strawberry Charlotte, 134
Strawberry Cream Cheese Pie, 64
Strawberry Cream Cheese Tart, 79
Strawberry Cream Puffs, 127
Strawberry Ice, 50
Strawberry Ice Cream Pie, 63
Strawberry Kiwi Glaze, 232
Strawberry Meringue Pie, 65
Strawberry Sauce, 224
Strawberry Slush, 22
Strawberry Smoothie, 22
Strawberry Sorbet, 51
Strawberry Yogurt Nog, 23
Strawberry-Banana Frozen Yogurt, 52
Strudel
apple filling, 77
apricot filling, 78
cherry filling, 77
phyllo, 76
prune filling, 78
Sweet "Sugar" Cookies, 207
Sweet Cakes with Warm Maple-Cinnamon
Topping, 107
Sweet Cherry Dessert Pie, 196
Sweet Corn Cake, 163
Sweet Crêpe Batter, 95
Sweet Potato Pie, 189
Sweet Potatoes, 189
Sweet Zucchini Bread, 165
Sweetened Citrus Peel, 222
Sweetened Whipped Topping, 231

T

Tangerine Cream Tarts, 113
Tart Cherry Ice Cream, 52
Tart filling, chocolate, 81
Tart Orange Coffee Cake, 150
Tart Orange Meringue Tarts, 112
Tarts
maple ice cream, 45
phyllo, 78
pistachio pineapple, 80
strawberry cream cheese , 79
tangerine cream, 113

tart orange meringue, 112
    Valentine, 112
Thanksgiving Pumpkin Mousse, 83
Tiramisu, 133
Toasted-Coconut Sauce, 227
Toasted-Walnut Chocolate-Chip Ice Cream, 53
Tofu, 11, 12, 36
Toppings
    chocolate-flavored nondairy whipped, 231
    fudge, 75
    maple-cinnamon, 107
    sweetened whipped, 231
Torte
    chocolate dream, 118
    lemon meringue, 118
    mocha, 182
    Schaum, 120
Tortoni, 53
Traditional Cream Puffs, 126
Traditional Pavlova, 114
Trifle
    individual strawberry, 137
    Jamaican, 136
Triple Sherbet Dessert, 54
Tropical Punch, 23

V

Valentine Tarts, 112
Vanilla, 24, 86, 102, 208
Vanilla Shake, 24
Vanilla Wafers, 208
Virgin Piña Colada, 24
Wafer Crust, 193

W

Waffles
    pumpkin, 109
    strawberries and cream, 109
Walnut Roll-Up Cookies, 94
Washington's Birthday Napoleon, 71
Watermelon Sorbet, 54

Yogurt, 11, 23, 25, 27, 49, 56
Yogurt Orange Whip, 27

Z

Zucchini, 165